Yankeys Now

NBER Series on Long-term Factors in Economic Development
A *National Bureau of Economic Research Series*
Edited by Claudia Goldin

Also in the series

Claudia Goldin
Understanding the Gender Gap: An Economic History of American Women
(Oxford University Press, 1990)

Roderick Floud, Kenneth Wachter, and Annabel Gregory
Height, Health and History: Nutritional Status in the United Kingdom,
1750–1980 (Cambridge University Press, 1990)

Robert A. Margo
Race and Schooling in the South, 1880–1950: An Economic History
(University of Chicago Press, 1990)

Samuel H. Preston and Michael R. Haines
Fatal Years: Child Mortality in Late Nineteenth-Century America
(Princeton University Press, 1991)

Barry Eichengreen
Golden Fetters: The Gold Standard and the Great Depression, 1919–1939
(Oxford University Press, 1992)

Ronald N. Johnson and Gary D. Libecap
The Federal Civil Service System and the Problem of Bureaucracy: The
Economics and Politics of Institutional Change (University of Chicago
Press, 1994)

Naomi R. Lamoreaux
Insider Lending: Banks, Personal Connections, and Economic Development
in Industrial New England, 1784–1912 (Cambridge University Press,
1994)

Lance E. Davis, Robert E. Gallman, and Karin Gleiter
In Pursuit of Leviathan: Technology, Institutions, Productivity, and Profits in
American Whaling, 1816–1906 (University of Chicago Press, 1997)

Dora L. Costa
The Evolution of Retirement: An American Economic History, 1880–1990
(University of Chicago Press, 1998)

YANKEYS NOW

Immigrants in the
Antebellum United States,
1840–1860

Joseph P. Ferrie

New York   Oxford
Oxford University Press
1999

Oxford University Press

Oxford   New York
Athens   Auckland   Bangkok   Bogotá   Buenos Aires   Calcutta
Cape Town   Chennai   Dar es Salaam   Delhi   Florence   Hong Kong   Istanbul
Karachi   Kuala Lampur   Madrid   Melbourne   Mexico City   Mumbai
Nairobi   Paris   São Paulo   Singapore   Taipei   Tokyo   Toronto   Warsaw

and associated companies in
Berlin   Ibadan

Published by Oxford University Press, Inc.
198 Madison Avenue, New York, New York 10016

Oxford is a registered trademark of Oxford University Press

Library of Congress Cataloging-in-Publication Data
Ferrie, Joseph P.
Yankeys now : immigrants in the antelbellum U.S., 1840–1860
Joseph P. Ferrie
p.   cm.
Includes biographical references and index.
ISBN 0-19-510934-1
1. United States—Emigration and immigration—History—19th
century. 2.Immigrants—United States—History—19th century.
JV6451.F47   1997
304.8'4073—dc21   97-16780

9 8 7 6 5 4 3 2 1

Printed in the United States of America
on acid-free paper

For My Parents

Relation of the Directors to the Work and Publications
of the National Bureau of Economic Research

1. The object of the National Bureau of Economic Research is to ascertain and to present to the public important economic facts and their interpretation in a scientific and impartial manner. The board of Directors is charged with the responsibility of ensuring that the work of the National Bureau is carried on in strict conformity with this object.

2. The President of the National Bureau shall submit to the Board of Directors, or to its Executive Committee, for their formal adoption all specific proposals for research to be instituted.

3. No research report shall be published by the National Bureau until the President has sent each member of the Board a notice that a manuscript is recommended for publication and that in the President's opinion it is suitable for publication in accordance with the principles of the National Bureau. Such notification will include an abstract or summary of the manuscript's content and a response form for use by those Directors who desire a copy of the manuscript for review. Each manuscript shall contain a summary drawing attention to the nature and treatment of the problem studied, the character of the data and their utilization in the report, and the main conclusions reached.

4. For each manuscript so submitted, a special committee of the Directors (including Directors Emeriti) shall be appointed by majority agreement of the President and Vice Presidents (or by the Executive Committee in case of inability to decide on the part of the President and Vice Presidents), consisting of three Directors selected as nearly as may be one from each general division of the Board. The names of the special manuscript committee shall be stated to each Director when notice of the proposed publication is submitted to him. It shall be the duty of each member of the special manuscript committee to read the manuscript. If each member of the manuscript committee signifies his approval within thirty days of the transmittal of the manuscript, the report may be published. If at the end of that period any member of the manuscript committee withholds his approval, the President shall then notify each member of the Board, requesting approval or disapproval of publication, and thirty days additional shall be granted for this purpose. The manuscript shall then not be published unless at least a majority of the entire Board who shall have voted on the proposal within the time fixed for the receipt of votes shall have approved.

5. No manuscript may be published, though approved by each member of the special manuscript committee, until forty-five days have elapsed from the transmittal of the report in manuscript form. The interval is allowed for the receipt of any memorandum of dissent or reservation, together with a brief statement of his reasons, that any member may wish to express; and such memorandum of dissent or reservation shall be published with the manuscript if he so desires. Publication does not, however, imply that each member of the Board has read the manuscript, or that either members of the Board in general or the special committee have passed on its validity in every detail.

6. Publications of the National Bureau issued for informational purposes concerning the work of the Bureau and its staff, or issued to inform the public of activites of Bureau staff, and volumes issued as a result of various conferences involving the National Bureau shall contain a specific disclaimer noting that such publication has not passed through the normal review procedures required in this resolution. The Executive Committee of the Board is charged with review of all such publications from time to time to ensure that they do not take on the character of formal research reports of the National Bureau, requiring formal Board approval.

7. Unless otherwise determined by the Board or exempted by the terms of paragraph 6, a copy of this resolution shall be printed in each National Bureau publication.

(Resolution adopted October 25, 1926, as revised through September 30, 1974)

Preface

This book is the direct result of my dissatisfaction with the quality of data available to assess the economic mobility of Americans—particularly the mobility of immigrants—in the nineteenth century. In the process of trying to improve the information about these people and their progress and trying to re-answer many old questions with new data, I have incurred a great many debts, both intellectual and personal. Though they are far too numerous to list adequately here, I must nonetheless acknowledge the most substantial.

The first scholars whose work influenced this project were the members of my doctoral committee at the University of Chicago: Robert Fogel was never too busy to offer frequent and penetrating criticism; and David Galenson, the committee chair, sparked my initial interest in this subject, read and thought about each page and idea with a care I can only hope to approach in my own supervision of doctoral students, and offered his patient encouragement, gentle prodding, and constant friendship throughout. I also had the benefit of the comments of members of the Economic History Workshop at the University of Chicago who taught me how to think like an economic historian.

The collection of data underlying this work would have been impossible without the generous assistance of other scholars who gave me unlimited access to their own data in the best spirit of intellectual cooperation: Ronald Jackson (who provided indexes to the 1850 and 1860 U.S. population census manuscripts and mortality data from the 1850 census), Ira Glazier (who provided Irish passenger ship lists), Gary Zimmerman and Marion Wolfert (who provided German passenger ship lists), and Robert Swierenga (who provided Dutch emigration records and passenger ship lists). The task of processing the census indexes was made possible by the assistance of Clayne Pope and the Economics Department at Brigham Young University.

Early versions of parts of several chapters appeared in scholarly journals, the editors and referees of which greatly improved the cogency of my ideas and the clarity of my presentation: *Historical Methods* (Chapter 2); *Research in Economic History* (Chapter 4); *Explorations in Economic History* (Chapter 5); the *Journal of Economic History* (Chapter 6); and the *Journal of Interdisciplinary History* (Chapter 7). I also had the benefit of presenting my work in numerous forums where scholars from a variety of disciplines provided valuable insights: the annual meetings the Economic History Association, the Social Science History Association, and the Program in the Development of the American Economy at the National Bureau of Economic Research; and economic history workshops at Northwestern, Harvard, UCLA, Iowa, Indiana, Yale, Illinois (Urbana and Chicago), Queens (Canada), McGill, Arizona, Brigham Young University, Vanderbilt, and USC.

The number of people who have offered detailed comments on my work is enormous. My greatest debts in this regard are to Stan Engerman, Robert Margo, Claudia Goldin, Ken Sokoloff, Clayne Pope, Jeremy Atack, Lee Alston, Larry Neal, and my colleagues at Northwestern, Joel Mokyr, Lou Cain, and Alan Taylor, who also offered their encouragement throughout the book's long gestation. I am grateful as well for the generous financial support that made an extremely data-intensive project like this possible: a faculty research fellowship from the Olin Foundation that relieved me of my teaching responsibilities for the 1993–94 academic year, a quarter-time appointment at Northwestern University's Institute for Policy Research since 1995, and two grants from the National Science Foundation (Nos. SES 9309689 and SBR 9511344). The book would also have never seen the light of day without the assistance and substantial forbearance of Herb Addison and the production staff at Oxford University Press.

Finally, my greatest debts are personal: to my wife Mari whose patience with this project knew no bounds and whose unwavering support made it possible to maintain the focus necessary to bring the work to a satisfying conclusion; and to my parents—to whom I dedicate this work—whose love of learning surely sparked my own and whose constant encouragement and curiosity surely hastened the book's completion.

Chicago, Illinois   J.F.
December 1998

Contents

Yankeys Now

1

Immigrant Origins and the "Saltwater Curtain"

The Issues

In December of 1872, Joseph Hartley and his wife Rebecca wrote to friends in Yorkshire, England. Joseph had left West Riding in early 1858, sailed from Liverpool to New York, and eventually settled in Lockport, a stone quarrying town in upstate New York. Rebecca had left Cambridgeshire in 1857. The friends and family they left behind held out the hope that the Hartleys would one day return to their native country. But fifteen years after their departure from England, Joseph and Rebecca had come to see themselves as Americans:

> You see we have plenty to heat and drink. You want us to come home. I dont think we Could live in England know. We are yankeys now. England is the place if you have plenty of money but America is the place for a poor man to get a home. Here is a home for every man if he is stedy.[1]

For the Hartleys, the time between their departure from England and the day when they could describe themselves as "yankeys" was fifteen years. In that time, they had experienced a number of changes in their circumstances. They left New York City quickly and lived for a time in Medina, another quarrying town in New York, before settling for good in Lockport. Joseph had moved up in occupation from an often-unemployed quarry laborer to boss of the Lockport quarry. And he and Rebecca had a farm of thirty acres and four children as the fruits of their labor in America.[2]

Few immigrants left as detailed a record of their life in the United States as did Joseph and Rebecca Hartley in their letters back to England. But all experienced migration to America as a process of transformation. At the most fundamental level, the move to America transformed the relationship between the migrant and

1. Drake, "We Are Yankeys Now," p. 255.
2. Ibid., pp. 224–225.

his physical and economic environment. Though immigrants often sought out locations that seemed familiar in America, the places where they settled must have nonetheless been different from the places they left in important ways. If this were not the case, we would be surprised that so many chose to make the hazardous, costly, and uncertain journey across the Atlantic.

Migration also produced a transformation in the migrants themselves. Debate rages even today about the extent to which new arrivals can or should assimilate into the culture and economy of the country they have chosen as their new home. Such discussion has continued since the colonial period. It clearly shaped America's closing of the "Golden Door" at the beginning of the twentieth century, when immigration was restricted. But there can be no doubt that some such adaptation occurred, if only as a matter of survival: some old skills had to be discarded and new ones learned, a few phrases of English acquired for dealings outside the immigrant community, and at least a rudimentary sense of the rules by which people interact in a new society obtained. Perhaps over time, these transformations were only slight; perhaps they were quite substantial. But they clearly occurred, and shaped the relationship between immigrants and the people with whom they chose to live.

Finally, migration also brought about changes in the places the immigrants entered. Whether for good or ill, the arrival of strangers altered the circumstances in which the rest of the population lived. Immigrants brought new ideas, new attitudes, new foods, and new faiths. The skills they brought had the potential to transform whole industries for the benefit of all or undermine the economic position of native-born workers.

This book argues that the analysis of immigration to the United States in the years before the Civil War misses much of this process of transformation. Conventional historical sources are inadequate for understanding how immigrants were changed by their time in America and how America was changed by its immigrants because such sources seldom reveal more than a momentary glimpse of the circumstances of most Americans. We may see them as an entry in the census manuscripts, as the subject of a newspaper story, or as a name in a city directory, but none of these sources tells us more than how they looked at a single point in time. To see the process of transformation, we need more. At the very least, we need to know what immigrants looked like when they arrived (their economic conditions, their family situation, their first location in the United States), what they looked like at some later date, and the amount of time between those two observations. If we think of the immigrant as a projectile in flight, we cannot say very much more than where the projectile is at a single moment using the snapshot provided by conventional sources. With a series of snapshots taken at known intervals, and knowledge of where the projectile began its flight, we can say much more. In doing so, we can begin to understand migration as the process of transformation experienced by migrants.

This is not a novel notion. More than thirty years ago, Frank Thistlethwaite urged historians to throw back the "salt water curtain inhibiting [American] understanding of European origins."[3] He suggested that we "treat the process of migration as a complete sequence of experiences."[4] A number of scholars took up his challenge. Studies of German, Swedish, Norwegian, and Dutch immigrants appeared in the 1970s and 1980s, all of which went to great lengths to uncover the circumstances in which immigrants came to America and how they were changed over the course of their time here by the migration experience.[5]

The circumstances that made this work possible, however, were somewhat unusual. Each of these studies is based on a population that migrated from a well-defined and easily identified community in the country of origin and settled in a narrowly circumscribed location in the United States. This made it possible to follow specific individuals through the migration process by locating them in civil and church records at their place of origin and doing the same in their United States community. The depth of information these studies explore is stunning: they examine the lives of immigrants quite literally from the cradle to the grave. They explore family formation, fertility, geographic mobility, property acquisition, farming practices, inheritance patterns, political affiliations, and mortality. What these studies do not reveal is how the millions of immigrants who did not tread such well-marked paths fared in the migration process. These studies tell us a great deal about particular communities and particular migration streams, but they may tell us very little about most immigrants at the middle of the nineteenth century.[6]

It is possible to examine for other immigrants many of the same characteristics that changed for the Hartleys in the years after arrival in the United States and that have been examined in community-based studies. This book does just that for a new sample of more than two thousand European immigrants who came to the United States during the 1840s. This new sample makes it possible to trace patterns of geographic, occupational, and financial mobility from an immigrant's arrival in the United States until up to twenty years later. The sample was constructed by locating in the manuscript schedules of the 1850 and 1860 federal censuses of population 2,600 immigrants listed in passenger ship arrival records for the port of New York during the years 1840 to 1850. A companion sample was also created to serve as a source of comparison: 4,900 natives and immigrants present in the 1850 federal census of population and located in the 1860 census. Both samples contain information on each individual's location, occupation, and wealth in 1850 and 1860. The sample linked from the ship lists also contains unique information on each immigrant's date of arrival and characteristics at arrival (such as family structure and occupation).

The following chapters describe and explain the changes in location, occupa-

3. Thistlethwaite, "Migration," p. 32.

4. Ibid.

5. Kamphoefner, *Westphalians*; Ostergren, *Community Transplanted*; Gjerde, *Peasants to Farmers*; Swierenga, "Dutch International Migration and Occupational Change."

6. Kamphoefner, *Westphalians*, pp. 170–200, discusses the likely differences between the chain migrants who are the focus of community-based studies like his own and the rest of the immigrant population.

tion, and wealth of immigrants arriving in the first great wave of nineteenth-century European migration to the United States. The goal is a better understanding of the process of transformation—for both immigrants and the United States—brought about by immigration in the antebellum United States. Similar work has already been done on immigration later in the nineteenth century. A number of benefits will result from the focus here on the period before 1860.

The period 1840 to 1860 represents a distinct and important part of the larger story of nineteenth-century immigration. This period includes the crest of the century's first great wave of migration, which began in the years following the end of the Napoleonic Wars, and as such is interesting in its own right. It was also an era when immigrants were key actors in the events of the day: the opening of the West, the rise of modern industry, and the economic and political realignments that culminated in the Civil War.

But this period is also important for the comparisons it can yield. Many of the circumstances surrounding this migration—such as the origins of the migrants and the state of development of the U.S. economy—were different from those at the time of the next great wave in the late nineteenth and early twentieth centuries. An examination of immigration in this period might reveal how these different circumstances led to differences in the experiences of antebellum migrants and later immigrants. It can also tell us whether the patterns—such as settlement paths or occupational trajectories—seen among later "new" migrants were set much earlier, during this first wave of "old" European migration.

The best way to see the differences in the experiences of immigrants followed from ship records to census manuscripts is to consider brief biographical sketches of three representative immigrants from the sample.

1. *Edward Shuttleworth.* Shuttleworth was born in England in 1814 and described himself as a cloth dyer when he sailed from Liverpool to New York in March 1840. He was accompanied on the journey to the United States by his wife Elisabeth (age 26) and two sons, John (age 4) and James (age 1). Ten years later, in 1850, they were living in Woodbridge Township, in Middlesex County, New Jersey, roughly twenty miles from where they had first set foot in the United States. Edward was still employed as a dyer and possessed $300 in real estate. The family had grown to number seven with the addition of two sons, Edward (age 9 in 1850) and Thomas (age 7), and a daughter, Jane (age 5), all three of whom were born in Rhode Island. Both young Edward and Thomas had attended school in 1850. After another ten years, in 1860, the family had returned to Rhode Island and was living in North Providence. Edward was still employed as a dyer, though his holdings now included $1600 in real estate and another $1000 in personal property. The composition of his family had not changed since 1850. None of the five children attended school in 1860.

2. *John Claxton.* Claxton was born in 1815 in Ireland. He described himself as a domestic servant when he departed, unaccompanied, from Liverpool in May 1841. In 1850, he was living in Whitestown, a small village in Oneida County, New York, with his wife Maria (age 35), who had been born in England, and four

children, Mary (age 10), Elisabeth (age 9), William (age 4), and Emma (age 2), all of whom had been born in the state of New York. John was working as a miller and owned no real estate. The three older children attended school in 1850. By 1860, the family had moved to Nunda, a small town in McHenry County, Illinois. John was a farmer, and had amassed $1750 in real estate and $400 in personal property. His family now consisted of himself, his wife Maria, and children Mary, William, Emma, and John (who had been born in 1858 after the family's move to Illinois). The three older children attended school in 1860.

3. *Nathan Bing.* Bing was a 37-year-old laborer when he and his son Moses (age 5) sailed from Bremen in July 1844. Six years later, in 1850, he was living with Moses and his German-born wife Caroline (age 44) in the second ward of Cincinnati and working as a merchant. He owned no real estate and his son Moses (now age 11) did not attend school. He and his family were still in Cincinnati in 1860, though they had moved to the fourteenth ward. Nathan was still working as a merchant and had by now accumulated $1000 in personal property, but no real estate. His family had grown with the arrival in the United States of sons Isaac (age 17) and Samuel (age 16), both born in Germany before Nathan's departure, and sons Dena (age 9) and Benjamin (age 7), both born in Ohio. Moses, the eldest son, owned $500 of personal property in 1860, while Samuel, Dena, and Benjamin all attended school in 1860.

Though these immigrants appear to have been quite ordinary, they are noteworthy in one important respect. We know many of the details of their experiences during their first two decades in the United States: where they moved after arriving at New York, what occupations they pursued, and how their wealth changed as they moved from the East to the West, or rose from servant, to miller, to farmer, and as their age and length of residence in the United States increased. For most of the more than six million immigrants who came to the United States between 1820 and the Civil War, it is impossible to document geographic, occupational, and financial mobility in such detail for the years immediately after arrival.

These brief family histories suggest a number of questions regarding the location, occupation, and wealth of antebellum immigrants. Though we may never know the answers to these questions for particular families, with a sample of the sort described here, we can sketch out patterns of geographic, occupational, and financial mobility based on central tendencies.

All three families were located outside New York City by 1850. How quickly did immigrants leave the port where they arrived? Were some immigrants more likely to remain in New York for some time after their arrival? Did the unskilled or financially strapped remain, unable to afford to go farther? Were the Irish or Germans whose countrymen formed large immigrant communities in New York more likely to remain there? Shuttleworth initially settled in central New Jersey, Claxton in upstate New York, and Bing in a large midwestern city. What characteristics of these individuals and places led them to match up in this way? Were there intervening stops before an 1850 location was reached? Recall that though

Shuttleworth was living in New Jersey, all three of his children had been born in Rhode Island. If there were intervening stops, which immigrants were more likely to make such stops?

Of the three families, Bing remained in the same city between 1850 and 1860, while Shuttleworth moved from a rural location, to an eastern urban location and Claxton left the East for the rural Midwest. How common were urban-to-rural and rural-to-urban moves? How often did migrants spend time in an urban center before acquiring land and moving to a rural area? Why did some migrants who had started out in an urban center (New York) and probably passed through other urban centers on their way to a rural location then subsequently return to an urban center? What were the 1850 characteristics associated with these changes? Were those in particular occupations—such as retailing—more likely to remain in the same location? Were the less successful more likely to move on? Neither Claxton nor Bing had accumulated any real estate by 1850, yet one moved and the other stayed. What were the 1860 characteristics associated with those changes? Claxton's real estate wealth rose from nothing to $1750 after his move, while Bing remained in the same city and had amassed $1000 in personal property by 1860.

Only Shuttleworth had the same occupation at arrival, in 1850, and in 1860. Claxton moved from servant to miller to farmer, while Bing moved from laborer to merchant. How common were upward and downward moves in occupational status between arrival and 1850? Were immigrants who made downward moves between arrival and 1850 able to move back up in occupational status by 1860? Which immigrants were most likely to make each type of move?

Shuttleworth remained in the same occupation while relocating from rural New Jersey to urban Rhode Island, Claxton changed occupation going from rural New York to rural Illinois, and Bing remained in the same occupation and the same city. How often were changes in occupation associated with changes in location? Were those who moved out of a location more likely to move up in occupational status as well? Previous work on nineteenth-century occupational mobility has been hampered by an inability to follow those who left the location on which a particular study was based, leaving this an open question.

Only Shuttleworth had accumulated any real estate wealth by 1850, but he had also arrived with the largest family (a wife and two children), arrived earliest, and arrived with a skill. How well do characteristics at arrival account for 1850 wealth? How much was it worth in terms of 1850 wealth to have arrived with a family? Arrival with a family may have indicated superior wealth before departure, since moving an entire family at once may have been more costly than moving in stages as the Bing family did. How much was it worth to have arrived with a skill? After accounting for all other influences on 1850 wealth, what was the value of an additional year of residence in the United States?

By 1860, all three families had amassed some wealth, with Shuttleworth having the highest total wealth ($2600), Claxton the next ($2150), and Bing the least ($1000). How well do characteristics at arrival account for 1860 wealth? How important were 1860 characteristics? After accounting for all other 1860 characteristics, how valuable was an additional year in the United States by 1860?

How much of the return to duration in the United States in 1860 resulted from duration in a specific location and how much resulted from duration in the United States generally? Other studies have found large returns in terms of 1860 wealth for immigrants who had been present in the same location since 1850, though these returns vary by the specific location studied.

In order to make sense of the patterns that emerge in response to these questions, we need to know more about the native-born population and its behavior over the same period. For example, finding that immigrants moved up in occupational status only slowly may be less an indictment of immigrant failure than an indication of hard times felt more generally if natives moved up only at the same slow rate. Along the way to answering how immigrants did in the antebellum period, then, it will be necessary to say how natives fared. In the process, this study will provide some unique data on the experience of natives, particularly intercounty migrants, over the 1850s.

The immigration that began in the 1840s and peaked in the 1850s provoked a sharp political backlash. Fear that immigrants were stealing the jobs of native workers fueled the growth of the Know-Nothings and prompted much discussion of immigration's impact. Just as it is difficult to understand the performance of immigrants in isolation without knowledge of the performance over the same period of native-born workers, so too is it difficult to appreciate the immigrant experience in the antebellum period without knowing how immigrants affected natives in the nation's labor markets. To understand the discrimination many immigrants, particularly the Irish, faced in this period, we need to know more about the basis for that discrimination. We will thus need to assess the impact of immigration on natives in the U.S. labor market.

The following chapters take up each of these questions in turn. Chapter 2 describes the construction of the sample and tests its representativeness. Chapter 3 provides some background on the circumstances faced by immigrants in Europe and America, and the place of antebellum immigration in the broader context of immigration to the United States over the nineteenth and twentieth centuries. Settlement patterns, particularly the timing of departure from New York and the volume of movement to the western states, are described in chapter 4. The extent and causes of immigrant occupational mobility in the years immediately after arrival are analyzed in chapter 5. Chapter 6 examines immigrant wealth accumulation. The subsequent experiences of immigrants between 1850 and 1860 are explored in chapter 7. Chapter 8 focuses on the changes in the fortunes of native-born workers caused by this period's massive immigration. The final chapter offers a summary of the main findings and some more general conclusions.

2

The Data

Two New Samples

The experience of migration as a process of transformation can only be seen in data that allow us to follow specific individuals from their departure from Europe until some time after their arrival in the United States. The lack of information on immigrants' characteristics at their arrival prevents us from distinguishing their experience in Europe from their experience in the United States. In measuring occupational skills or wealth, for example, we are unable to separate what immigrants brought from what they subsequently gained. This may lead us to misinterpret the experiences of different immigrant groups: Was the successful German artisan in 1850 Milwaukee a recent, skilled arrival, or an early, unskilled arrival? Was the propertyless Irish laborer in 1850 New York poor because he had come with little and only recently arrived, or because he had come with nothing and accumulated nothing over his years in the United States? At the same time, the immigrant experience cannot be adequately understood without an appreciation for how the native-born population performed over a comparable period.

The data employed in this study were designed to meet these needs. Two samples were created: (1) one of 2,595 European immigrants linked from 1840–50 passenger ship arrival records to the 1850 and 1860 United States federal census manuscripts (which we will refer to as the "Ship List Sample"), and (2) one of 4,271 native-born Americans and 667 immigrants linked from the 1850 sample of the Public Use Microdata Series (PUMS) of the United States federal censuses to the 1860 United States federal census manuscripts (which we will refer to as the "PUMS Sample"). Though the details of the collection of these bodies of data are somewhat involved, the plausibility of the conclusions drawn from the data is only as great as the reader's belief in the representativeness of the data. This chapter describes the process by which the samples were created and tests how well they represent the populations from which they were drawn (the population of

European immigrants who arrived at New York during the 1840s and the total population of the United States between 1850 and 1860).

Linking Immigrants From Ship Lists to the Census

The manuscript schedules of the federal censuses of population are the richest source of data on immigrants in the nineteenth century. But the nineteenth-century census provides information on immigrants only at the time of the census. No background information other than country of origin was collected. For example, the federal census did not begin to ask immigrants their year of arrival in the United States until 1890.

The greatest—and still least exploited—source of information on the characteristics of immigrants at their arrival is the collection of passenger ship lists maintained by the United States State Department from 1820 onward.[1] Though the lists tell us about immigrants at arrival and allow us to calculate the duration of residence of those who survived to some later date, they tell us nothing about immigrants after they entered the United States. This sample was constructed to overcome the shortcomings of the census manuscript schedules and the passenger ship lists by yoking these two rich sources: tracing immigrants located in the ship lists into the census.

This sample was created by attempting to locate in the 1850 and 1860 manuscript census schedules a sample of 23,799 European immigrants—5 percent of all male family heads and unaccompanied males listed in passenger ship lists of arrivals at New York over the period 1840 to 1850. This produced a linked sample of 2,595 unaccompanied males and male family heads, as well as the family members who accompanied them: 1,456 located in 1850, 1,647 located in 1860, and 508 located in both censuses. The information at arrival on each includes port of embarkation, country (and in some cases village) of origin, date of arrival, age at arrival, family size and structure at arrival, and occupation at arrival. The information in 1850 or 1860 on each individual includes place of residence, age, family size and structure, occupation, wealth holdings (real wealth in 1850, real and personal wealth in 1860), literacy, and school attendance. In both the ship lists and the census, family structure was inferred, since family relationships were seldom explicitly described. Each group of people listed consecutively with a common surname was considered a family, with the first individual listed considered the head of the family.

The information on date of arrival is unique for most of the nineteenth century. Though it is possible to infer immigrant family heads' year of arrival for pre-1890 censuses by examining the pattern of birthplaces recorded for the family's children, this is of little practical value for immigrants arriving in the middle of the nineteenth century. The volume of immigration of unaccompanied persons

---

1. The collection of these lists and their quality are discussed in Hutchinson, "Immigration Statistics."

and families with no children in this period means that the resulting sample would be both small and biased toward older, more established families. For example, of the family heads traced in the present sample, only 22 percent arrived with children and had additional children subsequently. Thus, only 22 percent of the family heads in the sample could have had their duration of residence ascertained with any precision from the census. None of the older subordinate family members or unaccompanied males who had formed their own families by 1850 could have had their duration of residence ascertained in this way. Even among those for whom a date of arrival could be inferred in this manner, the reliability of that inference depends crucially on the spacing of births, the survival of children born immediately before and after migration, the probability that family heads and their offspring arrived together, and the age when children left home. At the same time, the positive relationship between wealth and marital fertility observed in the nineteenth century means that the inferred duration might incorporate a significant wealth bias. Finally, even if duration of residence could be determined in this way, the census contains no information on immigrants prior to their arrival, such as occupation, family structure, or exact place of origin.

Collecting the Passenger Ship List Sample

The first step in constructing the linked sample was drawing a sample of male immigrant family heads and unaccompanied male immigrants from passenger ship lists of ships arriving at New York during the period 1840–50. The years from 1840 to 1850 were chosen for practical reasons. The census began to collect information on country of origin (a key variable in the linkage process) and wealth (a key variable in the analysis) in 1850. At the same time, national indexes to the 1850 and 1860 censuses have now been created. The census stopped asking about wealth holdings after 1870, while late nineteenth-century censuses are indexed by state rather than nationally. Thus, 1840–60 is the only time in the nineteenth century when it is possible without great cost to link passenger ship arrival records to manuscript schedules of the federal censuses of population that contain wealth data. New York was chosen as the port to focus on for two reasons: during the 1840s it increasingly dominated all other ports in the volume of immigrants passing through it; and in studying patterns of settlement, it seemed reasonable to concentrate on immigrants beginning from a common point of arrival. The principal bias that could result from this focus on New York is the omission of the poorest immigrants. For example, it has been estimated that before 1865, roughly half of all U.K. immigrants in the United States had come through Canada, because the passage fare to Canadian maritime ports was less than half that to American ports.[2] German immigrants were often advised to travel through New Orleans if their destination was in the Midwest, since fares to the upper Midwest by way of New Orleans were also less than half the fare via New York.[3]

2. Ibid., p. 975; Mageean, "Irish Emigration," p. 54.
3. See chapter 4 in this volume.

The filing of these lists beginning in 1820 was required by the Passenger Ship Act of 1819. The master of each ship calling at a U.S. port was to file with the Customs House for the port a list or manifest, "in which list or manifest it shall be the duty of said master to designate, particularly, the age, sex, and occupation, of the said passengers, respectively, the country to which they severally belong, and that of which it is their intention to become inhabitants."[4] It appears that these lists were compiled at the port of origin, possibly as transcriptions of ship company records onto U.S. government forms. This conclusion follows from three observations: the almost exact correspondence in the spelling and order of names in cases where it has been possible to compare the lists with the ship company's records; the emendations to the lists ("born at sea," "died at sea," "boarded late"), usually appearing at the end of the list, indicating that the lists were prepared before the ship embarked and added to as circumstances dictated; and the similarity of the handwriting on lists from different ships traveling from the same port.[5]

Though the lists vary in quality—for example, most give only "United States" as the destination while some give the names of specific cities, and most give only a country as a place of origin while some give specific villages—they represent the most broadly based source of information on immigrants prior to their arrival.[6]

For the period 1840–45, a 5 percent sample of male immigrant family heads and unaccompanied male immigrants was drawn. Every twentieth distinct surname was examined. If there were no immigrants with the same surname following immediately on the list, the individual was assumed to be unaccompanied. If the unaccompanied person was a male, he was taken into the sample. If the unaccompanied person was a female, the next distinct surname was examined instead.[7] If at least one person followed in the list with the same surname, it was inferred that this was a family.[8] The first individual with that surname was considered the head of the family. If the family was headed by a male, the head of the family was taken into the sample, along with information on all the members of his family. If the family was headed by a female, the next distinct surname was examined instead.

Finally, a male family head or unaccompanied male was included in the sample only if he gave a full first and last name, age, and country of origin. This restriction led to the exclusion of immigrants on lists of several ships that were copies of originals. In the transcription process, individuals' first names were re-

4. Hutchinson, "Immigration Statistics," p. 998.
5. Mageean, "Irish Emigration," compares the ship company records and the passenger ship lists.
6. The difficulties with the lists and the potential biases they might induce if sampling were done to avoid them are discussed in Erickson, "Emigration from the British Isles to the U.S.A. in 1831" and "Uses of Passenger Lists," and Swierenga, "Dutch International Migration Statistics."
7. Female heads of families and unaccompanied females were excluded because linkage to the census manuscripts was done on the basis of first and last name. The possibility that females would change their names upon marriage or remarriage, or that females were traveling to rejoin males who had previously migrated, argued against their inclusion in the sample.
8. On some lists, males and females were listed separately, or family heads and family members were listed separately. For these lists, the original family structure was inferred before the list was examined for sampling.

placed with initials. Given the apparently random occurrence of these bad lists, this does not seem a major shortcoming. At the same time, such bad lists also seemed to have the most careless listing of occupations, with whole ships listed simply as farmers or laborers, so their exclusion probably enhances the accuracy of reported occupations in the ship list sample.[9]

Two further samples of arrivals at New York, also drawn from passenger ship lists, were added to extend coverage to the period 1846–50: a sample of immigrants from the United Kingdom (England, Scotland, Wales, Ireland, and unspecified Great Britain) arriving during 1846–50, and a sample of immigrants from Germany arriving during 1847–50.[10] Male family heads and unaccompanied males were taken from these samples in the manner described earlier. Since U.K. and German migration accounted for at least 90 percent of all immigration into the United States in the 1840s, the combination of these three samples gives a fairly comprehensive picture of European immigration over the period. In order to keep the sample to a reasonable size and assure that the massive Irish and German immigration after 1847 would not dominate the results, these two later samples were drawn to represent roughly 2.5 percent (rather than 5 percent) of European immigrant male family heads and unaccompanied males over the period they cover. Every fortieth distinct surname was examined rather than every twentieth as had been done for 1840–45.

The German post–1845 sample has four peculiarities: it contains no immigrants for 1846; it covers only immigrants sailing from Bremen; it includes only immigrants giving a place of origin more specific than "Germany" (for example, a principality, region, city, or village); and it does not include information on occupation. The first of these is not a serious flaw, since in all the subsequent analysis we shall control for year of arrival. The second is likewise not crucial, since Bremen was itself a major German port of embarkation: by 1850 it accounted for nearly a third of all German arrivals at New York. The only other major port for Germans sailing to the west, Le Havre, accounted for another 40 percent, with the remainder coming from a variety of smaller ports. The one bias that might result from the fact that all the German immigrants in the sample after 1845 sailed from Bremen is a disproportionate number of immigrants from northern and eastern Germany. Since migration from Germany after 1840 was increasingly from these regions, this does not seem a major difficulty. At the same time, since these lists (and many of those for Germany in the 1840–45 sample) tell us exactly where in Germany these immigrants began their journey, we can take account of this bias.[11]

The third peculiarity, the concentration on those giving specific points of ori-

9. Other lists with full first and last names recorded also often contained either entirely farmers or entirely laborers. Cohn, "Occupations of English Immigrants," has shown, however, that the ages and family structures of immigrants on these lists suggest that they were in fact predominantly farmers or laborers.

10. These lists appear in Glazier, *Famine Immigrants*, and Zimmerman and Wolfert, *German Immigrants*. Both authors graciously provided their lists in machine-readable form.

11. Glazier and Filby, *Germans to America*, p. xiii.

gin, might seem a more serious flaw. In examining lists of immigrants from the United Kingdom, Erickson found that such good lists were a biased sample from the universe of all ship lists: they covered only a few ports and thus misrepresented the true distribution of occupations and places of origin among immigrants.[12] These difficulties do not arise in the case of the Bremen ship lists. No doubt in part as a result of Germany's political fragmentation before 1871, a large number of Germans leaving both Bremen and Le Havre gave their principality, region, city, or village as their origin. For Bremen, such immigrants amounted to 30 percent of the total over 1847–50.[13] Further, among German immigrants traveling from Le Havre over the period 1840–45, there are no apparent differences between those giving Germany and those giving a more specific location as their origin. The lack of information on occupation in the Bremen lists, though also an apparently major flaw in this sample, was easily remedied: after the sample was traced to the 1850 and 1860 censuses, each individual successfully linked was then located in the original passenger ship lists, where their occupation could be determined.

Representativeness of the Passenger Ship List Sample

The sample that resulted from this procedure consisted of 6,211 male family heads and 17,588 unaccompanied males, along with information on the 22,000 family members accompanying the male family heads. Figure 2-1 shows the number of immigrants in the sample and in the published total for immigrant arrivals at New York by year. The sample tracks actual immigration quite well for the period 1840–44, but diverges from the published trend in 1845. After 1846, where the break in the figure corresponds to the collection of a one-in-forty sample rather than the one-in-twenty sample used for 1840–45, the sample again tracks the published series quite well.

The characteristics of the ship list sample are shown in Table 2-1. The male family heads and unaccompanied males who arrived over this period are young on average (26.7 years), and concentrated in farming, skilled occupations, and unskilled labor. Three quarters of those in the sample were traveling unaccompanied. The average age is similar across countries of origin, but there are some differences in the occupational structure, the family structure, and the distribution of ports of embarkation.

The Irish were more concentrated in the unskilled labor group than either the British or the Germans.[14] The Germans were seldom found among the unskilled laboring group. Among those who arrived with families, the Germans had the

12. Erickson, "Emigration from the British Isles to the U.S.A. in 1831," p. 193.

13. Of course, this is just the opposite of the problem described above with U.K. immigrants, too many of whom were given the imprecise origin of "U.K." because of the region's political unity or the carelessness of the compilers of the lists.

14. The distribution of ship list occupations for the Germans is for those who were linked to the census and then again located in the ship lists. The distributions for the English and Irish are for all immigrants in the ship list sample, whether or not they were subsequently linked to the census.

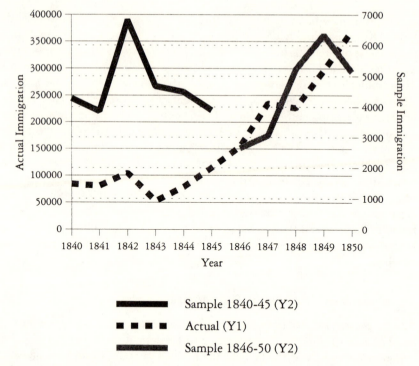

Figure 2-1. Actual immigration to the United States from Europe by year and immigration in the sample by year. *Source:* U.S. Department of the Treasury, *Immigration into the U.S.*, pp. 4345–4346.

highest average number of children, and the Irish the fewest. Most of the Irish sailed from Liverpool, as did most of the British, though a large number of British (27 percent) also sailed from other smaller ports, such as Glasgow, Portsmouth, Bristol, Hull, and Cardiff. The Germans sailed from Le Havre and Bremen, while smaller numbers departed from Hamburg and the Low Countries.

Table 2-2 compares the distribution of the immigrants in the sample with the published immigration figures for each year of arrival.[15] The unit of observation in the published figures is the individual, so the characteristics of all individuals in the sample—family heads, family members, and unaccompanied individuals—

15. There remains some question as to the reliability of the published figures. Both Erickson, "Emigration from the British Isles to the U.S.A. in 1831," p. 180, and Swierenga, "Dutch International Migration Statistics," p. 450, and "Reply," p. 1598, offer estimates of how many immigrants were undercounted—included in passenger ship lists but excluded from published totals ostensibly derived from those lists. Erickson shows that arrivals for only five months in 1831 calculated from the ship lists total more than the published figure for the entire year. Swierenga finds that total Dutch immigration over the period 1840–49 was underestimated by at least 70 percent. These studies suggest that discrepancies between the published immigration figures and figures based on well-designed samples of ship lists are possibly the result of errors in the published figures.

Table 2-1. Characteristics of a sample of immigrant arrivals
at New York, 1840–50.

		Origin		
Characteristic	Total	Irish	British	German
Age	26.7	25.7	26.5	27.7
Years in U.S.	5.0	3.5	6.2	4.6
Occupation (%)				
White Collar	12.5	14.3	12.3	11.2
Skilled	18.2	6.0	22.9	28.7
Farmer	26.4	12.1	19.9	52.0
Unskilled	42.3	67.2	42.5	7.6
Other or none given	0.2	0.2	0.3	0.0
Family structure				
Alone (%)	73.8	74.0	69.9	79.7
Accompanied (%)	26.1	26.0	30.1	20.3
Married (%)	20.3	19.0	23.6	16.5
W/children (%)	20.1	18.1	23.4	16.7
No. of children	2.2	1.7	2.2	2.5
Embarkation port (%)				
Liverpool	53.0	88.6	72.5	0.7
Bremen	18.3	0.0	0.0	63.0
Le Havre	9.8	0.0	0.1	22.0
Other	18.9	11.4	27.4	14.2
No. of obs.	23,799	6,776	9,022	6,871
Percent (%)	100.0	28.5	37.9	28.9

Source: Sample of male household heads and unaccompanied males in passenger ship arrival records at port of New York, 1840–1850.

Note: All characteristics are as reported in the passenger ship lists, except "Years in U.S." which is measured in 1850. Occupational categories are described in Appendix E.

are used in Table 2-2. Immigrants from Ireland, England, Scotland, and Wales are grouped together as "Ireland and Great Britain." This is done because the passenger ship lists were often imprecise as to the exact country of origin of Irish and British immigrants, often stating simply "U.K." (which would have been correct) or "Great Britain" (which would not have been) for Irish immigrants. The exact country of origin was later determined for all immigrants linked to the census.

For the entire sample period, there is a good correspondence between the sample and the published figures. The most worrisome exceptions to this are the underrepresentation of farmers and of those from countries other than Ireland, Britain, and Germany. The underrepresentation of farmers results from the fact that the sample includes no Germans for 1846 (and Germans were disproportionately farmers in the ship lists), while the sample of Germans who sailed from Bremen in the 1847–50 period did not include their occupations, so they fall into the "Other or None" category for 1847–50. As a result, the sample has the ap-

Table 2-2. Representativeness of a sample of immigrant arrivals at New York, 1840–50 (index of representation).

Characteristic	Total	Year of Arrival		
		1840–44	1845–46	1847–50
Age				
Under 15	105	127	105	79
15 to 40	100	89	102	112
Over 40	88	112	78	68
Origin				
Ireland or Britain	116	114	140	115
Germany	110	115	71	124
Other	29	44	40	0
Occupation				
Farmer	74	108	78	38
Unskilled	110	117	157	111
Other or none given	103	96	95	110

Source: Sample of male household heads and unaccompanied males in passenger ship arrival records at port of New York, 1840–1850, and U.S. Census Bureau, *Historical Statistics*, series C 140–142, C 91–95, and C 120–137.

Note: The index of representation is calculated as the fraction possessing a characteristic in the sample divided by the corresponding fraction in the published figures multiplied by 100. Values above 100 indicate that a characteristic is overrepresented in the sample and values below 100 indicate underrepresentation. For example, the value of 105 for under age 15 in the "Total" column means that the fraction of arrivals for the whole period who were under age 15 is 5 percent greater in the sample than the fraction shown in the published figures. For 1840–42, figures are for year ending December 31; for all other years, for year ending September 30. Occupational categories are described in Appendix E.

propriate percentage of farmers for 1840–44, a slight underrepresentation for 1845–46 (since German farmers are included in 1845, but no Germans are included in 1846), and a gross underrepresentation for 1847–50. As was noted earlier, once German arrivals from the Bremen sample were located in the census manuscript schedules, the original passenger ship lists were searched to find their occupations.[16] The underenumeration of those from countries other than Ireland, Britain, and Germany results mainly from the inclusion in the published immigrant figures of arrivals from British America, the West Indies, and South America.

Linking the Passenger Ship List Sample to the Census Manuscripts

After the sample was drawn from the passenger ship lists, the next step was to locate immigrants in the national index to the 1850 federal census of population.[17]

16. The published immigration figures do not give a breakdown of occupation by origin for this period, so it was not possible to calculate an index of representation only for Irish and British farmers, unskilled workers, and others.

17. Jackson, "Index to the Seventh Census."

The 1850 index contains only family heads and subordinate family members with surnames different from that of the head. Thus, it was not possible to search for every individual in the ship list sample. Instead, only family heads at arrival, unaccompanied males, and males who would have been age fifteen and over by 1850 were sought. The latter were included to capture those who arrived with their family but had left their parents' homes by 1850.

The list of the individuals from the ship lists meeting these criteria was arranged alphabetically and permutations of each surname were generated using the Soundex system. The resulting list was compared name by name with the index to find the location in the census of these immigrants.[18] This procedure was repeated for the 1860 census, making use of the 1860 census index.[19] The individuals sought were again male family heads at arrival, unaccompanied males at arrival, and subordinate family members who were age 15 and over in 1860.[20] This second search both created a group of immigrants linked from arrival to the 1850 and 1860 censuses and allowed us to capture some immigrants who had been present in 1850 but who had escaped enumeration then.

The census index gives only the name and the page number in the census manuscripts for an individual. No identifying information other than the name—for example, age, country of origin, or names and ages of other family members—is provided, so linkages could not be verified until the census manuscripts were consulted for each immigrant located in the index. In order to keep the searches in the manuscript pages to a reasonable number, only three types of linkages to the census index were pursued into the manuscripts: an exact match of first and last name, where one individual in the sample was traced to exactly one individual in the index; an inexact match of first or last name or both, where the exact first name or last name or both could not be located, but only one individual with the most likely alternative spelling could be located; and a multiple exact or inexact match, where either of the two preceding conditions held, but the individual could be linked to more than one but not more than three individuals in the index (with either the same first and last name or the most likely alternative spelling of it).

Thus, only those with three or fewer matches in the index were checked in the census manuscripts. Each potential match was checked in the manuscript pages to see which if any corresponded to the immigrant in question. Any individual with more than three matches in the census index was not pursued. The only exception to this was made for individuals with first and last names that appeared more than once in the sample. For each of these, enough matches were taken from the index to permit a maximum of three matches per individual.[21]

18. The 1850 census index was published on 400 sheets of microfiche, so this search was performed manually.

19. Jackson, "Index to the Eighth Census."

20. Jackson provided the computer tapes used to create the microfiche indexes for 1860. The Soundex system was used to code the names in both the index and the list of immigrants sought, and the computer was instructed which potential matches to accept and which to reject. The 1860 index also contained household heads and all individuals whose surnames differed from that of the household head.

21. That is, if a name appeared three times in the sample and nine times in the index, this

When the census manuscripts were examined to verify matches, age and country of origin were the primary identifying criteria used. A match was successful if
the age in the census and the anticipated age based on the reported age in the ship
lists were within five years of each other. For country of origin, it was necessary to
make some allowance for the inexact reporting of origin in the ship lists for immigrants from the United Kingdom. Thus, an immigrant who was described as
from the United Kingdom or from Great Britain in the ship lists and who matched
the age of an immigrant in the manuscripts reported to have come from Ireland
was considered a successful match.

The names and ages of other family members were used only in cases where
more than one immigrant in the manuscripts matched the age and origin of an
immigrant in the ship lists. Family characteristics were never the primary criteria
used in making matches since family structure could change over time as immigrants married and as family members arrived to join relatives who had previously
arrived in the United States. For example, an immigrant accompanied by a particular family in the ship lists might appear with a different family in the census
if he had remarried between arrival and 1850. An immigrant without a family in
the ship lists might appear with a foreign-born wife and foreign-born children in
the census if the wife and children sailed separately.

The "Common Name" Problem

Since our linkage procedure eliminates those with the most common names, we
must ask what effect this will have on the characteristics of the resulting linked
sample. First, note that not all common names are excluded—only the most common combinations of first name and surname. Thus, though "John Smith" would
not wind up in the linked sample, there is a very good chance that "Napoleon
Smith" would (as he did).

Second, the common name problem affects the entire sample—the Irish,
English, and Germans all have a few combinations of first names and surnames
that are quite common. The differences are a matter of degree: the English probably have the least variety and the Germans the most. We might then expect this
procedure to result in fewer English and more Germans than in our original sample, with the share of Irish closer to the share in the ship list sample. But since the
subsequent work on the linked sample will be disaggregated by country of origin,
this is not a serious difficulty. Within national groups, there is little reason to suspect that the elimination of common names will seriously bias the sample with
respect to any of the variables of interest.

Table 2-3 shows the distribution of the number of matches in the 1850 census
index for a sample of 400 immigrants in the passenger ship list sample. Twenty-

---

was considered a potentially successful match. All nine entries were checked in the manuscripts to
see which matched the immigrants in question. If the name appeared three times in the sample and
ten times in the index, the immigrants with this name were not pursued and did not enter the linked
sample.

Table 2-3. Number of appearances in the 1850 census index for combinations of surname and given name in a sample of 400 immigrant arrivals at New York, 1840–50.

Number of appearances	Total		U.K.		Germany	
	N	%	N	%	N	%
None	169	42.2	75	30.4	94	61.4
One to three	110	27.5	72	29.2	38	24.8
Four to ten	50	12.5	41	16.6	9	5.9
Over ten	71	17.8	59	23.9	12	7.8

Source: Random sample of 400 individuals from sample of male household heads and unaccompanied males in passenger ship arrival records at port of New York, 1840–1850, sought in index to 1850 federal census of population.
Note: "U.K." includes Ireland.

eight percent of those sought in the 1850 index had one to three matches, whereas just over 30 percent had more than three matches. The question of the extent of the bias that results from excluding those with common names comes down to a question of how different are the immigrants in these two groups.

To assess these differences, a logistic regression was estimated in which the dependent variable was whether an immigrant's name appeared three or fewer times in the census index or whether the immigrant's name appeared more than three times; the independent variables were all of the individual's characteristics from the ship lists. Separate regressions were estimated for each country of origin. None of the characteristics was found to be either statistically or substantively significant, so we can have some confidence that concentrating on those with fewer than four appearances in the census index does not impart a bias to the resulting linked sample. When the sample had been traced to the 1850 census manuscripts, the same exercise was performed on the successfully linked immigrants. The dependent variable was whether the immigrant's name had only one or more than one appearance in the 1850 census index, and the independent variables were the individual's 1850 characteristics. Again, none of the characteristics was associated with being in either of these groups.

The only other study to explore the relationship between the commonness of names (combinations of first names and surnames) and characteristics such as occupation, wealth, and location found no link between either occupation or wealth and the commonness of names.[22] Steckel defined common as more than 10 matches in a state index (a definition that will classify fewer individuals as having common names than the linkage procedure used here). Though he detected a link between location and commonness—common names were twice as likely in cities with populations over 75,000 and were 40 percent less likely in the

22. Steckel, "Census Matching."

South—this result follows from the sample design: the study used separate indexes for each state, but states varied in the size of their population.[23] Thus, southern states (with lower populations) and less urban states (with lower populations) should have fewer names repeated in the index. Since the sample used here is national in scope, this problem does not arise. The ranking of different nationalities by commonness of names can be calculated from Steckel's figures. The predicted probability of having a common name was 7.5 percent for the English, 4.6 percent for the Irish, and 1.6 percent for the category "other foreign-born," which included Germans.

Representativeness of the Linked Sample

Of the 23,799 individuals sought in the 1850 and 1860 censuses, 1,456 were successfully located in the 1850 census manuscripts, 1,647 were located in 1860, and 508 were located in both. Though the percentage linked to either 1850 or 1860 (10.6 percent) might seem low, several factors could account for this linkage rate.

The first is inaccuracies in the ship lists. Based on a comparison of the ship lists with Dutch emigration records, Swierenga estimates that actual Dutch immigration through U.S. ports was two to three times greater than that contained in existing ship manifests, with at least 5 percent of this difference accounted for by mistakes made by clerks preparing the ship lists.[24] This figure must be adjusted downward somewhat for U.K. and German immigration if Swierenga is correct that "the smaller and less distinctive the nationality group, the greater is the likelihood of such oversight."[25] A further source of consolation in this respect is his finding that, at least for the Dutch, there was no correlation between such oversight and the characteristics of those overlooked.[26]

The second source of linkage failure is return migration. Since the United States kept no record of emigration until 1908, it is difficult even to guess how large a role this played in the linkage failures. For the years 1908 to 1914, there was fewer than one alien departure for every two alien arrivals in the same year, but it would be difficult to infer from this a rate of return migration for any year in the nineteenth century for two reasons.[27] First, the extent of return migration in the early twentieth century is likely to have been substantially greater than that in the middle of the nineteenth century when there were still large areas of the United States left unsettled and relatively greater passage fares. The second difficulty—which also plagues the other estimates described below—is that this figure tells us how many immigrants left for every hundred who arrived in a particular year, but it does not say when those departing immigrants originally arrived. For our purposes this is crucial: for example, if an immigrant who arrived in 1845

23. Ibid., Table 1.

24. Swierenga, "Dutch International Migration Statistics," p. 462; Swierenga, "Reply," p. 1597.

25. Swierenga, "Dutch International Migration Statistics," p. 465.

26. Ibid., pp. 462–465.

27. U.S. Census Bureau, *Historical Statistics*, p. 119.

did not leave until 1851, he was at risk to have been linked to the 1850 census but not the 1860 census.

Willcox suggests that for the period 1840–50, return migration was roughly 10 percent of immigration.[28] Unfortunately, this is not based on an enumeration but is simply an informed guess, based on a backward extrapolation of the observed ratio of return migration in a year to immigration in that year of 39 percent at the end of the nineteenth century, with the extrapolation designed to fit the actual increase in the foreign-born population between census years.

Kamphoefner has developed alternative estimates of return migration, employing the methodology of Kuznets and Rubin.[29] This method uses life tables and figures for actual immigration to derive the number of immigrants who would have survived to a census date and compares that number with the number actually present to estimate return migration as the deficit. Kamphoefner's calculations suggest that the return migration rate (again, returns as a fraction of total arrivals) was 12 percent for the Germans, 6 percent for the Irish, and 30 percent for the British during the 1850s.[30]

For the Germans at least, Kamphoefner then shows that these figures are implausibly high, since they count immigrants merely visiting their country of origin as return migrants, even though they might have returned only to retrieve additional family members. He suggests a rate of roughly 2 percent as more reasonable. Even this figure might be too high, though, to the extent that immigrants were more likely than natives to be missed in the federal census enumerations.[31] Since the Kuznets-Rubin method takes the number of likely survivors to the census date and subtracts the actual number of resident immigrants to estimate returns, underenumeration of immigrants would mean that many of those counted as returns were simply missed by the census.

Finally, Baines uses British census data to estimate returns to England and Wales from abroad. His method avoids the shortcomings of an approach based on often incomplete immigration records and United States census records, and eliminates the need to assume a particular mortality regime for immigrant arrivals. He finds returns to have been 19 percent of outward-bound passengers for the decade 1861–70.[32] His calculations suggest a sharp rise in the return rate to 50 percent by the 1870s.

Another source of linkage failure is mortality in the United States. Little is known about the mortality experience of immigrants in the nineteenth-century United States. It is possible, however, like Kuznets and Rubin, to use life table methods to estimate the number of immigrants arriving in each year who would have survived to be enumerated in the 1850 census. If we assume a mortality schedule which corresponds to West Level Twelve—with an expectation of 43 additional years at

28. Willcox, *American Demography*, p. 390.
29. Kamphoefner, "Return Migration"; Kuznets and Rubin, *Immigration*.
30. Kamphoefner, "Return Migration," p. 295.
31. The issue is discussed in greater detail below.
32. Baines, *Migration*, p. 136.

age 20—we would expect that 78.5 percent of those sought in the index (male family heads, unaccompanied males, and males who arrived in families and would have been age 15 or older by 1850) survived to be enumerated in the 1850 census.[33]

Appendix C presents new estimates of mortality in 1850 by nativity, based on a sample from the mortality schedules of the 1850 federal census of population. These figures suggest that Vinovskis's estimates may substantially overstate the probability of survival to be enumerated in the census. The life expectation of 44 years at age 20 in Massachusetts is based primarily on small towns and rural places. The estimate in Appendix C for immigrants is substantially lower: only 36 years. This corresponds to a West Level Nine mortality schedule.

"Age-heaping" in the ship lists and in the census may account for additional linkage failures. Since age was one of the variables used to verify matches, misreporting of ages in either source would diminish the number of successful linkages. To reduce this problem, an immigrant in the census was considered a match for a ship list immigrant if he corresponded in other particulars (first and last name and country of origin) with the difference in ages no greater than five years. Knights reports that 11 percent of those located in the 1850 and 1860 censuses of Boston had their ages misreported by more than five years.[34] More than 1,000 unique matches in the census index failed to yield a unique match in the census itself, usually because the census age was more than five years different from the ship list age.

Since only those immigrants who appeared in the census could be successfully linked, underenumeration in the census presents another difficulty. A number of studies have attempted to assess the accuracy of the census by searching for individuals in the schedules who were known to have been residents of a particular area at the time of the census, such as state legislators. Steckel reports that estimates of losses calculated in this way range from 9 to 19 percent in the 1850 and 1860 censuses.[35] These figures are, in general, calculated for groups such as state legislators and voters who were probably more likely to be enumerated than immigrants, so they probably represent a lower bound on the underenumeration of immigrants.

The failure to record immigrants' information accurately in the ship lists or census would also make linkage less likely. The first difficulty in communication the immigrants in the sample might have experienced would have been with those compiling the passenger ship lists. If their characteristics were incorrectly recorded here, then no matter how accurate the census data in which they were sought, the chances of their being located were slim. Fortunately, as was discussed

---

33. These calculations are based on Coale and Demeny, *Model Life Tables*, pp. 2–13. West Level Twelve was used since its e_{20} of 43 years is roughly the same as the e_{20-29} of 44 years calculated by Vinovskis, "Mortality Rates," p. 211, for Massachusetts in 1860. Though his figures are for both natives and immigrants—and thus probably overstate life expectancies for immigrants alone—Massachusetts seems representative of the locations in which immigrants were found by 1850: it had a large and growing urban center which received many immigrants, a number of smaller industrializing cities, and a sizable rural population.

34. Knights, "Age Reporting."

35. Steckel, "Quality of Census Data," Table 1.

earlier, the lists appear to have been constructed at the port of embarkation, so Irish and English immigrants were recorded by English-speaking clerks, and Germans were recorded by German clerks (or French clerks, in the case of those sailing from Le Havre).

In the census, two difficulties arise: immigrants having difficulty communicating with the census marshals early in their time in the United States, and immigrants having "Americanized" their names later in their time in the United States. Steckel reports that immigrants present in 1860 and known to have been present as well in 1850 were 20 to 45 percent less likely than natives to be successfully linked to the 1850 census.[36] Since Steckel was tracing individuals backward, these losses cannot be due to return migration or mortality. His individuals must have been present in 1850, but since they were closer then to their time of arrival, the chances that they had not yet changed their name or had difficulty communicating with the census marshals were greater. If we assume that the 9 to 19 percent underenumeration rate described recently applies to natives and use Steckel's rate of additional misenumeration for immigrants, then the underenumeration rate for immigrants was between 17 and 34 percent.

Even if an individual was accurately recorded in the ship lists and census, he would not be successfully linked if he did not also appear accurately in the census index. A study of the accuracy of the index to the 1850 census was conducted by the Genealogical Library of the Church of Jesus Christ of Latter-Day Saints in 1982. By comparing the actual census manuscripts for a sample of counties with the indexes, it was possible to determine how many individuals did not appear in the indexes. Some were missed in the index because of simple transcription errors, but other sources of loss were more serious. The most glaring of these—omissions from the index—were found to amount to between 11 and 19 percent.[37]

In order to assess the accuracy of the 1860 indexes, I undertook a study using the same procedure: drawing samples of 100 individuals from each of eight places, chosen to represent a cross section of the places in which significant numbers of immigrants were located in 1860.[38] Of the 800 individuals in the sample, only 12 (1.5 percent) either were omitted outright from the index or had their names so garbled as to prevent a match.[39] It thus seems safe to conclude that inaccuracies in the census index might represent a significant source of loss between arrival and 1850, but the 1860 index was considerably more accurate.

Finally, those with common names could not be pursued. As Table 2-3 indicates, of those who had at least one match in the 1850 census index, 53 percent

36. Steckel, "Census Matching," Table 3.
37. Flick, "Reliability of Census Indexes."
38. The places chosen were five rural counties (Adams and La Salle in Illinois, Wyoming in New York, and Huntingdon and Sullivan in Pennsylvania) and three cities (St. Louis, Albany, and Hartford).
39. For example, one individual whose name was "Lapham" in the census was recorded as "Lathrop" in the index. It was possible to locate such individuals for this exercise since I was able to obtain the 1860 index in machine-readable form. Thus, it was possible to locate all the individuals in the index who were drawn from the page in the manuscripts where an individual was located, and determine which of those individuals was closest to the individual drawn from the manuscripts.

had more than three matches and were thus not linked. The combination of these factors could account for almost all of the observed rate of success in linkage. If we assume an error rate of 5 percent in the ship lists, a return migration rate of 5 percent, a 21.5 percent mortality rate, a census underenumeration rate for immigrants of 17 to 34 percent, an 11 percent rate of age misreporting in the census, an error rate for the index between 11 and 19 percent, and the exclusion of 53 percent of the sample because of the commonness of their names, the expected linkage rate is between 15 and 22 percent. More liberal allowance for immigrant mortality alone would bring these figures very close to the actual 10.6 percent linkage rate obtained.

The linked sample itself provides a means of checking the reasonableness of two of these estimates of factors preventing linkage to the census. Of the 1,647 immigrants located in the 1860 manuscript schedules, only 508 (31 percent) were successfully located in 1850 as well. Since all 1,647 immigrants were present in the United States in 1850 as well, this means that 69 percent of the immigrants located in 1860 must have escaped enumeration in the 1850 census or the 1850 census index. How does this estimate compare with rates of underenumeration for the census and index discussed above? The combined effect of the high estimates for immigrant 1850 census underenumeration and 1850 index underenumeration is a total underenumeration rate from these two sources of 46.5 percent.[40]

The ship list characteristics of immigrants located in the census manuscripts are compared in Table 2-4 with the ship list characteristics of those who were not located. Several differences are immediately apparent. Immigrants linked only to 1850 are slightly older, more likely to be married and have children, have slightly larger families, and arrived in the United States earlier than those not linked. Immigrants linked only to 1860 had lower levels of these characteristics than those not linked. Immigrants who were linked at all were more likely to be skilled and less likely to be unskilled than those who were not linked at all. The linked and not linked groups contained roughly the same fraction of white collar workers and farmers.

It is difficult to say how important any one of these factors is by itself in determining whether an individual was successfully linked to the census. To explore this issue further, a regression analysis was performed. The results suggested that only age and time since arrival had a statistically or substantively significant positive impact on the probability of being linked. When the sample was confined to those for whom occupations were found in the ship lists, this effect of age and time since arrival turns out to have been more the result of occupation: those in com-

---

40. This is calculated as the product of the 66 percent census enumeration rate (one minus the underenumeration rate) derived from Steckel, "Census Matching," and the 81 percent census index enumeration rate (one minus the underenumeration rate) estimated by Flick, "Reliability of Census Indexes." One minus this product is the estimated rate of combined underenumeration in the census itself and in the census index. Note that problems such as mortality and the commonness of names could not account for the failure to have located in 1850 those immigrants successfully located in 1860. These immigrants must have been alive in 1850, and their names must have been less than common, since they were located in 1860.

Table 2-4. Characteristics of immigrant arrivals at New York, 1840–50, by linkage to 1850 and 1860 manuscript census schedules.

Characteristic	Not Linked	Linkage		
		1850 only	1860 only	1850 & 1860
Age	26.8	27.7	23.3	25.4
Years in U.S.	5.0	5.7	4.9	5.3
Occupation (%)				
White collar	12.6	14.6	10.1	12.9
Skilled	17.6	25.2	20.5	24.6
Farmer	26.4	27.6	26.8	22.8
Unskilled	42.9	32.2	41.8	39.4
None given	0.2	0.0	4.4	0.0
Family structure				
Alone (%)	74.0	66.9	83.2	75.0
Accompanied (%)	26.0	33.1	16.8	25.0
Married (%)	20.2	28.3	13.0	19.3
W/children (%)	20.2	25.6	11.7	16.7
No. of children	2.2	2.3	1.3	1.8
Origin (%)				
Ireland	28.5	25.2	30.5	30.7
Britain	37.9	41.8	29.6	40.2
Germany	28.7	29.0	35.7	27.2
Other	4.9	4.0	4.3	2.0
Embarkation port (%)				
Liverpool	53.1	52.0	47.4	58.3
Bremen	18.1	17.5	23.0	18.5
Le Havre	9.9	9.7	10.4	6.7
Other	18.8	20.7	19.2	16.5
No. of obs.	21,204	948	1,139	508
Percent (%)	89.1	4.0	4.8	2.1

Source. Sample of male household heads and unaccompanied males in passenger ship arrival records at port of New York, 1840–1850.

Note: All characteristics are as reported in the passenger ship lists, except "Years in U.S." which is measured in 1850. The distribution of occupations does not include Germans from the Bremen sample (see text). Occupational categories are described in Appendix E.

mercial, skilled, farming, and mining occupations in the ship lists were more likely to have been located than those who were unskilled workers.[41]

The only important respect in which the sample of those who were linked to at least one census differs from those who were not linked at all, then, is the pres-

41. Though there was a statistically significant effect from arriving as a farmer, its substantive impact was negligible, amounting to a difference of only 1.5 percentage points in the probability of being linked. The probability that the true coefficient on those in professional occupations was zero was less than 10 percent as was the probability for the coefficient on "commercial."

ence of higher percentages of commercial workers, skilled workers, and miners among the linked group. In the subsequent analysis, the fact that the sample is selected for those who stayed must be kept in mind. If the return migrants were different from those who stayed in respects related to the characteristics being examined, then our conclusions will apply only to immigrants who came to the United States and stayed.

A final issue regarding the linked sample is the characteristics of its three components: those linked only to 1850, only to 1860, and to both 1850 and 1860. The census characteristics of these three groups are shown in Table 2-4. The main differences among the groups seem to be average age and family structure. For example, the "1850 only" group is three years older on average in 1850 than the "1850 & 1860" group. The "1860 only" group is two years younger on average in 1860 than the "1850 & 1860" group. The "1850 only" group is less likely to have a family present or be married, and has a lower average number of children than the "1850 & 1860" group. Again, the reverse is true for the comparison between the "1860 only" group and the "1850 & 1860" group.

One possible source of the difference between the "1850 only" and the "1850 & 1860" groups is mortality: those who survived between 1850 and 1860 would have been younger on average in 1850 than those who did not. The differences in family structure might merely reflect this age difference. For the difference between the "1860 only" and "1850 & 1860" groups, the difference might result from the fact that younger, less attached, more footloose immigrants were less likely to be enumerated by the census. Thus, those enumerated twice, given that they had survived to 1860, would have been older on average than those who were enumerated only once and had survived to 1860.

To assess the extent to which the characteristics of immigrants differed by whether they were linked only to 1850, only to 1860, or to both 1850 and 1860, regressions were estimated in which the dependent variable was whether an immigrant had been linked twice. The only variables that consistently showed up as either substantively or statistically significant were age and family structure, which behaved as expected: older immigrants with families were less likely to show up in both 1850 and 1860 than only in 1850, while they were more likely to show up in 1850 and 1860 than only in 1860. None of the other variables that will be the objects of study in the following chapters—location, occupation, or wealth—was related to whether an immigrant was linked twice or only once.

A Linked Sample of Natives and Immigrants

Previous studies using individuals linked across the 1850s have used samples of individuals drawn from the 1860 census and sought in the 1850 census. This is because until recently the 1850 census was the only antebellum federal census that met two important criteria: it contained information on place of birth (which would be essential for successful matching) and it had been indexed. The indexes were created at the state level, however, and had not yet been collated into a national index.[42] This dictated the sampling strategy used in these studies: since it was necessary to trace individuals *into* the 1850 census (since it was indexed) and since the nearest census with information on place of birth was 1860 (such information was not included in 1840), individuals had to be traced backward from 1860 to 1850 rather than forward. Since the appropriate state index had to be chosen out of the collection of more than thirty indexes, the structure of an individual's family in 1860 was used to point to the most likely state index to search. This limited the base (1860) population to families with at least one child who was 10 years or older in 1860.

The new 1860 federal census index, however, is national in scope. This means that if a base population is chosen from the 1850 census, that population can be traced forward to 1860 without the need to focus on particular states or the need to limit the base sample to families with children of particular ages. Instead, all individuals who could have set up independent households by 1860 could enter the 1850 base population.[43] For this study, the the 1850 sample from the new Public Use Microdata Series (PUMS) of federal census of population samples was used. The 1850 sample—a nationally representative sample of 153,188 individuals in 27,095 families—was used as the base population.[44] The only restrictions placed on the individuals sought in 1860 were that they had to be males who were 10 years or older in 1850. Females were not sought, as the likelihood that they would change their name upon marriage was great, and younger individuals were unlikely to have left their parents' home by 1860. This resulted in a population of 55,055 males to be located in 1860.[45] The characteristics of these individuals are shown in the first column of Table 2-5.

The next step in the creation of the sample was locating these individuals in the 1860 census index.[46] The index includes the name and location in the manuscript pages of each household head and each individual living in a household whose name was different from that of the household head. Since no individual characteristic other than surname and given name were provided, it was necessary to locate an individual in the 1860 manuscripts and compare his age and birthplace with the corresponding characteristics of the individual from the 1850 PUMS being sought in order to determine whether the right person had been located. For individuals with common combinations of surname and given name, this meant that several hundred reels of microfilm might have to be searched to verify a single match.[47] To overcome this difficulty, only those individuals whose

42. Jackson, "Index to the Seventh Census."

43. The 1860 index contains the location in the census of every household head and every individual living in a household whose surname was different from that of the head. Thus, any individual observed in 1850 and sought in 1860 could be found if the individual had either set up a separate household or moved into the household of someone with a different surname.

44. This sample was created by the Social Science Research Laboratory in the University of Minnesota Department of History. The final sample is about 30 percent larger than the preliminary sample used here. The preliminary sample used here, though, is also nationally representative.

45. The sample is described in greater detail in Ferrie, "New Sample."

46. Jackson, "Index to the Eighth Census."

47. To account for minor variations in the spelling of surnames between 1850 and 1860 (as well

Table 2-5. Characteristics of males 10 years and older in 1850 Public Use Microdata Series, by commonness of name and linkage to 1860 manuscript census schedules.

Characteristic	All Obs.	Common Names	Uncommon Names	
			Not Linked	Linked
Age	29.7	29.8	29.8	28.9
Birthplace (%)				
U.S.	81.5	81.0	81.6	84.0
Foreign	15.3	15.8	15.1	12.9
America	1.1	0.9	1.4	0.6
Europe	14.2	14.9	13.7	12.3
Britain	2.8	3.3	2.3	1.7
Ireland	6.2	7.5	4.3	5.8
Germany	4.3	3.5	5.5	4.1
Other	0.9	0.6	1.6	0.7
Unknown	3.3	3.2	3.5	3.1
Family size	2.7	2.7	2.6	2.8
Married (%)	37.7	38.0	35.9	43.3
Literate (%)	94.3	94.1	94.2	95.9
Occupation (%)				
White collar	7.2	6.4	8.3	7.1
Skilled	12.1	12.1	11.9	13.0
Farmer	32.6	32.6	31.8	36.6
Unskilled	20.7	21.0	20.3	21.1
None given	27.3	27.8	27.7	22.2
Region (%)				
New England	14.3	14.5	12.9	18.8
Middle Atlantic	30.0	30.1	28.1	37.2
Midwest	25.8	26.4	25.9	22.3
Southeast	14.7	14.7	15.1	12.9
South Central	13.7	13.1	15.7	8.1
Far West	1.5	1.1	2.4	0.6
Size of Location (%)				
Under 2,500	79.4	79.4	79.1	80.8
2,500 and over	20.6	20.6	20.9	19.2
2,500-9,999	7.1	7.0	6.9	8.6
10,000-49,999	5.9	6.3	5.6	5.2
50,000-99,999	2.1	1.9	2.5	1.5
100,000 & over	5.5	5.4	5.8	3.9
Migrant	28.2	28.3	29.8	21.1
Real Estate ($)	641.33	633.95	636.36	708.91
No. of obs.	55,055	19,812	30,305	4,938

Source: Males 10 years and older in 1850 Public Use Microdata Series (Ruggles et al., 1995).

Note: All characteristics are as reported in 1850. "Common" names are those that appeared more than ten times in the 1860 census index. Occupational categories are described in Appendix E. "New England" is Connecticut, New Hampshire, Maine, Massachusetts, Rhode Island, and Vermont; "Middle Atlantic" is New Jersey, New York, and Pennsylvania; "Midwest" is Illinois, Indiana, Iowa, Kansas, Michigan, Missouri, Minnesota, Nebraska, Ohio, and Wisconsin; "Southeast" is Alabama, Delaware, Florida, Georgia, Kentucky, Tennessee, Maryland, Mississippi, North Carolina, South Carolina, and Virginia; "South Central" is Arkansas, Louisiana, and Texas; "Far West" is Arizona, California, Colorado, New Mexico, Oregon, Utah, and Washington. "Migrant" is an individual living in a state different from his reported state of birth.

combinations of surname and given name appeared fewer than ten times in the 1860 census index were sought in the 1860 manuscript census schedules.[48]

To assess the possible bias introduced in this sample by the exclusion of those with common names, I estimated a logistic regression in which an indicator of whether the individual had a common name (more than ten appearances in the 1860 census index) was the dependent variable and the individual's 1850 characteristics were independent variables. The results showed that there were some statistically significant relationships between an individual's characteristics and the probability that he had a common name. The sizes of the marginal effects, however, were generally quite small relative to the predicted mean probability. For example, though the coefficients on linear and quadratic age terms were both statistically significant at the 99 percent level, the impact of age on the predicted probability was small: the probability declined from 39 percent at age 20 to 37 percent at age 45, and then rose to 39 percent at age 75. The range of 2 percentage points represents just 5 percent of the total predicted probability. The same is true for the other continuous variables: family size and real estate wealth.[49]

Among the categorical variables used, only residence in the West (15 percentage points, or 41 percent, less likely to have a common name) had a substantial impact. None of the other categorical variables had an impact greater than 2.8 percentage points or 7.5 percent of the predicted probability. The effect of residence in the West is puzzling, but since only 1.5 percent of those in the 1850 PUMS were living in the West, the overall impact on the representativeness of the sample of those with uncommon names must be slight.

After eliminating 36 percent of the 1850 PUMS from further consideration because of common names, the remaining 35,243 individuals were sought in 1860.

---

as transcription errors in the creation of the 1850 PUMS and the 1860 census index), the actual surnames and given names were not used when individuals were sought in the 1860 index. Instead, surnames were coded according to the NYSIIS indexing system; Lynch and Arends, "Selection of a Surname Coding Scheme." This is similar to the Soundex system in that names are coded identically if they sound roughly the same. The NYSIIS system is thought to be slightly better than the Soundex system at coding foreign-sounding names. Using the NYSIIS system, the surnames "ABBOTT," "ABBOT," "ABOT," and "ABOTT" would all be assigned the same code: "ABAT." Given names were truncated after four letters to account for spelling variations. For example, "Charles," "Charlie," and "Charley" were coded identically. Names from both the 1850 PUMS and the 1860 index were coded in this way before both lists were sorted by NYSIIS code and truncated given name. It was at this point that individuals were sought in the 1860 index.

48. An exception was made for individuals whose combination of surname and given name appeared more than once in the base population (the 1850 PUMS): these individuals were sought if there were ten or fewer matches per individual. Thus, if a particular surname/given name appeared three times, those three individuals were sought if there were thirty or fewer matches in the index for that surname/given name combination. This exception was made because 5 percent of the individuals in the 1850 PUMS had the same combinations of NYSIIS code and truncated given name.

49. Someone with ten family members was 2.4 percentage points more likely to have a common name than someone with only two family members, a difference of 8 percent. Though the coefficient on real wealth was statistically insignificant, someone with $10,000 of real estate wealth in 1850 was 0.01 percentage point more likely to have a common name than someone with $100 in real estate in 1850, a difference of 0.03 percent.

Of these individuals, 20,793 (59 percent) had no potential matches in the 1860 census index and could not be pursued further. The remaining 14,450 individuals were sought in the 1860 manuscript schedules. These individuals generated roughly 94,000 potential matches. These searches resulted in 4,938 successful matches.

Since only 14 percent of those with uncommon names were successfully matched, it is necessary to ask how we can account for the apparently large number of individuals who were not matched and in what ways, if any, they differ from the matched population. The potential sources of linkage failure fall into two categories: mortality and problems in the 1850 census, the 1850 PUMS, the 1860 census, or the 1860 census index.

The new life tables in Appendix C were applied to the distribution of ages, regions, urban/rural locations, and nativities for the 50,055 males in the 1850 PUMS at risk to be linked to the 1860 census. The results suggest that survival rates in the 1850s may have been as low as 76 percent (for immigrants in urban places) and as high as 89 percent (for the native-born in the rural Northwest). The overall survival rate was 85 percent.

Given that an individual survived to 1860, his chances of being successfully linked depended next on the accurate transcription of the three characteristics used to verify matches in each of three sources: the 1850 manuscripts, the 1850 PUMS, and the 1860 manuscripts. If a name, age, or birthplace was misreported in any of these three sources, the probability of linkage would be reduced by an amount corresponding to the severity of the error. The linkage procedure was designed to mitigate the impact of some of these sources of error. NYSIIS coding of surnames and the use of only the first four letters of the given names should reduce the linkage failures from inaccurate name reporting and transcription. To reduce the failure rate attributable to inaccurate age information, a tolerance of 10 years was used in comparing the expected age in 1860 of an individual from the 1850 PUMS with the age of a potential match in the 1860 manuscripts (i.e., an absolute difference between expected and actual ages of 10 or fewer years was acceptable for a match along this dimension). Some leeway was allowed as well in the comparison of birthplaces, particularly for immigrants who may have reported a very specific birthplace in one source ("County Mayo, Ireland"), but only a very broad description in another ("U.K.").

These procedures, however, cannot account for more serious errors. Individuals who were omitted entirely from the 1860 census, for example, could never be linked. As in the linkage from the ship lists described earlier, linkage failure could result from underenumeration in the census, or misreporting of age or birthplace. It seems reasonable as a first approximation to use 85 percent as the enumeration rate for the 1860 census and 95 percent as the rate of accurate reporting for name, age, or birthplace in each of the three sources.[50]

The next source of linkage failure is the 1860 census index. My previous cal-

---

50. For simplicity, I will assume that these sources of error are independent, so that the probability that an individual's three characteristics were accurately reported in all three sources is $(0.95)^3 = 0.63$.

culations suggest that the accuracy rate was 95 percent for household heads. But not all the individuals from the 1850 PUMS who were sought in the 1860 census were household heads and therefore eligible to appear in the census index in 1860. Since we are seeking individuals who were as young as 10 years of age in 1850, and may not have set up independent households by 1860, and also some who were old enough to have retired and perhaps moved into the homes of siblings or children by 1860, perhaps only 95 percent of those who survived to 1860 and had their characteristics successfully recorded would have appeared in the census index.

A final source of linkage failure is inconclusivity. Some of these multiple potential matches might represent multiple enumerations of the same individual. Other individuals shared the same three characteristics—name, age, and birthplace—with at least one other individual in 1860. Perhaps only 95 percent of the cases that get to the point where characteristics in 1850 and 1860 can be compared actually result in a conclusive match.

The cumulative effect of these sources of linkage failure on the overall linkage rate can be calculated for a range of values for these sources of linkage failure. Two scenarios were calculated: an optimistic scenario using the somewhat conservative assumptions regarding the magnitude of the errors at each stage (which projects a linkage rate of 29 percent) and a pessimistic scenario which uses more liberal assumptions regarding the errors and reduces the accuracy rates at each stage by 5 percentage points (and projects a linkage rate of 12.7 percent).

Although it is possible that the sources of linkage failure described here are uncorrelated with an individual's characteristics, other studies suggest that some groups (immigrants, the unskilled, the poor, illiterates) were less likely to be enumerated at all or enumerated accurately.[51] One way to see whether individual characteristics are in fact associated with successful linkage is to compare the 1850 characteristics of those who were linked and those who were not linked. Table 2-5 shows these comparisons for the full 1850 PUMS (column 1) and the group that was linked to 1860 (column 4).

A regression was estimated to assess the separate impact of these factors. As expected, the probability of a successful link rose slightly with age in 1850 through age 27 and then declined. This probably reflects individuals setting up independent households between ages 20 and 27, and a combination of mortality and perhaps individuals moving into other households at older ages. Occupation had a clear impact on linkage, but the patterns were not what we would expect on the basis of the greater likelihood of linkage among more skilled workers. In fact, linkage was 2 percentage points (25 percent) less likely for white collar and skilled workers than for unskilled workers. As we shall see later, though, white collar and skilled workers were in many cases the most geographically mobile members of the labor force. Their low linkage rates may be the result of their low persistence rates. Conversely, farmers were considerably more likely to be located than unskilled workers, which may reflect their greater rates of geographic persistence.

---

51. The probability of survival clearly decreased with age, and the probability of appearing in the census index increased until middle age and then may have decreased.

The impact of 1850 region of residence on the probability of a successful match reflects two effects: the difficulty of enumerating individuals in frontier regions, and the high rates of geographic mobility among those in the West. The probability of successful linkage was not related to nativity, family size, marital status, literacy, urban residence, or real estate wealth.

Another way to assess the success of the linkage procedure is to compare the characteristics of those in the linked sample with other samples. Two samples to which the present one may be compared are the sample of males age 20 and over collected by Soltow, and the linked sample created by Steckel.[52] The average age in the 1850–60 Linked PUMS is identical to that in Soltow's sample and six years younger than in Steckel's sample. These age patterns are reflected in wealth-holding patterns in the three samples. The mean value of real estate in 1850 is slightly lower in the 1850–60 Linked PUMS, and slightly less wealth is held at the highest percentile than in Soltow's sample (though the fraction held by the wealthiest 30 percent is identical in the two samples). With more young men than Steckel's sample, the Linked PUMS and Soltow's sample display somewhat greater overall inequality (as indicated by the Gini coefficient) than Steckel's sample.

Mean wealth levels were again similar in the Linked PUMS and Soltow's sample in 1860; both were less than half as great as the levels in Steckel's sample. Soltow's sample had a less equal real estate wealth distribution than the 1850–60 Linked PUMS, which in turn had a less equal distribution than Steckel's sample. In total wealth, Steckel's sample again displayed less inequality, but the 1850–60 Linked PUMS and Soltow's sample had virtually the same degree of inequality.

Since Soltow's sample was a random sample of males age 20 and over, while Steckel's sample was composed of men who had married and begun a family by 1850, these comparisons are not surprising. They indicate that, in terms of age, real estate wealth, and total wealth, the 1850-60 Linked PUMS looks quite similar to a random sample of the nation's adult males. Despite the numerous steps in the linkage process, the biases seem to have canceled each other out overall, resulting in a sample that provides our best view yet of the economic mobility of average Americans over the 1850s.

52. Soltow, *Men and Wealth*; Steckel, "Census Matching."

3

The Context of
Antebellum Immigration

The two decades before the Civil War witnessed the first great wave of European immigration to the United States. As Figure 3-1 shows, from 1820 (the first year for which reliable data are available) through the mid-1840s, the annual volume of immigration remained well below 100,000, which translates into an immigration rate that remained between four and five per thousand.[1] The volume of immigration rose dramatically in 1847, in the wake of the failure of the potato crop in Ireland in 1846 and on the European continent in the following two years and Continental political turmoil in 1848. In 1850 alone, nearly 370,000 immigrants arrived in the United States, pushing the immigration rate above 15 per thousand for the first and only time in the nation's history. Three countries (Great Britain, Ireland, and Germany) accounted for 93 percent of all arriving immigrants in 1849. The rate of immigration seen in the mid-1850s has yet to be surpassed in U.S. history.

The United States that antebellum immigrants entered was still primarily rural. Of the free male native-born population age 20 to 65 in 1850, 83 percent lived in places of fewer than 2,500 persons, whereas only 9 percent lived in cities of more than 10,000 persons.[2] Immigrants were far more concentrated in cities than the native-born: more than 36 percent were living in places of more than 10,000 persons in 1850, while only 54 percent lived in rural locations (with populations below 2,500). In their choice of regions, immigrants were more concentrated in the Middle Atlantic states (43 percent) than natives (27 percent), and

1. U.S. Census Bureau, *Historical Statistics* and *Statistical Abstract*, series C 89 and A 6.
2. These figures and the figures in the following paragraph were calculated from the Public Use Microdata Series (PUMS) of the 1850 federal census of population; Ruggles et al., *IPUMS-95*.

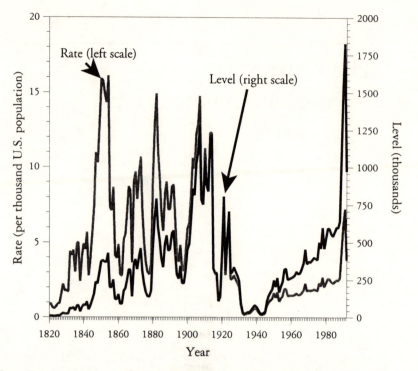

Figure 3-1. Immigration to the United States (rates and levels), 1820–1992. *Source:* U.S. Census Bureau, *Historical Statistics*, series C 89, A 6; U.S. Census Bureau, *Statistical Abstract.*

were only half as likely as natives to reside in the South. Half of the nation's immigrant population in 1850 resided in just three states: New York (27 percent), Pennsylvania (14 percent), and Ohio (9 percent). These differences suggest that if immigrants' arrival had an impact on natives' economic circumstances, that impact was probably concentrated in a few places: urban places in the Northeast.

In terms of its occupational structure, the United States that antebellum immigrants entered was one in which economic activity was still largely oriented toward small-scale production on farms or in artisan's workshops: 51 percent of native-born males age 20 to 65 were farmers in 1850, and 17 percent were skilled workers. Only 22 percent were common laborers or servants, and 11 percent were in professional or commercial occupations. By contrast, in 1849, 28 percent of immigrants who reported occupations at arrival reported they were farmers, 23 percent reported they were skilled workers, 46 percent reported they were common laborers or servants, and 3 percent reported they were in professional or commercial occupations. These differences suggest that immigrants should have had the greatest impact on skilled workers and common laborers.

Before we can make sense of the economic performance of immigrants in the years before the Civil War, we need to know more about the secular and cyclical trends in the macroeconomic environment that they faced. How easy a time they had in advancing economically should reflect, at least in part, the level of unemployment and the pattern of wage growth. To some extent, we can control for macroeconomic conditions in the following chapters by comparing the performance of immigrants to natives. If the difference in performance between immigrants and natives changes over time, we might attribute that change to conditions peculiar to either immigrants or natives, as changes that had an equal bearing on both would not change the difference between their performances. By looking at the change over time or across arrival cohorts in the difference between immigrants and natives along some dimension, we will control for economy-wide effects that had an impact on both. This "difference-in-differences" approach has been adopted in numerous studies of immigrant performance.

In terms of the business cycle, 1860 was considerably worse than 1850. The late 1840s exhibited above trend GNP growth, following the California Gold Rush. By 1850, growth was 4.5 percent above trend.[3] The following years included one sharp downturn, the Panic of 1857, with a slight recovery in 1858–1859. By 1860, the economy had entered a long slide into the pre-Civil War recession: growth in GNP was 2.5 percent below trend in 1860. Real wages did not grow over the 1850s for manufacturing workers in large urban firms in the Middle Atlantic states.[4]

These cyclical and short-run fluctuations in wages and prices occurred during a long-run growth of manufacturing and a shift of economic activity, particularly agriculture, to the West. Output per worker in manufacturing grew 30 percent or more in each region during the 1850s, and the size of farms, as measured by capitalization, grew 70 percent or more outside the South.[5] Over the same decade, the nation's center of population moved a greater distance west than over any decade from 1790 to 1930: the center crossed the Ohio River, from central West Virginia to central Ohio.

These sectoral and regional shifts were accompanied by shifts in employment: the share of unskilled laborers in the work force grew 10 percent between 1850 and 1860 (from 30.4 percent to 33.3 percent), the share of farmers grew 3 percent (from 20.8 percent to 21.4 percent), and the share of skilled and white collar workers fell 7 percent (from 48.8 percent to 45.3 percent). These figures were calculated using the tabulations of occupations published in the 1850 and 1860 census volumes. The number of farmers was taken to be the same as the number of farms (to classify farm tenants as laborers), and the number of unskilled workers was obtained by adding "laborers," "farm laborers," and other workers in the "unskilled" category in Appendix E. The work force was taken to be the male population age 15 and over. The white collar and skilled category was calculated as the residual after subtracting farmers and unskilled workers from the total work force.

These trends suggest that urban workers in the Northeast (particularly in man-

3. Berry, *Production and Population.*
4. See Sokoloff and Villaflor, "Market for Manufacturing Workers."
5. See Bateman and Weiss, *Deplorable Scarcity*, p. 17.

ufacturing) faced difficult circumstances throughout the decade. White collar workers (clerks) fared worse than artisans and unskilled workers throughout the country, and white collar and skilled workers represented a shrinking share of the total labor force. The growth of the West represented opportunity for many, particularly those with the financial resources to enter agriculture—a growing source of employment despite industrialization and the sector probably least affected by the price rises of the mid-1850s. Finally, the ranks of the unskilled were growing throughout the decade, so movement out of this group into white collar and skilled jobs or farm ownership was probably becoming more difficult, particularly in the Northeast.

Unfortunately, the period between 1840 and 1860 may be the time in U.S. labor history when the difference-in-differences approach is least applicable. New evidence on wages, prices, mortality, and stature suggest that native-born workers, particularly those in skilled occupations in the urban Northeast, suffered a "Hidden Depression" from 1843 to 1857.[6] The distress suffered by native workers in this period was the result of three forces: a downturn in railroad construction, rising prices for food and housing in eastern cities, and intense competition in the labor market from new immigrant arrivals. Immigrants, too, suffered from the drop in demand for unskilled railroad workers and the rising cost of necessities in places like New York and Philadelphia. But structural changes in the economy may have enhanced their ability to compete with native-born workers. These developments are taken up in greater detail in chapter 8.

---

6. Fogel, *Without Consent or Contract*, pp. 354–362, summarizes much of this evidence.

4

The Geographic Mobility of Immigrants after Their Arrival at New York

> Our boxes were unloaded, and now we stood beside them on the pier not knowing where to go.[1]

The immigrant who wrote these words in his diary in 1854 after the journey to America expressed the misgivings most immigrants must have felt at some point in their travels. But this immigrant and his family were not standing on the docks of lower Manhattan when he began to have his doubts. Instead, they were on the shores of Lake Michigan, having just been deposited by steamer at Milwaukee. Though he was unsure of what his next step would be, he had planned all along to travel to Wisconsin. He and his family arrived at New York, but left the same afternoon, bound immediately for the interior where they had heard opportunity lay.

Although much progress has been made over the last fifty years in measuring the geographic mobility of nineteenth-century Americans, we still know little of the paths followed by people like the immigrant described above in moving from one location to another. Both the earliest studies of geographic mobility by Malin, Curti, and Bogue that focused on the farming frontier, and more recent work on urban places in both the East and the West by Thernstrom, Katz, Griffen and Griffen, and Galenson, have focused on the experience of individuals located in documentary sources in the same location over several years.[2] These studies have calculated the fraction of the population observed in a place at one point in time that is still located in that place after a period of time, usually a decade (the decadal persistence rate), and examined the characteristics associated with the

1. Quoted in Lucas, "Journey of An Immigrant Family," p. 221.
2. Malin, "Turnover of Farm Population"; Curti, *Making of An American Community*; Bogue, *Prairie to Cornbelt*; Thernstrom, *Poverty and Progress* and *Other Bostonians*; Katz, *People of Hamilton West*; Griffen and Griffen, *Natives and Newcomers*; Galenson, "Economic Opportunity."

probability that individuals would remain in the same community. The experience of individuals who changed locations has been inferred from their appearance in and disappearance from these sources.

What none of the studies of mobility for either immigrants or the native born tells us, however, is how an individual who was located in someplace like 1850 Chicago got there, why they chose that location, why they left or stayed over the next decade, and how those who left fared compared with those who stayed. To provide some tentative answers to these questions, this chapter focuses on a group that was likely to have been the most mobile of nineteenth-century Americans: recently arrived European immigrants. It is possible to answer a number of questions regarding the geographic mobility of immigrants in the twenty years after their arrival. How long did they remain in New York? Why did some decide to stop and stay there, while others left quickly and headed for the interior? Where had they moved by 1850, and how quickly did they get there? How many stayed at the locations in the interior where they were located in 1850? How did they do there in terms of occupational mobility and wealth accumulation? In answering these questions, this study is the first to explore the experiences of individuals in a variety of locations who relocated over the course of a decade.[3]

New York City

New York was for John Reemus—the Dutch immigrant quoted earlier—as it was for most of the immigrants in the sample a place to change boats or catch a train to the interior, rather than a goal in itself, however temporary. But a small group of immigrants in the sample did remain in New York for a time after their arrival. Since the entire sample at least passed through New York, the logical place to begin in considering settlement patterns is with these immigrants who chose to settle—at least initially—in the first place they reached in the United States.

Table 4-1 shows the straight-line distance from New York City to where immigrants who arrived at New York between 1840 and 1850 were located in 1850. Of the 1,456 immigrants in the sample who were located in 1850, 13.6 percent were located in New York City; of the 1,647 who were located in 1860, only 10.7 percent were still located by then in New York.[4] Another 3.2 percent lived within 25 miles of New York in both 1850 and 1860. The British were only half as likely as the Irish or Germans to be found in New York City in either 1850 or 1860. More than 21 percent of Irish immigrants and 16 percent of German immigrants lived in 1850 within 25 miles of where they landed in America; by 1860, roughly 15 percent of both groups were living within 25 miles of New York. We will examine more closely those immigrants who moved past New York later in the chap-

---

3. Knights, *Yankee Destinies*, follows the careers of several thousand Boston residents who left Boston in the second half of the nineteenth century. Davenport, "Out-Migrants," does so for a rural county in upstate New York.

4. "New York City" includes New York County (Manhattan) and both Kings County (Brooklyn) and Queens County in the following discussion.

Table 4-1. Distance moved from New York City between arrival and 1850 among immigrant arrivals at New York, 1840–50.

Location	Total	Origin		
		British	Irish	German
In New York City (%)	13.6	7.2	17.7	14.5
Outside				
Under 25 miles (%)	3.2	3.2	4.1	2.0
25–49 miles (%)	1.6	0.9	3.4	0.5
50–99 miles (%)	9.2	8.8	11.9	6.8
100–249 miles (%)	25.6	28.7	35.1	11.6
250–499 miles (%)	16.4	17.6	10.6	22.2
500–999 miles (%)	27.3	31.7	14.4	38.5
1,000 miles+ (%)	3.0	1.8	2.8	3.9
Average distance	348.3	389.0	245.9	424.2
No. of obs.	1,456	442	536	441

Source: Male household heads and unaccompanied males in passenger ship arrival records at port of New York, 1840–1850, linked to 1850 manuscript census schedules.

Note: "In New York City" includes New York, Kings, and Queens counties.

ter. Here, we will consider why so many (particularly so many Irish and Germans) chose to stay there, and how long they took to move out.

New York offered a number of advantages to the immigrants whose ships docked at its piers. Perhaps the most important was a large labor market, with ready employment for the common laborer and the skilled artisan. At the same time, New York contained large concentrations of Irish (in the "Five Points" area of the Sixth Ward, where the population was 42 percent Irish in 1855) and Germans (in *Kleindeutschland*, an area of four wards on the Lower East Side which was more than 50 percent German in 1855).[5] The city offered both jobs and the company of one's countrymen.

The city presented a number of disadvantages to new arrivals as well. The continuous arrival of additional immigrants in response to the lure of jobs in the city assured that wages remained low in most of the occupations for which immigrants competed with their more recently arrived countrymen. At the same time, the countrymen who had preceded the immigrants often saw them as easy marks: New York was notorious in the antebellum period for the frauds perpetrated on immigrants by their own countrymen. The worst abuses in this respect were those of the boardinghouse "runners," who would accost immigrants on the docks in their native tongue, grab their luggage, and drag them to the boardinghouse offering the runner the highest bounty.[6] Contemporaries estimated that nearly a fifth of

5. See Ernst, *Immigrant Life*, pp. 39–42. An account of the development of *Kleindeutschland* is provided in Nadel, *Little Germany*.

6. See Kapp, *Immigration*, Chapter 4, for a description of these abuses, as well as the measures undertaken beginning in 1847 to mitigate them.

the money spent on transportation by immigrants after their arrival in the United States fell into the hands of the "runners."[7] It was not until 1855, with the opening of the immigrant landing depot at Castle Garden in lower Manhattan, that immigrants were shielded from all but officially sponsored agents.[8] Ellis Island was not opened as an arrival depot until 1892.

The general impression among those who watched the immigrant trade was that "the farther west one goes, the more this deviltry decreases."[9] Immigrant aid societies advised new arrivals to leave the city as soon as they were able, and often advanced them the funds to help them do so.[10] The guidebooks published in Europe to aid immigrants along every step of the way usually contained the admonition that "it will be best to hurry away from New York and on to the place of destination."[11] And letters sent back to Europe to advise potential immigrants urged them to flee New York "as you would the devil."[12] Most of the immigrants in the sample seem to have taken heed of this advice: in 1850, 86.4 percent of the arrivals over the preceding decade had already left New York; by 1860, this percentage had risen to 89.3 percent. Though this percentage fell among immigrants from all countries, it fell the most among the Irish: the percentage located in New York dropped from 17.7 percent in 1850 to 12.3 percent in 1860.

How many immigrants left the city immediately and went to the interior? How many left only after some time in the city? Figure 4-1 plots the percentage of immigrants at each time since arrival who were still located in New York in 1850. The first observation, those who had been in the United States less than a year, is problematic: though it is lower than many subsequent observations, this is probably the result of a selection problem. The most recently arrived immigrants may have been harder to locate and enumerate in New York City than elsewhere, so the percentage of recent arrivals located in New York is smaller than the percentage of earlier arrivals located in New York. Immigrants who were in the United States one year or less are excluded from the analysis in the balance of this section.

Apart from the first observation, a clear pattern emerges. About 65 percent of those who had just arrived were located outside New York. The percentage located outside New York rises by 4 percentage points for every year since arrival for the first five years immigrants are in the United States. After five years, the fraction of immigrants located outside New York still rises with greater duration in the United States, but the rise is much less rapid. As a result, 26.6 percent of those who arrived in the years 1846 to 1850 were still in the city in 1850, but only 14.6 percent of arrivals who had been in the United States more than five years were still in New York in 1850.[13]

7. Thompson, *Hints to Emigrants*, p. 93.
8. Ernst, *Immigrant Life*, pp. 31 and 231.
9. Ficker, "Friendly Adviser," p. 226.
10. Ernst, *Immigrant Life*, p. 62.
11. Ficker, "Friendly Adviser," p. 224.
12. Birch, "Editor and the English," p. 633.
13. These figures assume equal-sized arrival cohorts over the 1840s. They are calculated from a re-

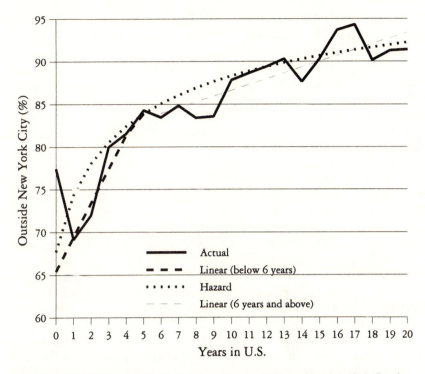

Figure 4-1. Percentage of 1840–50 arrivals at New York, located in New York City by years in the U.S. *Note:* See text for estimating procedure. *Source:* Male household heads and unaccompanied males in passenger ship arrival records at port of New York, 1840–1850, linked to 1850 and/or 1860 manuscript census schedules.

It is tempting to infer a time series pattern from this cross-sectional finding, saying that most immigrants who left the city after settling there initially left in the first five years after arrival, and only about half as many did so in the years after that. Before we can make such an inference, though, we must deal with two econometric issues. The first is the possibility that the observed cross-sectional pattern of departures from New York is produced by changes over the 1840s in the characteristics of subsequent cohorts of immigrants. If later arrivals are more likely to possess characteristics associated with persistence in New York, then Figure 4-1 is capturing the effect of changes in the propensity of successive cohorts of arrivals to settle in New York initially rather than the behavior of immigrants departing

gression in which the first observation from Figure 4-1 was excluded, and the percentage outside New York was modeled as a function of the number of years since arrival for a cohort. Years since arrival, a dummy variable for durations under five years, and an interaction between that dummy and the duration since arrival were used as regressors. The results show a clear break at five years. The increase in the percentage outside New York with increasing duration is both statistically and substantively significant at durations below five years; after that, the effect of duration is smaller in magnitude but also statistically significant.

from the city in the years after their arrival. This is an example of a more general problem: the inability to distinguish duration and cohort effects in a single cross section. In a single cross section, if earlier arrivals are more likely to have left New York at any time since arrival than more recent arrivals, we might mistakenly attribute the higher fraction outside New York among earlier arrivals to the fact that their duration in the United States is greater, when in fact the fraction of these immigrants living outside New York would be higher even if they were observed at the same duration in the United States as more recent arrivals.[14] This problem is discussed in greater detail in Appendix A.

In order to get around this problem, we will exploit the fact that some immigrants in the sample are observed in 1850, some are observed in 1860, and some are observed in both years. This will allow us to control for both duration in the United States and year of arrival. Each immigrant in the sample contributes one observation to the analysis. This means that a group of immigrants with the same year of arrival will contain some immigrants who have been in the United States t years and some who have been in the United States $t + 10$ years.[15] To determine the impact of duration in the United States on the probability of departing from New York, we estimate the parameters of the hazard function using dummy variables for year of arrival as the only covariates in the X vector and years since arrival in the United States for t.

An observation is considered to have moved out of New York only if any one of the following conditions is true: (1) the individual was observed only in 1850 and had moved out of New York by that date (so t is the time from arrival to 1850); (2) the individual was observed only in 1860 and had moved out of New York by that date (so t is the time from arrival to 1860); (3) the individual was observed in both 1850 and 1860 and had moved out of New York by 1850 (so t is again the time from arrival to 1850); or (4) the individual was observed in both 1850 and 1860, was still in New York in 1850, but had moved out by 1860 (so t is again the time from arrival to 1860). Individuals who were observed only in 1850 and were in New York in that year were considered not to have made a move, and the time from arrival to 1850 was used for t. Individuals who were observed only in 1860 and were still in New York in that year were considered not to have made a move, and the time from arrival to 1860 was used for t. Individuals who were observed in both 1850 and 1860 but were in New York in both years were considered not to have made a move, and the time from arrival to 1860 is used as the value for t.

The second difficulty is that while the sample tells us each immigrant's date of arrival and location in 1850 and 1860, we do not know the date at which moves out of New York occurred. We may know, for example, that an immigrant who arrived in 1840 had left New York by 1850, but we do not know when during the immigrant's ten years in the United States that transition occurred; all we know is how long the immigrant was at risk to make such a transition and whether it

14. See Heckman and Robb, "Using Longitudinal Data," for a discussion of these effects.
15. For example, if two immigrants arrived in 1845, and one had left New York by 1850 but the other did not leave until 1860, the sample would contain two 1845 arrivals, but the years since their arrival that would be used in the analysis would be 5 and 15, respectively.

occurred during that period. We also do not know the date at which immigrants who had not yet left New York by 1850 or 1860 would do so. These observations are right-censored.

A continuous-time duration model with discrete observations can address both of these problems. This method consists of estimating the following probability for each individual:

$$P_{jk}(t;X) = Prob[outside \ New \ York \ at \ time \ t \mid in \ New \ York \ at \ time \ 0;X] \quad (1)$$

The date of arrival is time 0 and the time since arrival is t; the vector X contains dummy variables for each year of arrival. Estimation of such a model will allow us to calculate the probability that an immigrant had left New York at various times after arrival, which in turn will allow us to infer a distribution and mean for the time between arrival and departure from New York. This technique compensates for the lack of information on each individual immigrant's date of departure from New York. Since the model utilizes information on both those who have left and those who have not by time t, it also surmounts the right-censoring problem.

To see how we can estimate this model, suppose that immediately after arrival, the immigrant is located in New York.[16] The immigrant can then either devote all his time to his job in New York or use some of his time to learn of opportunities outside New York. A maximization problem can be constructed in which the immigrant determines the intensity with which to seek information about other locations based on the costs and benefits of changing location. The result of this maximization will be a function $\theta(t;X)dt$ that describes the probability at each date since arrival in the United States that the immigrant will learn of an opportunity at a location outside New York in the interval $(t,t + dt)$. If $\gamma(t;X)$ represents the probability that such information is worth acting upon—that leaving New York would result in a higher present value of lifetime welfare—then the probability that the immigrant will leave New York in the interval $(t,t + dt)$ is $\lambda_{12}(t;X)dt = [\theta(t;X)][\gamma(t;X)]dt$, where the subscripts refer to the transition from location 1 (New York) to location 2 (outside New York). The function $\lambda_{12}(t;X)$ is known as the *hazard function*.

As Appendix B demonstrates, the hazard function for a sample of individuals is related to $P_{12}(t;X)$, the probability that the immigrant had left New York after t years in the United States, by the relationship

$$P_{12}(t;X) = 1 - \exp\left(\int_0^t -\lambda_{12}(u;X'\beta) \ du\right) \quad (2)$$

where β is a vector of parameters to be estimated. Appendix B derives the likelihood function that is used to estimate these parameters. We will assume that the

16. This motivation for the hazard model follows Lancaster, *Econometric Analysis*, p. 5.

hazard function follows either a *Weibull* distribution or a *log-logistic* distribution.[17] The line labeled "Hazard" in Figure 4-1 shows the results of this estimation procedure. It reveals the effect of time in the United States on the probability that an immigrant was located outside New York, controlling for the specific year in which each immigrant arrived. The pattern is similar to the pattern from the linear model with a structural break at five years, though the hazard model suggests a slightly higher percentage outside New York initially, and a more rapid rate of departure from New York in the first two years in the United States than the linear model. When the log- logistic hazard was used instead of the Weibull, the pattern was identical, suggesting that the results in Figure 4-1 are not due to the assumption of a monotonically increasing hazard function. The similarity of the hazard model results to those from the simple linear model demonstrates that the observed pattern of departures from New York results from immigrants actually moving out of New York as their time in the United States increased, rather than from changes over the 1840s in the propensities of successive cohorts of immigrants to spend any time in New York.

Before we turn to a consideration of how individual characteristics influenced the decision to move past New York, it is worth noting some differences by country of origin in the pattern of departure from New York. The hazard model was estimated separately for British, Irish, and German immigrants, with controls for the specific year of arrival included for each. The results are shown in Figure 4-2. The Germans were the least likely to remain in New York at arrival: 70 percent were located outside New York City within a very short time of arrival, as opposed to 65 percent of British immigrants and only 57 percent of Irish immigrants. But the British and Irish left New York more rapidly than the Germans. After twenty years in the United States, only 8 percent of Irish and German immigrants and 4 percent of British immigrants were still located in New York. When the coefficients for the specific years of arrival are examined, there are no clear patterns. It thus appears that there were no substantial, secular changes over the 1840s in immigrants' propensity to spend any time at all in New York.

Some of the differences in the percentage settling initially in New York and in the subsequent rate of departure from New York might reflect differences across origin groups in the possession of characteristics associated with the desire or ability to move immediately past New York. In order to adjust for changes in the mix of characteristics in the sample, we will also include each immigrant's personal characteristics as elements of the vector X. The sample contains information on a number of immigrant characteristics at arrival. How are these characteristics correlated with an immigrant's decision to remain in New York?

The prevailing wisdom among those offering advice to arriving immigrants was that those who were able to leave New York should do so. We expect, then, that immigrants who arrived with the means to proceed past New York would have

---

17. The formula for each function appears in Appendix B. The single-parameter Weibull and log-logistic functions are used rather than more complicated functions (such as the gamma function or a piece-wise linear hazard function) to make estimation of the hazard easier with the relatively small sample sizes employed here.

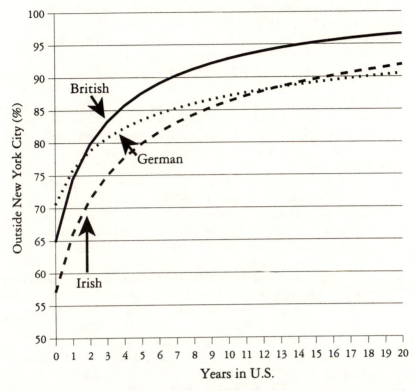

Figure 4-2. Percentage of 1840–50 arrivals at New York located in New York by years in the United States and origin. *Note:* See text for estimating procedures. *Source:* Male household heads and unaccompanied males in passenger ship arrival records at port of New York, 1840–1850, linked to 1850 and/or 1860 manuscript census schedules.

done so, absent a compelling reason to remain. The *Irish American*, reporting this tendency, said,

> The pith and marrow of Ireland, with money and value—averaging between 100 and 5,000 dollars each family—have arrived, within the past two years, in our seaboard cities. These emigrants do not stop in cities to spend their monies and fool away their time. They go directly into the interior to seek out the best locations as farmers, traders, and so forth. (August 26, 1849)

Although the sample contains no direct evidence of immigrants' wealth at arrival, a reasonable proxy might be whether an immigrant arrived with wife and family in tow, after controlling for age. The direct cost of transporting an entire family to the United States was greater than the cost of traveling alone (though not proportionately so, since children traveled at a reduced fare). The indirect cost of moving to the United States might have been higher as well for an entire family, since more mouths had to be fed until a permanent job had been found and a home established. Those traveling alone were either unmarried or unable to afford to move an entire family at once. It may also have been more costly for those with larger families to remain in New York because of higher food and housing costs.

An immigrant's occupation may have also played a role in determining whether he would remain in New York. Immigrants in commercial occupations, such as merchants and clerks, often arrived in New York with a letter of reference from their employer at home to the New York merchant with whom that employer did business.[18] Since most trade at this time was carried on through large port cities such as New York, instead of directly between European merchants and U.S. merchants in the interior states, most arriving merchants and clerks would have sought out employers in New York.

For other occupations, though, New York was clearly less desirable. Skilled workers could earn considerably more in the West than they could on the East Coast. The average daily wage of a carpenter (without board) in 1850 was below the national median of $1.40 in New York state, whereas interior states such as Illinois, Missouri, Iowa, Wisconsin, and Minnesota all offered wages considerably above the median.[19] At the same time, prices for food and rent were also higher in New York.[20] The market for labor in other skilled occupations was also glutted in New York. The *New York Tribune* reported a great oversupply of shoemakers in the city in 1845, for example (September 9, 1845). Unskilled workers were also victims of oversupply in the New York labor market, but the difference between what they could earn elsewhere and their depressed wages in New York was probably well below the difference experienced by skilled workers. In 1850, the wages of common day laborers in New York state were above the national median, while carpenters' wages were below the median. An immigrant who arrived as an unskilled worker should have been less likely to be located outside New York than an immigrant who arrived with a skill.

As Figure 4-2 shows, nationality may have played a role in the ability to leave New York. Large communities of both Irish and Germans were present in the city by the beginning of the 1840s. But the Germans were more prosperous and cohesive as a community. They formed a powerful mutual aid society, the German Society, which put immigrants in contact with employers in the interior and helped finance movement out of New York. The Irish Emigrant Society was considerably less effective.[21] The flight from famine in the late 1840s also probably left many Irish immigrants too impoverished or too ill-informed for travel past New York.

Table 4-2 presents the results of estimating equation (2) on the sample of immigrants who arrived between 1840 and 1849. Immigrants who were observed only in 1850 and arrived less than twelve months before the 1850 census are excluded from the analysis. The excluded categories are unmarried, British, illiterate, unskilled worker, and 1840. Many of the anticipated differences are apparent. Immigrants who were younger at arrival, employed previously in white collar jobs, literate, and

18. Ernst, *Immigrant Life*, p. 64.
19. U.S. Census Office, *Compendium of the Seventh Census*.
20. U.S. Senate, *Wholesale Prices*.
21. Ernst, *Immigrant Life*, pp. 64–65.

Table 4-2. Estimates of the parameters of the hazard function for leaving New York among immigrant arrivals at New York, 1840–50.

Variable	Mean	$\delta P_{12}/\delta X$	Probability
Age	24.141	0.006	0.018
Age^2 × 10^{-2}	6.691	−0.007	0.088
Married	0.241	0.032	0.151
Family size	1.673	0.003	0.656
Origin			
Irish	0.416	−0.102	0.001
German	0.298	−0.068	0.001
Other	0.026	−0.060	0.193
Literate	0.931	−0.051	0.079
Occupation			
White Collar	0.062	−0.073	0.017
Skilled	0.244	−0.001	0.937
Farmer	0.232	−0.016	0.428
Year of Arrival			
1841	0.082	0.018	0.580
1842	0.159	−0.010	0.723
1843	0.096	0.040	0.220
1844	0.098	0.031	0.329
1845	0.084	0.053	0.114
1846	0.039	0.026	0.522
1847	0.042	0.093	0.026
1848	0.106	0.036	0.265
1849	0.124	0.071	0.025
1850	0.068	0.090	0.011
ln(Years in U.S.)	2.320	0.096	0.001
$\bar{P}_{12}$		0.870	
Log-likelihood		−918.205	
No. of obs.		2,532	

Source: Male household heads and unaccompanied males in passenger ship arrival records at port of New York, 1840–1849, linked to 1850 and/or 1860 manuscript census schedules.

Notes. "$\delta P_{12}/\delta X$" is the impact of a one unit change in a variable on the probability that the individual was located outside New York, evaluated at the mean probability in the sample. It is calculated as $\delta P_{12}/\delta X = (\beta\alpha)(-\bar{P}_{11})(\log(\bar{P}_{11}))$, where β and α are estimates of the parameters from the Weibull hazard function (equation B8 in Appendix B) obtained by maximum likelihood,

$$\bar{P}_{11} = \sum_{i=1}^{N}[\exp(-\exp(X_i'\beta)t_i)^{\alpha}]/N$$

is the average probability in the sample that an individual was still located in New York, and $\bar{P}_{12} = 1 - \bar{P}_{11}$. For "ln(Years in the U.S.)" $\beta = 1$. "Probability" is the probability that the true $\delta P_{12}/\delta X$ is equal to zero. All characteristics are as reported in the passenger ship lists, except "Years in U.S." and "Literate" which are measured in 1850 or 1860 (see text). The omitted categories are "Unmarried," "British," "Illiterate," "Unskilled," and "1840 arrival."

Irish or German were considerably less likely to be found outside New York. For example, an immigrant who was able to read or write was 5 percentage points less likely to be found outside New York than one who was not. Both family size and marital status have the anticipated sign, though neither is statistically significant.

Evidence on the role of poverty in preventing immigrants from leaving New York is provided by a simple comparison of the 1850 real estate wealth of immigrants in and outside New York who had arrived in the 12 months before the 1850 census. Though this comparison does not control for other influences on wealth-holding such as age or occupation, the results are suggestive: 9 of the 115 immigrants located outside New York in 1850 owned real estate, while none of the 21 located in New York did so. The average wealth owned among those outside New York was $58.91.

To see whether the pattern in Figure 4-1 results from changes in sample characteristics over the 1840s, we can compare the patterns of departure from New York with and without controls for personal characteristics. The coefficient on "Log(Years in U.S.)" in the hazard estimate shown in Figure 4-1 is 0.085, whereas the corresponding estimate in Table 4-2 is 0.096. The predicted percentage located outside New York using the parameters in Table 4-2 is 60.0 at arrival and 87.9 at 10 years. Controlling for personal characteristics, then, leads to a slight increase in the overall rate of departure from New York and a somewhat lower rate of departure at arrival, suggesting that the pattern in Figure 4-1 reflects the arrival late in the 1840s of a disproportionate number of immigrants who were younger, less literate, and less likely to have experience in white collar jobs.

It is possible to compare the actual increase in the foreign-born population of New York between 1845 and 1850 with the total number of immigrant arrivals at New York over this period that these figures suggest would have remained in the city.[22] A total of 620,724 immigrants arrived at New York between the 1845 state census of New York and the 1850 federal census of New York. Using the pattern of departures based on the hazard model in Figure 4-1, the estimated number of these who would have still been located in New York by the 1850 census is 161,433. The actual foreign-born population increase for New York over the same period was 112,497. The estimate predicts 43 percent more immigrants would have remained in the city than actually did so. This difference could be accounted for by mortality—the estimates of the rate of departure from New York made above are based on immigrants having survived to be enumerated in 1850—and under-enumeration in the 1850 census. For example, Figure 4-1 suggests that the rate of census enumeration among immigrants in the United States less than one year is roughly 85 percent. If we assume that the survival rate among the 1845–50 arrivals was 80 percent and that 85 percent of immigrants who arrived in the 12 months before 1850 were enumerated in the 1850 federal census, the predicted increase in New York's immigrant population between 1845 and 1850 falls to 125,004, an overestimate of 11 percent.

22. It is necessary to use 1845 rather than 1840 since the 1840 federal census of population did not collect information on country of origin. The 1845 figure is drawn from the 1845 New York state census.

Another check on the estimates of the rate of departure from New York is provided by New York's City Inspector. Of the 105,162 immigrant arrivals in 1860, half stated that they planned to settle in New York. The inspector later estimated, though, "that only 15,000, or about 14 per cent, chose to stay in the Empire City."[23] This is the same as the proportion of all 1840–50 arrivals in the sample still located in New York City in 1850 (Table 4-1).

A final question regarding immigrants who located in New York is what became of those who settled there initially? How many stayed and how many later decided to leave the city? Where did they go? Were they more or less successful (in occupational status or wealth) than those they left behind? Though these questions have been asked about nineteenth-century immigrants and natives, the inability to follow migrants who left one location for another over the course of a decade has left most answers in the realm of speculation. Since the immigrants in the present sample who were located in New York in 1850 were sought again in 1860, it is possible to provide more concrete answers here.

Two measures of persistence will be employed here, as well as below when we consider persistence between 1850 and 1860 in locations outside New York. One (the "unconditional" measure) is the conventional measure: the fraction of individuals sampled in a location (in this case New York) who were found in that same location ten years later. Those who did not persist either were not enumerated at the second date (because of their death in the intervening years or because they were simply missed in the census or the census index) or moved to another place.[24] This is the measure reported in most nineteenth-century persistence studies. The second measure of persistence (the "conditional" measure) uses only those immigrants sampled at a location in 1850 who were also positively located somewhere in 1860.[25] This rate is conditional on survival to 1860 and on enumeration in the 1860 census and the 1860 census index.

For the present sample, the unconditional measure of persistence in New York is 15.2 percent (N = 198), while the conditional measure is 44.8 percent (N = 67). The unconditional measure is quite low in comparison with other studies of other nineteenth-century U.S. cities. Boston and Philadelphia, for example, had rates of 39 and 32 percent, respectively.[26] The unconditional persistence rate for New York calculated here is in fact only slightly higher than the lowest rate found for any nineteenth-century American city—the 14 percent rate for Chicago between 1850 and 1860.[27]

Three factors might help account for the low unconditional rate. The first is the extent of immigrant mortality in New York. But as we shall see below, persistence rates for the sample in other communities were correspondingly low, so immigrant mortality must have been high even outside New York if mortality is the whole story. The second factor is that immigrants in this sample must have been

23. Board of Aldermen, *Documents*, p. 30.
24. For a discussion of these issues, see Galenson and Levy, "Note on Biases."
25. I am grateful to Jonathan Pritchett for suggesting this terminology.
26. Thernstrom, *Other Bostonians*, pp. 222–223.
27. Galenson, "Economic Opportunity," p. 584.

enumerated in both the census and the census index before they would have been successfully located in 1860. Other studies, in which the entire sample of 1850 residents was matched against the entire 1860 census enumeration for a community, would have missed fewer people. A third possible explanation is that this study examines only immigrants, whereas studies such as Thernstrom's looked at both immigrants and natives. One of the best predictors of nonpersistence is whether an individual had made a previous move, which all the members of this sample had obviously done in coming to the United States.

Immigrants who left New York between 1850 and 1860 went to the same locations as those who had never settled in New York: 51.3 percent were located elsewhere in the Northeast in 1860, 18.9 percent had moved to Ohio, Indiana, or Michigan, and another 16.2 percent went to the Northwestern states of Illinois, Iowa, Wisconsin, and Missouri. As we shall see later, this was the pattern of settlement for the entire sample in 1850. Those who were located in the city in 1850 and elsewhere in 1860 were more likely than those who had bypassed New York to be located in urban places in 1860: 64.9 percent were located in 1860 in places of more than 2,500 people, while less than half of the entire sample were located in such places.

The immigrants who settled in New York initially and moved out during the 1850s fared as well in terms of occupational mobility as did those who remained in New York and only slightly worse than those who left New York soon after arrival. If we confine ourselves to those who arrived before 1846 (so we are comparing those who settled in New York for a time with those who did not), we can compare the percentages moving up and down in occupation for persisters, nonpersisters, and those who never settled in New York.[28] Of the persisters, 33 percent moved up in occupation, while 24 percent moved down. Among those who settled in New York and moved out, 30 percent moved up and only 11 percent moved down. Of the immigrants who never settled in New York, 59 percent moved up over the same period, while 13 percent moved down. The only one of these differences that is statistically significant, however, is the comparison between the percentage moving up for nonpersisters and the percentage moving up for those who never settled in New York.

Among persisters, only 10 percent owned any property in 1850, compared to 5 percent of nonpersisters, both of which were significantly below the 36 percent figure for those who had not settled in New York. By 1860, 30 percent of persisters owned real estate, as did 37 percent of nonpersisters, and 50 percent of those who did not settle in New York. Those who left New York after initially settling there did worse in acquiring any property than either those who persisted or those who never settled in New York. The average amount of real property gained between 1850 and 1860 was highest among those who persisted in New York. This group increased its real estate wealth by $1,170 on average between 1850 and 1860. Those who left New York between 1850 and 1860 saw their real estate wealth rise an average of only $463, while those who had never settled in New

28. An upward move is defined as movement from unskilled to any other occupation. A downward move is from any other occupation into unskilled.

York saw theirs rise by $1,044 over the same period. None of these differences was statistically significant, however.

Immigrants Bypassing New York: Numbers and Trends

The calculations in the preceding section suggested that roughly 65 percent of immigrants passed through New York without stopping for a significant amount of time. This fraction was probably slightly higher for arrivals in the late 1840s than it had been for those earlier in the decade. Part of this difference is accounted for by the arrival late in the 1840s of cohorts that had large numbers of young, illiterate, nonwhite collar immigrants. But several developments in the United States over the 1840s made it easier for immigrants to leave New York quickly and probably helped arrivals in the late 1840s avoid having to spend time in New York.

One development that made it easy for immigrants to leave New York rapidly was increased communication between employers in the interior and immigrant arrivals in New York. By the late 1840s, employers who required large amounts of labor—particularly unskilled labor—were beginning to station recruiters in New York City. Many railroad and canal workers found employment in this way, but so too did more skilled workers recruited for work in factories from New England to the Midwest. Smaller employers were also able to satisfy some of their demand for labor by recruiting in New York, through advertisements in the immigrant press.[29]

In 1847, the Commissioners of Emigration of New York made recruitment even easier. By corresponding with labor contractors in the interior, they were able to secure jobs for boat and train loads full of unskilled workers.[30] A labor exchange was established at which newly arrived immigrants could see posted "help wanted" notices from employers throughout the country. The number of immigrants who found jobs through the exchange rose steadily in the years after its inception, reaching more than 18,000 by 1851.[31] During the 1850s, branch offices were established in seven states to channel information to immigrants arriving at New York.[32]

These developments made it easier for immigrants to spend a few hours or days in New York, find an employer, and move on. But there was a trend as well in the number of immigrants who knew even at the time of their departure that they *wanted* to move through New York quickly. The passenger ship lists recorded immigrants' intended destinations. Though most simply reported "U.S.," there was an increasing tendency among those who reported a specific location to report a place other than New York. In 1846, 57 of the 1,511 immigrants in the sample reported a destination other than "U.S."; 93 percent of these gave "New York" as a response. In 1850, when 392 out of 2,640 immigrants reported a specific destination other than "U.S.," the fraction giving "New York" had fallen to 73 percent.[33]

29. Ernst, *Immigrant Life*, p. 64.
30. Commissioners of Emigration, *Annual Report*, pp. 78–79, 116.
31. Kapp, *Immigration*, p. 115.
32. Ernst, *Immigrant Life*, p. 65.
33. A χ^2 test was significant at the 99% level for the comparison of these percentages.

Like John Reemus, the Dutch immigrant quoted earlier, many immigrants had at least some idea where they hoped to go—even if they lacked the resources to get there—and it was increasingly somewhere other than New York as the 1840s passed.

Many of these immigrants who had specific ideas about where they were going were helped to reach those destinations by remittances sent back to Europe by those who preceded them. The U.S. Treasury estimated that remittances from the United States to England totaled $14.3 million in the years 1848 to 1851.[34] This amounts to an average of $11.23 per immigrant arrival over these four years, enough to finance travel from New York to most interior locations, as we shall see below.[35] The Irish alone remitted $21.7 million in 1853–54, and $238 million between 1847 and 1887.[36] At the same time, it was also possible for immigrants to travel on tickets that had been paid for in America. More than a third of those traveling from Ulster in the years 1847 to 1849 were on prepaid tickets.[37] This left these immigrants with greater resources to join family and friends in the interior.

Two other factors made it easy for immigrants to bypass New York, and made it increasingly easy to do so by the late 1840s and early 1850s: the volume of information they received both before and after their arrival about alternative locations in the United States and the relatively low passage fares to the interior. We will consider the sources and extent of information available to immigrants before departure and the cost of moving directly to the interior before turning to the resulting distribution of immigrants after they passed through New York.

Information About Locations in the Interior

Although we cannot know how much information about the United States immigrants possessed, it is clear that a great deal of information was in circulation in Europe during the first half of the nineteenth century. The principal sources that immigrants such as those in the sample could have been exposed to were published guidebooks and newspaper accounts of life in the United States, advertisements by shipping companies and by railroads and state governments promoting settlement on their lands, and letters from friends and family who had already relocated to the United States.

The exhortations of shipping and railroad companies were probably of the least use to immigrants. Their vested interest in selling tickets and land made their information somewhat suspect.[38] Advertising by state governments, through the distribution of pamphlets at European ports and in New York, through notices in

34. U.S. Census Office, *Seventh Census*, p. 123.

35. Page, "Economic Aspects of Immigration," p. 1025, quotes a figure of $19.4 million for 1848–52.

36. Ibid., p. 1024; Taylor, *Distant Magnet*, p. 101.

37. Mageean, "Irish Emigration," p. 284.

38. See Gates, *Illinois Central*, for the role of the Illinois Central Railroad in promoting immigration, and the exaggerations and outright falsehoods in its claims.

European and American newspapers, or through the importunings of agents in Europe and New York, were only slightly more reliable. In any case, few of the immigrants studied here could have seen such state-sponsored promotion, since it did not begin in earnest until 1845.[39]

The information conveyed in guidebooks was probably of more use to immigrants. Taylor catalogs several hundred such guides published in Europe in the first half of the nineteenth century.[40] These books conveyed a range of information: the provisions that should be carried during the voyage, innkeepers to be trusted on the way to the interior of the United States, soil types and farm prices, and even descriptions of the political systems and economies of different states. This source had its shortcomings as well. In order to reach as wide an audience as possible, guidebooks often covered large areas of the United States in fairly general terms. The information on land prices and availability was often out of date by the time the published volume was in the hands of a potential migrant in Europe.

A good example of the broad coverage of some of these guides is Christian Traugott Ficker's "Friendly Adviser for All Who Would Emigrate to America and Particularly to Wisconsin," published in Leipzig in 1853. Ficker discusses the particulars of the transatlantic voyage and the trip to the interior, the difficulties of starting a farm, and topographical and climatic features of the northwestern states, and includes a long discussion of the extent of public works and the job market, as well as information on the political system and the different religions practiced and tolerated.

By far the most reliable source of information on conditions and opportunities in the United States was correspondence from family and friends who had gone on to America. Letters provided a more truthful and timely assessment of circumstances in the United States, and also contained information likely to be of the greatest use to potential immigrants: names of countrymen with whom to stay along the way, how closely the expectations of those who had previously migrated were matched by experience, and how similar a location was to a potential immigrant's village of origin.[41]

An additional benefit of reliance on family and friends was that an immigrant had a ready source of support at arrival. Family and friends could shepherd the new arrival through the entire settlement process, meeting them in New York or somewhere in the interior, helping them find a home and a job, and offering assistance through the early years in the United States. The New York Commissioners of Emigration reported that as many people were greeted in New York by friends and relatives as were helped by the commissioners' labor exchange in finding jobs in the interior of the United States.[42]

39. Michigan sent an agent to New York in 1845 and published a small handbook extolling the state's resources, which was distributed in New York and Europe; Jenks, "Michigan Immigration," pp. 69–70. The most successful state promotion, Wisconsin's, did not begin until 1852.

40. Taylor, *Distant Magnet*, p. 67.

41. For examples of such letters, see Erickson, *Invisible Immigrants*; Drake, "Yankeys Now"; Conway, "New Orleans"; and Kamphoefner et al., *News*.

42. Commissioners of Emigration, *Annual Report*.

The Cost of Traveling Past New York

The immigrants in this sample arrived at a time of great change in the system of transportation between New York and the rest of the United States. Immigrants who wanted to settle along the Atlantic coast could still sail directly from New York to ports such as Boston, Providence, and Baltimore, as had been the case for more than a hundred years. But those who arrived in the 1840s and sought transportation to the interior found a growing range of options. There were three routes from which to choose: to the Upper South or Midwest via New Orleans; west across Pennsylvania to Pittsburgh, and then into Ohio and the West; and from New York to Buffalo and then into the West through the Great Lakes. Before 1846, these were essentially water routes; after 1846, part of the trip via Buffalo was by rail, with the same true after 1853 of the Pennsylvania route.

The least popular route was to sail from New York to New Orleans and then travel by flatboat up the Mississippi. Though this was the cheapest route to St. Louis or even Illinois, it was time consuming and exposed the immigrant to the dangerous disease environment of New Orleans, a particular hazard in the summer months. Immigrants were advised by both friends and published sources to avoid this route unless traveling with a large amount of baggage to a location in the South.[43] Though we do not know the cost of sailing from New York to New Orleans, the cost of travel from Liverpool to the Upper South via New Orleans was seldom more than $35.00 per person, roughly the cost of the transatlantic passage to New York alone.[44]

A second route in the years before the completion of railroad lines to the interior was to travel by train from New York to Columbia, Pennsylvania, via Philadelphia, and from Columbia to Pittsburgh by canal. The travel time was from six to eight days, and the journey cost $6.00 in 1845. By 1855, the entire trip could be made by rail in two days, at a cost of only $4.50.

The most popular route was from New York to Albany, from Albany to Buffalo, and thence to ports along the Great Lakes. Before the completion of the railroad line between Albany and Buffalo, the trip was made entirely on water: to Albany by steamboat in 10 hours, and then along the Erie Canal to Buffalo in another seven or eight days, at a total cost of $5.00. Steamships then distributed the immigrants throughout the Upper Midwest. More than 60,000 immigrants were traveling via the canal by 1844.[45] After 1846, with the opening of the first trunk rail line between Albany and Buffalo, immigrants could travel either entirely by water, or avoid the Erie Canal and travel by rail instead from Albany to Buffalo in only 30 hours. Immigrants were advised to avoid the canal. Given only the slight difference in the cost of going from Albany to Buffalo by rail, the greater time spent in traveling by canal was seen as a major disadvantage of this route.[46]

The cost of travel from New York to points in the interior via Albany and

43. Conway, "New Orleans," pp. 3–4.
44. Ibid., p. 3.
45. Page, "Distribution of Immigrants," p. 688.
46. Ficker, "Friendly Adviser," p. 226.

Table 4-3. Passage fares from New York
City to interior U.S. locations in 1847.

Destination	Mode of Transportation	
	Water	Water & Rail
Buffalo	$5.00	—
Cleveland	5.50	$9.00
Chicago	10.00	12.00
Cincinnati	12.00	12.50
Louisville	13.00	13.50
St. Louis	14.00	14.50
Detroit	—	9.25
Pittsburgh	—	10.50
Milwaukee	—	9.50

Source: Kapp, *Immigration*, pp. 70–71.

Buffalo is shown in Table 4-3. It was possible throughout the 1840s for immigrants to book their passage for the entire length of these journeys before their departure from Europe. Fraud was a frequent problem, though: immigrants who had paid for their entire trip through a forwarding agent in Europe were often told that their tickets were worthless when they reached New York. Similarly, those who booked through agents in New York were required to make additional payments at Albany or Buffalo.[47] These charges raised the actual cost paid by many immigrants above the figures quoted here.

The most expensive destination was St. Louis, which could be reached more cheaply by traveling from Europe to New Orleans directly and then up the Mississippi. Other destinations, such as Chicago, could be reached by water or by rail and water for only a third more than the $35.00 the immigrant had probably paid to get from Europe to New York in the early 1840s.[48] Immigrants traveling in the late 1840s faced a comparatively greater cost of travel to the interior: many had paid only around $15.00 to travel from Liverpool to New York in steerage, while it would cost them nearly that again to travel to the interior.[49]

When seen in light of the resources with which immigrants arrived, the cost of travel to the interior was not a tremendous burden: the average amount of money with which immigrants arrived in the 1840s was probably above $60.00, though the Irish were no doubt somewhat below this average.[50] And differences in the cost of reaching various interior points was not great: for example, it cost

47. Kapp, *Immigration*, p. 68; Ernst, *Immigrant Life*, pp. 27–28.
48. The standard fare from Liverpool to New York aboard a packet was $35.00 in 1840; Taylor, *Distant Magnet*, p. 94.
49. Ibid.
50. The issue of how much wealth immigrants brought with them to the United States is taken up in greater detail in chapter 6. The figures given here are only meant to demonstrate that travel to the interior was within the reach of most arriving immigrants.

only $4.00 more to get to Milwaukee than it cost to travel only to Cleveland. Among those who hoped to set themselves up in urban employments, then, the choice of where to go was probably determined more by the contacts or opportunities at a particular location than by the direct cost of getting there.

A far more onerous expense for those who hoped to enter or reenter farming was that of setting up a farm. In the 1840s, estimates suggest that an arriving immigrant needed at least $400 to buy and clear a 40- to 80-acre tract of land in the West and provide for himself and his family until he was able to bring in his first crop.[51] Many of those who arrived as farmers would have lacked the resources for such an undertaking.[52]

The Distribution of Immigrants

Where immigrants were located by the time of the 1850 census is conveyed in Tables 4-4 and 4-5 and Figure 4-3. Nearly three quarters were found in the Middle Atlantic and Midwest regions alone, while more than half were found in just three states—New York, Pennsylvania, and Ohio. Smaller numbers were found in New England and the states closest to the frontier, while very few immigrants were found in the South and Far West. Comparison of this distribution with the distribution of the total U.S. population reveals that immigrants were far more concentrated in their settlement than Americans in general: for every state in Table 4-4 except Missouri, the immigrant share is greater than the share of the total U.S. population. In New York, immigrants were overrepresented by a factor of more than two, while in Wisconsin their share was nearly seven times the total U.S. population share. These disparities are even more striking than they at first appear. To the extent that immigrants exhibited higher fertility rates than natives even after their arrival, the ratio of immigrant share to native share might be biased toward parity for the following reason: places with large concentrations of immigrants would also have had larger concentrations of children, since the native population in a location included the native-born children of immigrants. Places with big immigrant shares would thus to some extent have had larger native shares.[53]

Most of this disparity between the native and immigrant distribution by region is eliminated if the South is excluded: though the South contained nearly 39 percent of the total U.S. population, it received only 8 percent of the immigrants in the sample. If we restrict our attention to the nonsouthern total U.S. population

51. Kremers, "Letters," pp. 80–81; Page, "Distribution of Immigrants," p. 691; Taylor, *Distant Magnet*, p. 96.

52. For the 1850s, Atack and Bateman, *To Their Own Soil*, p. 144, calculated a range of farm-making costs. The low end of their range—under $1,000—was for farms under 40 acres in areas with population densities up to 30 persons per square mile. A similar size farm in a more thickly settled region might cost more than $2,000 to start.

53. The evidence on the higher overall fertility of nineteenth-century immigrants has recently been challenged by King and Ruggles, "American Immigration."

Table 4-4. Distribution of immigrant arrivals at New York, 1840–50, by region and state, 1850.

		Sample			
	Total U.S. (%)		Origin		
Location		Total (%)	British (%)	Irish (%)	German (%)
Region					
New England	11.8	13.7	12.7	24.4	2.5
Middle Atlantic	25.4	47.8	44.6	55.0	42.9
Midwest	23.3	30.2	38.0	12.7	43.1
Southeast	20.0	3.6	1.6	4.1	5.0
South Central	18.6	4.0	2.3	3.4	5.9
Far West	0.4	0.6	0.9	0.4	0.7
State					
New York	13.4	30.8	26.9	36.9	27.7
Pennsylvania	10.0	13.1	13.1	13.2	13.4
Ohio	8.5	10.0	9.3	3.2	18.8
Wisconsin	1.3	9.0	15.8	2.8	10.0
Massachusetts	4.3	7.0	5.7	12.5	1.8
Illinois	3.7	5.0	6.6	3.2	5.2
New Jersey	2.1	3.8	4.5	4.9	1.8
Michigan	1.7	2.3	4.1	0.2	3.4
Connecticut	1.6	1.9	1.6	3.5	0.5
Missouri	2.9	1.7	0.2	1.5	3.4
Other	50.5	15.4	12.2	18.1	14.0
N	23,191,876	1,456	442	536	441

Source: Male household heads and unaccompanied males in passenger ship arrival records at port of New York, 1840–1850, linked to 1850 manuscript census schedules; U.S. Census Office, *Seventh Census.*

Note: For definition of regions, see Table 2-5.

and nonsouthern immigrant destinations, then the only region with an overrepresentation of immigrants is the Middle Atlantic, with 41 percent of the total nonsouthern population but 52 percent of the immigrants in the sample. If we exclude the South, the share of the total nonsouthern population in the Midwest is 38 percent, while the share of the immigrants in the sample is 33 percent. Immigrants, then, were somewhat more likely than the total nonsouthern population to be found in the Middle Atlantic states, but slightly less likely to be found in the Midwest.[54]

Immigrants were clearly overrepresented in cities and small towns: although 85 percent of the total U.S. population in 1850 lived in places of fewer than 2,500 people, only 38 percent of the immigrants in the sample were found in such places.

54. Because of the small number of immigrants who were located in the South and the Far West, the following discussion of settlement patterns will be confined to an examination of those who settled in the Northeast, Midwest, and Far West states.

Table 4-5. Distribution of immigrant arrivals at New York, 1840–50, by city and size of location, 1850.

| | Total | Sample | | | |
| | | Origin | | | |
Location	U.S. (%)	Total (%)	British (%)	Irish (%)	German (%)
City					
New York	2.2	10.0	3.8	12.1	13.4
Philadelphia	1.8	4.7	4.8	5.0	4.5
Cincinnati	0.5	3.3	1.1	1.3	8.2
Buffalo	0.2	2.5	0.7	0.2	7.5
Brooklyn	0.4	2.2	1.8	3.7	0.7
Milwaukee	0.1	2.1	1.1	0.7	4.8
Providence	0.2	1.0	0.9	1.9	0.0
St. Louis	0.3	0.8	0.0	0.6	1.8
Boston	0.6	1.5	0.9	2.4	1.1
Pittsburgh	0.2	0.8	0.9	0.6	1.1
Other	90.8	70.9	83.9	71.5	56.9
Size of location					
50,000 and over	6.3	25.1	13.6	27.4	33.6
10,000–49,999	5.1	15.9	13.3	13.6	21.8
2,500–9,999	3.9	20.8	26.2	25.2	10.7
Under 2,500	84.7	38.2	46.8	33.8	34.0
N	23,191,876	1,456	442	536	441

Source: Male household heads and unaccompanied males in passenger ship arrival records at port of New York, 1840–1850, linked to 1850 manuscript census schedules.; U.S. Census Office, Seventh Census.

Part of this disparity might result from the fact that many cities were transportation hubs through which immigrants had to pass before they could reach the interior where most natives were located. As Table 4-5 shows, immigrants were indeed overrepresented in New York City, Philadelphia, Cincinnati, and Buffalo, all of which served as gateways to the interior. But this does not account for the concentration of immigrants in smaller cities, places with fewer than 50,000 people, which Table 4-5 also shows.

Even the earliest arrivals in the sample were more concentrated in cities than were natives, which suggests that immigrants were attracted to urban centers for reasons other than the fact that they had to pass through them to get anywhere else. The obvious attraction of cities was the high level of average wages—natives were attracted to the cities as well, as indicated by the fact that net internal migration from 1850 to 1860 among natives was from rural to urban places.[55] The particular advantages of cities to immigrants included ready sources of employment for the un-

55. Patterns of internal migration between 1850 and 1860 among both immigrants and natives are explored in greater detail in chapter 7.

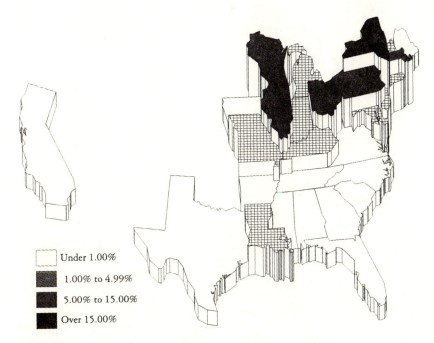

Under 1.00%

1.00% to 4.99%

5.00% to 15.00%

Over 15.00%

Figure 4-3. Distribution of immigrants by state (1850). *Source:* Male household heads and unaccompanied males in passenger ship arrival records at port of New York, 1840–1850, linked to 1850 manuscript census schedules.

skilled and, in many cases, the presence of large numbers of one's countrymen—an important source of both potential employers and potential customers.

Though we cannot know exactly when immigrants in the sample reached their observed 1850 locations, we can estimate how quickly they reached those places. Comparison of early and recent arrivals suggests that immigrants reached their observed 1850 regions soon after their arrival, if we assume that regions of initial settlement changed little over the decade. It is possible, however, that regions of initial settlement *did* change over the 1840s, as those who arrived late in the 1840s followed the advice of those who arrived earlier and took advantage of their assistance. In the presence of such "chain migration," we can infer nothing about how long it took immigrants to reach their observed 1850 locations from their distribution at a point in time by time since arrival. Though the most recent arrivals may have reached their 1850 locations quickly, the earlier arrivals on whom they relied to reach those locations may have spent several years reaching *their* 1850 locations if they were the first links in the migration chain.

In the absence of such complications, the data suggest that immigrants reached their 1850 locations rapidly. For example, 36 percent of those who arrived before 1845 were located by 1850 in the Midwest, but so too were 30 percent of the 1845–50 arrivals. The difference in mean duration in the United States between those in the Northeast and Midwest amounts to just over five months, but this

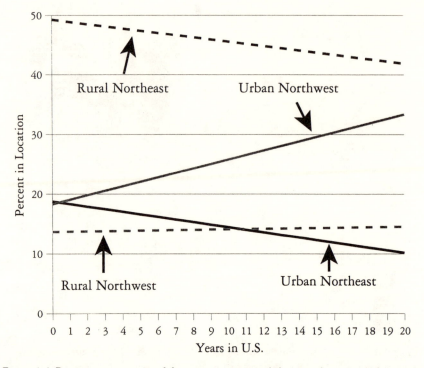

Figure 4-4. Regression estimates of the percentage in each location by years in the United States. *Source:* Male household heads and unaccompanied males in passenger ship arrival records at port of New York, 1840–1850, linked to 1850 and/or 1860 manuscript census schedules.

difference is statistically insignificant. Similarly, 40 percent of early arrivals were located in places with fewer than 2,500 people, but so too were 38 percent of the most recent arrivals. The differences in average duration between those in cities and in such rural places, though statistically significant, was only six months.

Another way of looking at how quickly immigrants reached their 1850 locations is to examine the fraction of the sample located in various locations for all times since arrival, which is done in Figure 4-4. This shows the percentage of the sample located in the Northeast (outside New York City) and Northwest (Midwest and Far West) for each time since arrival. These percentages were calculated by pooling observations from 1850 and 1860, calculating the fraction in each of the four locations at each full year since arrival, and regressing the percentage against the years since arrival.[56] The percentage of the sample located in the urban Northeast outside of New York City and the rural Northeast decreases with increasing duration in the United States, while the shares in the urban and rural Northwest rise. It thus seems safe to conclude that most immigrants quickly reached a location of the size

56. The coefficients on years since arrival were statistically significant for both rural locations and insignificant for both urban locations.

Table 4-6. Native-born children of immigrant arrivals at New York, 1840–50, born outside state of residence, by region and size of location, 1850.

Region	No. of Families with Native-Born Children	Families with Native-Born Children Born Out of State (%)	Native-Born Children Born Out of State (%)
Northeast	320	12.2	12.3
Urban	75	11.0	10.3
Rural	245	16.0	18.0
Northwest	449	19.3	21.0
Urban	151	21.3	25.3
Rural	298	18.5	19.6

Source: Male household heads and unaccompanied males in passenger ship arrival records at port of New York, 1840–1850, linked to 1850 manuscript census schedules.

Note: "Northeast" includes New England and Middle Atlantic. "Northwest" includes Midwest and Far West. "Urban" is a census subdivision (city, town, township, etc.) with an 1850 population over 2,500.

in which they were found by 1850, though there was subsequent movement within that size class from the Northeast to the Northwest.[57]

A study of immigrants in Wisconsin in 1850 suggests yet another way of assessing how quickly immigrants reached their observed 1850 locations. By examining immigrant families with children born in the United States, Schafer concluded that most Germans reached Wisconsin quickly, while the Irish made intervening stops after their arrival in the United States.[58] In 979 German families with 531 native-born children, 25 of the children (4.7 percent) were born outside Wisconsin. In 276 Irish families with 184 native-born children, 93 (50.5 percent) were born outside Wisconsin.[59]

The same exercise was performed for the present sample. The results are presented in Table 4-6. Overall, the impression of few intermediate stops between landing at New York and arrival at an 1850 location is confirmed. Only 10 to 12 percent of the native-born children in the sample were born outside the state where they were located with their families in 1850. There are differences by urban/rural and region, however. In the Northwest, 19.6 percent of native-born children in rural places were born outside the state where they were found, while this was true of 25.3 percent of those in urban places. Similar differences were ap-

57. These patterns, like the pattern of departures from New York described above, might have resulted from changes in the propensities of successive cohorts to locate originally in particular regions, as well as from interregional movement over time.

58. Schafer, Four Wisconsin Counties, pp. 85–89.

59. Atack and Bateman performed a similar exercise for 1860. They found that the percentage of native-born children born outside the state of 1860 residence increases as one goes farther west; Atack and Bateman, To Their Own Soil, p. 79.

parent in the Northeast as well, though the magnitudes were smaller. This supports the conclusion that movement after arrival was generally movement across regions within the same size of location class (urban or rural).[60]

The speed with which immigrants reached the places in which they were located in 1850 is not surprising. As we saw previously, at their arrival in New York, immigrants faced a variety of relatively inexpensive routes to the interior of the United States, which many had arranged to employ even before their departure from Europe. The total fare from Europe to Buffalo, Cleveland, or Detroit was probably only one fourth greater than the $35.00 fare to New York City alone, with the total fare to Chicago and interior points such as Cincinnati, Pittsburgh, and Louisville only a third more than the fare to New York alone.

Who Went West?

We now consider in more detail who went where. For example, who were the immigrants who located in the Midwest, Southwest, and Far West states? The West offered the availability of land and the opportunities presented by booming cities such as Chicago and Milwaukee. Other considerations may have been important to immigrants, though. Urban centers in both the East and the West offered the comfort of large concentrations of one's countrymen as company, customers, or employers, which may have been important for professionals, proprietors, skilled workers, and laborers. Rural places in the more thickly settled Northeast exhibited fewer of the disamenities associated with life on the Northwest frontier, and allowed farmers to purchase already established farms. For those who sought the company of their countrymen and planned to enter farming, the North Central and Northwest offered a number of communities of immigrants. Immigrants traveling in groups to establish such communities were likely to have looked to the West as well, where land was more plentiful and less expensive than in the East. The immigrants seen in the Northwest, then, have forsaken the economic and physical safety of a more settled area and survived the rigors of life on the frontier. What were the characteristics of these immigrants? More generally, what accounts for where we observe immigrants located in 1850?

Perhaps the simplest explanation of the pattern of settlement for immigrant arrivals, given how quickly they seem to have gotten to where we observe them in 1850, is that they simply settled close to the conventional routes to the interior. Immigrant diaries are full of stories of immigrants finding places along the way to the interior that struck them as particularly like home, buying a plot of land, and settling there. One particularly astute observer was able to determine how close the climate was to his own village's along the route from Baltimore to Ohio by the speed with which trees he recognized had borne fruit. He avoided several loca-

60. When the sample is disaggregated by region and country of origin, the finding of Schafer is replicated, though not in such striking terms. In the West, German families with native-born children had 8 percent of those children born outside their 1850 state; more than 27 percent of Irish and English native-born children in the West were born outside their 1850 state.

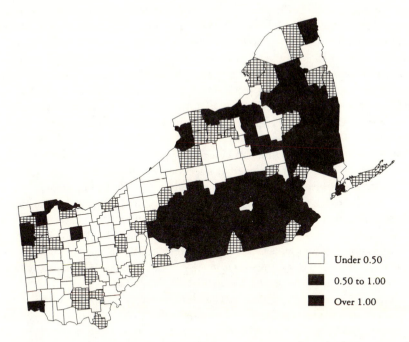

Figure 4-5. Distribution of immigrants in New York, Pennsylvania, and Ohio, compared to the distribution of native-born interstate migrants, by county (1850). The figure shows the ratio of the share of the immigrants in the sample in each county in the three state area to the share of the native-born interstate migrant population in each county in the three state area. A ratio over one indicates that immigrants are overrepresented relative to native-born interstate migrants; a ratio below one indicates they are underrepresented. *Source:* Male household heads and unaccompanied males in passenger ship arrival records at port of New York, 1840–1850, linked to 1850 manuscript census schedules; U.S. Census Office, *Seventh Census.*

tions early in his trip because the fruit has only begun to ripen in late August, indicating a shorter growing season than back in Germany.[61] Immigrants may have also been able to learn something about the state of the labor market in the cities through which they passed more easily than they could learn about more distant urban places.

The pattern of settlement by county for New York, Pennsylvania, and Ohio—which received the bulk of the immigrants in the sample—suggests that this took place but was probably of little importance in shaping the national pattern of immigrant settlement. Figure 4-5 shows the pattern of settlement among 1840–50 arrivals by county, compared to the patterns for native-born interstate migrants. Most of the counties that received the heaviest concentrations of arrivals relative to native-born interstate movers are located along the Hudson River Valley between New York and Albany, along the route of the Erie Canal between Albany

61 See the account of Christoph Munk in Mahr, "Down the Rhine."

and Buffalo, and along the canal and rail route from Philadelphia to Pittsburgh. It is not clear, though, whether immigrants settled in these places because of their proximity to the route they were traveling and the relative ease with which information about them could be gathered while *en route* to the interior, or simply because these were places that were desirable locations in any case, as demonstrated by the fact that canals and railroads had been built to reach them. Once immigrants had reached the West (e.g., Ohio), such patterns are less apparent. That immigrants were overrepresented relative to native-born interstate movers in these places suggests that the ease with which information could be gathered along the way or the desirability of these places because of their proximity to transportation may have been of particular importance to immigrants.

The counties with an overrepresentation of immigrants among in-migrants are also among the longer-settled counties in the region and the counties most likely to have sent interstate migrants to the West. This suggests another explanation for immigrants' choice of these locations: the desire of at least some immigrants to avoid a frontier existence to which they were not at all accustomed. Many may instead have chosen to take up farms in these older, established counties and "fill in" the spaces left by those who had gone west.

A number of immigrant characteristics have been suggested as determinants of where immigrants went. The most common perception was that the Irish clung to the cities of the Northeast, either too poor to escape the ports where they landed or too discouraged by their previous experience with agriculture to want to move back into farming. In describing antebellum migration patterns, Commons suggested that "the German immigrants moved westward and were hardly noticed. The Irish, however, congregated in the large cities."[62] The English were thought to favor locations in the Northeast, particularly upstate New York.[63]

The pattern of immigrant settlement, though, is less clear-cut than this. Many Irish did leave New York and headed west or to rural places in the East. Though 60 percent were found in eastern cities in 1850, the balance escaped such places. They were largely "rootless, unmarried men and husbands who returned [to cities in the East] in the off seasons to their families and acquaintances in New York and other large cities."[64] The high farm wages of the rural East and the less thickly settled western states and the high urban wages of booming cities were an attraction for many, an opportunity to earn the capital that would permit the purchase of an independent farm or urban business.[65]

Table 4-7 compares the arrival characteristics of immigrants by region and urban/rural location. The group most concentrated in the East was the Irish. More than 84 percent of Irish immigrants were found in 1850 in eastern states. At the same time, many of the Irish were also found in rural locations in 1850—in each region, they are a larger fraction of the rural population than of the urban population. Of the Irish who went west, most went to rural places. Germans were the

62. Commons et al., *History of Labour*, p. 414.
63. Ernst, *Immigrant Life*, p. 70.
64. Ibid., p. 63.
65. Kapp, *Immigration*, p. 118.

Table 4-7. Characteristics at arrival of immigrant
arrivals at New York, 1840–50, by region and size
of location, 1850.

Characteristic	East		West	
	Urban	Rural	Urban	Rural
Age	25.3	26.5	25.8	27.0
Married (%)	23.4	28.6	22.0	33.2
Family size	1.6	2.0	1.6	2.5
Literate (%)	91.6	92.6	96.7	96.3
Occupation (%)				
White collar	7.9	5.2	8.8	4.9
Skilled	30.8	23.4	34.1	28.3
Farmer	18.8	22.9	24.7	36.6
Unskilled	42.5	48.5	32.4	30.2
Origin (%)				
Britain	27.6	27.3	20.9	38.1
Ireland	45.3	53.2	16.5	17.8
Germany	25.6	16.5	58.8	34.5
Other	1.5	3.0	3.8	3.1
Years in U.S.	5.9	6.0	5.2	6.5
No. of obs.	718	231	182	325
Percent (%)	49.3	15.9	12.5	22.3

Source: Male household heads and unaccompanied males in passenger ship arrival records at port of New York, 1840–1850, linked to 1850
manuscript census schedules.

Note: "East" is New England, Middle Atlantic, and Southeast.
"West" is Midwest and Far West. All characteristics are as reported in
the passenger ship lists, except "Years in U.S." and "Literate" which are
measured in 1850.

most likely group to be found in the West—half were in the Midwest, Far West,
or Southwest states, compared to 16 percent of the Irish and 42 percent of the
British. But this figure contains roughly equal numbers of Germans in western urban places and western rural locations. Germans clearly favored the West, and
more so than the other groups tended to cluster in its cities, such as Cincinnati,
St. Louis, and Milwaukee. The fraction of Germans found in eastern cities,
though, was only slightly below that for the British.

The oldest immigrants at arrival were most likely to be found by 1850 in the
rural West. This may reflect several factors. One is the fact that older immigrants
may have arrived with greater wealth than younger immigrants, while most accounts suggest that "those who had the means to go west did so."[66] The fact that
those who described themselves as farmers at arrival dominated the occupational
distribution of those in rural western places lends some credence to this view:

66. Ernst, Immigrant Life, p. 61.

Table 4-8. Estimates of the parameters of the hazard function for entering the West among immigrant arrivals at New York, 1840–50.

Variable	Mean	$\delta P_{12}/\delta X$	Probability
Age	24.218	0.003	0.455
Age$^2 \times 10^{-2}$	6.728	−0.001	0.815
Married	0.241	0.033	0.242
Family size	1.672	0.011	0.138
Origin			
Irish	0.419	−0.232	0.001
German	0.301	0.071	0.007
Other	0.025	0.068	0.231
Literate	0.929	0.032	0.483
Occupation			
White collar	0.062	−0.069	0.126
Skilled	0.247	−0.051	0.078
Farmer	0.230	0.009	0.753
Year of arrival			
1841	0.080	0.000	0.994
1842	0.155	0.028	0.497
1843	0.094	0.116	0.006
1844	0.095	0.090	0.042
1845	0.082	0.073	0.124
1846	0.039	0.073	0.306
1847	0.041	0.092	0.137
1848	0.103	0.196	0.001
1849	0.121	0.243	0.001
1850	0.089	0.242	0.001
ln(Years in U.S.)	2.121	0.179	0.001
$\bar{P}_{12}$		0.387	
Log-likelihood		−1559.011	
No. of obs.		2,594	

Source: Male household heads and unaccompanied males in passenger ship arrival records at port of New York, 1840–1850, linked to 1850 and/or 1860 manuscript census schedules.

Notes: "$\delta P_{12}/\delta X$" is the impact of a one unit change in a variable on the probability that the individual was located in the Midwest or Far West, evaluated at the mean probability in the sample. It is calculated as $\delta P_{12}/\delta X = (\beta\alpha)\,(-\bar{P}_{11})\,(\log(\bar{P}_{11})$, where β and α are estimates of the parameters from the Weibull hazard function (equation B8 in Appendix B) obtained by maximum likelihood,

$$\bar{P}_{11} = \sum_{i=1}^{N}[\exp(-\exp(X_i'\beta)t_i)^{\alpha}]/N$$

is the average probability in the sample that an individual was still located in the Northeast or Southeast, and $\bar{P}_{12} = 1 - \bar{P}_{11}$. For "ln(Years in U.S.)" $\beta = 1$. "Probability" is the probability that the true $\delta P_{12}/\delta X$ is equal to zero. All characteristics are as reported in the passenger ship lists, except "Years in U.S." and "Literate" which are measured in 1850 or 1860 (see text). The omitted categories are "Unmarried," "British," "Illiterate," "Unskilled," and "1840 arrival."

those who reported their occupation as farmer at arrival may have arrived with the greatest assets, after liquidating their holdings before their departure from Europe.

Finally, the rural West also drew those who arrived with the largest families. To the extent that family size and wealth are positively correlated, those who went to the rural West may have been wealthier than the more numerous arrivals who settled in the rural East. There is another way to interpret the lure of the West for large families. Perhaps those who made their way to the rural West with large families were those with the financial resources to buy large farms, but perhaps just as important, they also had the human resources to work them in an area where hired labor was scarce and wages for farm laborers were high.

In order to separate the influences of factors such as origin, age, family structure, and occupation on the decision to locate in the West, Table 4-8 presents the results of estimating a hazard model like that used to estimate the timing of departures from New York earlier in this chapter. The econometric problems here are the same as those in Table 4-2: the need to separate the effect of time in the United States from changes across arrival cohorts in the propensity to move west, and the need to account for the lack of information on the time at which moves occurred.

Overall, those who arrived with larger families, farmers and unskilled workers, those who were married at arrival, and the British and Germans are more likely to have been found in the West. There are also some clear differences by year of arrival: immigrants who arrived in 1848, 1849, and 1850 were 50 percent more likely to be found in the West by 1850 than earlier arrivals. This change may be the result of improved transportation to the West (cutting the travel time from Albany to Buffalo from a week to 30 hours after 1846), or the result of changes in the characteristics of immigrants at arrival that reflect circumstances at their places of origin (the Irish famine beginning in 1846 and the crop failures and political turmoil that swept Germany in the last years of the 1840s). Finally, the greater numbers moving west in the late 1840s may reflect the poor conditions in eastern labor markets glutted by the arrival of previous waves of immigrants.

These results do not reveal why those with larger families went west. Since we are unable to control for wealth at arrival, the effect of family size at arrival may be merely the best proxy for the financial resources with which immigrants arrived, rather than a sign in itself of the importance of human resources among those going to the West. If we restrict our attention to immigrants who were in the United States fewer than two years in 1850, and who would have had relatively little time to accumulate wealth since their arrival, we may be able to get a better sense of the role of wealth at arrival. Among those in this group who stayed in the East, only 4 percent owned real estate in 1850, with an average value of $33.32; among those who went west, however, the percentage owning any property was nearly five times greater, 20 percent, and the average amount owned was $355.44. Both the difference in the proportion owning wealth and the difference in average wealth are statistically significant at the 5 percent level.

Another piece of evidence that points to the role of wealth in shaping the decision to go west is provided by the reports of Michigan's Commissioner of Immigration. In 1859 and 1860, the commissioner reported the average wealth of arriving German immigrants who went on to Michigan (ostensibly as a result of his successful recruitment of them).[67] The average was between $90 and $150. At their departure from Germany, the average wealth of immigrants recorded by officials of several German principalities was from $90 to $150 in the late 1850s. Since at least some of those examined at their departure had yet to pay their passage fare (probably $40 per person), the Germans sent to Michigan by the state's agent in New York were probably in the upper tail of the distribution of wealth at arrival.

Conclusion

When they set foot on the docks of lower Manhattan, antebellum European immigrants faced a wide array of possibilities: they could remain in New York City or take one of several routes to the interior of the United States where there were literally thousands of places in which they could settle. Most of those who arrived between 1840 and 1850 left New York quickly. The poor, the Irish, and the commercial class stayed behind to begin their lives in America only a few miles from where they first landed. The rest—perhaps three of every five arrivals—moved on after no more than a few weeks to the cities and towns that beckoned. They made few stops between the port where they began and the places in which they were found in 1850, moving with a deliberateness that suggests the care with which many planned their journeys and the volume of information about opportunities in America that was available to them before their departure.

More than half of these immigrants settled in just three states: New York, Pennsylvania, and Ohio. They were more strongly attracted to cities than the native-born, but they were also more likely than the native-born to be found in urban places just behind the frontier. All three groups were partial to the urban Northeast: 45 percent of the British, 60 percent of the Irish, and 41 percent of the Germans were found there in 1850. The Germans were the only group in which half settled in the West. Within the West, half of the Germans were found in rural places and half were found in urban places, where they dominated the immigrant communities that sprang up in western cities like Cincinnati, St. Louis, and Milwaukee. The British also went to the West in substantial numbers (42 percent), but were three times more likely to go to rural places there as they were to go to urban places. Immigrants who arrived latest in life and came with the largest families were the most likely to settle in the western states, perhaps because they possessed the financial and human resources to take advantage of the West's large expanses of unsettled farmland.

67. Jenks, "Michigan Immigration," p. 81.

5

Occupational Change
at Arrival

The research of a generation of economic and social historians has given us considerable insight into the occupational mobility experienced in the United States by immigrants in the first half of the nineteenth century. This work has shown that upward occupational mobility was infrequent during the careers of first-generation immigrants in the United States: no more than a third of immigrants who began their careers in the United States as unskilled workers in cities as different as Newburyport, Boston, Poughkeepsie, and South Bend were able to rise into the ranks of skilled or white collar workers, even after several decades in the United States.[1] This poor performance seems inconsistent with the belief expressed by many immigrants that the United States was a place where economic advancement—particularly occupational mobility—was likely. This apparent paradox may result from a censoring problem in these studies: they examine immigrants' U.S. occupations using sources such as the U.S. census, city directories, and local tax records, while immigrants were probably least likely to be enumerated in such sources in their first years in the United States. As a result, these studies may miss a great deal of occupational mobility if mobility was most likely in the first years after arrival. Even if occupational mobility was genuinely infrequent among recent arrivals, immigrants' optimism may have been justified if some of those observed as white collar, skilled workers, or farmers in the United States had been unskilled workers before they left Europe. To see whether either of these is the case, we need to know how immigrants' postmigration occupations changed as their time in the United States increased, and how their premigration and postmigration occupations compared.

1. See Thernstrom, *Poverty and Progress* and *Other Bostonians*; Griffen and Griffen, *Natives and Newcomers*; and Esslinger, *Immigrants and the City*.

The more accurate picture of immigrant occupational mobility that such information would provide may help us to understand not only the optimism that prompted many immigrants to incur the substantial costs of migration but also the full benefit that the United States derived from immigrants' arrival. Several studies have examined the premigration occupations of nineteenth-century immigrants to assess the value of the human capital transfer their arrival produced.[2] If immigrants stating they possessed some sort of human capital before their arrival (white collar, skilled workers, and farmers) were unable to put that capital to use after arrival and remained unskilled workers throughout their careers in the United States, measures of the human capital transfer induced by immigration will be upward biased. If immigrants were prevented by institutional forces (such as the presence of guilds and rigid apprenticeship systems, or the presence of rigidities in the land market resulting from feudal ownership patterns) in the country of origin from entering occupations there that made full use of their innate skills, and were able to move into such jobs in the United States, the human capital transfer will be understated by the occupations immigrants reported at their arrival. To see whether the distribution of premigration occupations overstates or understates the human capital transfer brought about by immigration, we need to know how the probability that immigrants were employed in their premigration occupation changed as their time in the United States increased.

Recent research on contemporary immigrants to the United States has shown that occupational mobility is often rapid early in immigrants' time in the United States and that many immigrants pursue occupations in the United States different from those they pursued in their country of origin.[3] Moreover, this research suggests that these patterns are not uniform across all immigrants: the ability to employ premigration skills after arrival in the United States is greater for immigrants coming from places more like the United States in terms of their degree of economic development than for immigrants from places less like the United States. This research suggests both the possibility that country of origin may be an important determinant of occupational mobility in the antebellum period and the mechanism that might account for differences in performance by country of origin.

This chapter uses the sample of immigrants linked from passenger ship records to the census manuscript schedules to answer three questions: (1) How much occupational mobility occurred between arrival and when we next observe immigrants in the 1850 or 1860 census? (2) How soon after arrival did immigrants change occupations? (3) And how can we account for this mobility? This sample allows us to examine such patterns for the first time for a group representative of the population of immigrants who arrived from Europe in the years before the Civil War.

---

2. Kapp, *Immigration*; Uselding, "Studies"; Neal and Uselding, "Immigration."
3. Chiswick, "Occupational Mobility."

Previous Research on Immigrant Occupational Mobility

For the nineteenth century, it has been difficult to study the occupational mobility of immigrants between their arrival and their appearance in U.S. sources. Such an undertaking requires knowledge of an immigrant's occupation in Europe, which is absent from nineteenth-century censuses, city directories, and tax and poll records. Several samples of immigrants linked from records in their community of origin to the U.S. census have permitted such work, but the circumstances that allowed such linkage are unusual.[4] Previous studies in which linkage of this sort was done were possible because the immigrants studied traveled from a narrowly circumscribed area of origin and settled in narrowly circumscribed areas within the United States, and because detailed point-of-origin occupational information was collected.

Among Germans who emigrated from Lippe-Detmold to St. Louis and two adjacent rural counties between 1832 and 1860, Kamphoefner found significant movement from European occupation to U.S. occupation in 1860, with most arrivals able to improve upon their occupational status in Europe. Twenty-eight of the 30 immigrants (93.3 percent) who were unskilled workers in Germany had risen in status by the 1860 census, of whom 22 had become independent farmers. Only 2 of 29 artisans (6.9 percent) had fallen to the status of unskilled worker by 1860, while 4 of 25 proprietors (16.0 percent) had fallen.[5]

Swierenga cast a wider net, examining the occupational mobility of all Dutch immigrants to the United States. Among those who arrived over the period 1841–50, he found more movement downward to unskilled worker and less upward from unskilled worker than Kamphoefner had found. Of 1841–50 arrivals who were in white collar occupations in Holland, 23 percent were described as unskilled workers in the 1850 census. Twenty-two percent of those who were skilled workers in Holland were unskilled workers in 1850.[6] Of 1841–50 arrivals who were unskilled workers or farm laborers, or stated no occupation upon arrival, 51 percent had moved up in status by 1850.

The fact that the groups studied by Kamphoefner and Swierenga went to narrowly circumscribed areas in the United States might have made their experiences different from the experiences of the British, Irish, and Germans who arrived in the antebellum period and settled in widely disparate locations. For example, 72 percent of the 9,000 Dutch immigrants present in the United States in 1850 lived in only 16 counties. The cohesiveness of the Dutch community might account for the fact that so few of those in white collar and skilled occupations in Europe appeared as unskilled workers in the United States, and for the fact that those who were unskilled workers in Europe were so likely to move up into skilled and white collar jobs in the United States. As Chiswick notes, "Among immigrants with

4. Two studies that have used such samples are Kamphoefner, *Westphalians*, and Swierenga, "Dutch International Migration and Occupational Change."

5. Kamphoefner, *Westphalians*, p. 153.

6. Swierenga, "Dutch International Migration and Occupational Change," p. 107.

limited destination language skills, geographic concentration can serve as a shelter between the origin and destination labor markets."[7] He notes further, however, that there may be a negative relationship between immigrants' labor market outcomes and their geographic concentration if concentration results in the provision of "ethnic goods" that immigrants value and immigrants are willing to trade off some improvements in labor market outcomes for these goods.

The present sample includes immigrants who settled in more than 500 counties. Though some no doubt took advantage of the safety that migration to an existing immigrant community afforded, many of those in the present sample struck out on their own without the benefit of such ties.

In the absence of detailed information on individuals linked from their place of origin to the census, historical researchers have instead relied on the record of mobility in individual local economies within the United States based on sources such as the decennial federal census, city directories, and local tax and poll records in which individuals can be linked across successive years. These studies have generally found little upward mobility among immigrants. Among Irish immigrants in Poughkeepsie who first appeared in the U.S. census as unskilled workers, only 26 percent escaped blue collar occupations during their careers in the city. No more than 30 percent of immigrants in South Bend, Indiana, who first appeared in the U.S. census as manual workers (skilled workers and unskilled workers) were able to move into nonmanual (white collar) occupations during their careers in the city.[8] In Newburyport, Thernstrom found that only 20 percent of foreigners who were in unskilled occupations in the 1850 U.S. census were able to reach skilled or white collar occupations by 1860.[9] For a slightly later period in Boston, Thernstrom found that no more than a third of the foreign born whose first observed occupation in the United States was blue collar (unskilled manual or skilled manual) were in white collar (nonmanual) occupations at the end of their careers in Boston.[10]

Since these studies were unable to control for an immigrant's time in the United States and since recent migrants were less likely to be enumerated by census takers, directory publishers, and tax collectors, these studies have understated mobility if mobility was most likely among recent arrivals. Since these studies contain no information on occupation prior to arrival, they also miss what may have been the single biggest change the immigrant worker would have ever made: his introduction into the U.S. economy. Since these studies are based on specific communities and can trace occupational mobility only for those individuals who remained in the community over a decade, they are also unable to take account of immigrants who moved up by moving out and relocating to another city or a rural area where greater opportunities beckoned. In chapter 7, we will examine occupational mobility between 1850 and 1860 for those immigrants in the sample linked to both censuses and avoid this pitfall. As we shall see, many of the

7. Chiswick, "Performance of Immigrants," p. 105.
8. Bodnar, *Transplanted*, summarizes these city studies.
9. Thernstrom, *Poverty and Progress*, p. 100.
10. Thernstrom, *Other Bostonians*, p. 117.

most successful immigrants were those who changed location. The extensive upward mobility in the Kamphoefner and Swierenga studies points to the possible
magnitude of such transitions in the population of all immigrants.

The reliability of the occupation information in the passenger ship lists, however, has been questioned by a number of researchers.[11] Since this information is
an important element of the story told here, it is worth exploring the reliability
of these data in more detail. One difficulty is the often haphazard recording of occupations: some lists contain nothing but farmers or laborers, and whole pages of
a ship's list sometimes contain nothing but ditto marks in the column for occupation. Based on a comparison of the age and family structure of those on such
"poor" lists with other immigrants on lists where occupation seems to have been
recorded with greater care, Cohn concludes that the immigrants on the poor lists
were probably in fact farmers and laborers.[12]

A more serious problem with the lists is that the Passenger Ship Act of 1819
did not specify whether immigrants' actual occupations in Europe or their anticipated occupations in the United States should be reported by the ship's captain.
Since there was no penalty for failure to report occupations accurately, immigrants
might have merely given optimistic statements of their prospects rather than true
statements of their occupations in Europe. What is necessary in order to get a
sense of how serious a problem misreporting represents in the lists is a sample of
immigrants linked to passenger ship lists from a source that describes their occupation in Europe with greater reliability than the ship lists.

In the course of tracing Dutch immigrants from Dutch municipal emigration
records into the U.S. census, Swierenga created just such a sample.[13] These Dutch
records were collected annually in cities, towns, and villages by local officials, who
then forwarded them to the Interior Ministry at The Hague.[14] Table 5-1 presents
a comparison of occupations stated in the passenger ship lists with occupations
stated in the Dutch emigration records for 878 Dutch immigrants who arrived between 1841 and 1850. The occupations are grouped into four broad categories:
white collar, skilled, farmer, and unskilled.[15] The only occupation in which a majority of Dutch immigrants appears to have given an incorrect occupation in the
passenger ship lists is farmer: more than 60 percent of those who described themselves in the passenger ship lists as farmers were known to Dutch municipal au-

11. Erickson, "Emigration from the British Isles to the U.S.A. in 1841"; Cohn, "English Immigrants."
12. Cohn, "English Immigrants."
13. Swierenga, "Dutch International Migration and Occupational Change." The patterns of
Dutch occupational mobility between departure from Europe and arrival in the United States described above are based on these Dutch municipal records, rather than the information from the ship
lists. Swierenga used the Dutch records because they included all the data on the ship lists as well as
information not available in the ship lists, such as reasons for emigration and religious affiliation.
14. Swierenga graciously provided this linked sample to me. The calculations that follow and any
conclusions drawn from them are my own handiwork, and Swierenga should in no way be implicated
in them.
15. The specific occupational titles that fall into each category are shown in Appendix E. This is
the categorization of occupations used by Thernstrom, *Poverty and Progress,* and the other studies of
occupational mobility cited above.

Table 5-1. Occupations reported by Dutch immigrants to the United States
in Dutch emigration lists compared to their occupations reported
in U.S. passenger ship arrival records, 1841–50.

Occupation in U.S. Passenger Ship Arrival Records	N	Occupation in Dutch Emigration Lists			
		White Collar (%)	Skilled (%)	Farmer (%)	Unskilled (%)
White collar	35	82.9	11.4	0.0	5.7
Skilled	225	3.6	77.3	6.2	12.9
Farmer	547	7.7	15.5	38.6	38.2
Unskilled	71	7.0	28.2	9.9	54.9

Source: Sample of Dutch Immigrants to the United States, 1841–1850, linked from Dutch municipal emigration records to U.S. passenger ship arrival records, provided by Robert Swierenga.
Note: Occupational categories are defined in Appendix E.

thorities by another occupational title. Most of those incorrectly identified in the ship lists as farmers were described by Dutch authorities as unskilled workers—common laborers or farm laborers. In contrast, 83 percent of those in white collar occupations in the ship lists and 77 percent of those in skilled occupations in the ship lists were known to be in those occupations before their departure from Holland. Fifty-five percent of those in unskilled jobs in the ship lists had also been in unskilled jobs in Holland.

The occupation in the ship lists for those stating they were white collar or skilled thus seems a reasonably proxy for occupation before departure, albeit one measured with error. There does not appear to be any systematic change over the 1840s in the extent of that error, though. For example, there is no trend over the 1840s in the percentage of unskilled workers in the Dutch ship lists who were actually white collar, skilled, or farmers in the Dutch emigration records, or in the percentage of white collar, skilled workers, or farmers who were actually unskilled workers. Differences in misreporting by country of origin are probably insignificant as well. The British and the Irish in the sample sailed from the same ports—most left from Liverpool or London—so the same clerks compiled the ship list occupations for both groups. As a result, they should be measured with roughly equal error. We do not know how the accuracy of the occupations reported for the British and Irish compare to the accuracy for the Germans in the sample. The accuracy of the lists reflects both the probability that immigrants would report their true occupation and the probability that they would have their occupations recorded correctly by those creating the ship lists. The fact that the Germans did not speak English is not likely to have been a great source of inaccuracy in compiling the German lists, since the lists were apparently compiled at the port of origin.

Farmers are more problematic. This is probably less the result of carelessness on the part of those compiling the lists than it is the result of the presence of large numbers of farm tenants in Europe and the absence of the term "tenant" in the ship lists. An individual who was a farm tenant in Europe would thus have been described as either a farmer or a laborer in the ship lists. Since there were no clear guidelines by which farm tenants were assigned to either group in the ship lists, we cannot separate those who were farm tenants in Europe (who were probably more akin to laborers in the amount of capital they possessed and the amount of supervision they received) from independent farmers. Similarly, some of those reported as laborers in the ship lists may have been farm tenants rather than farm laborers in Europe.

The Extent of Occupational Mobility
from Arrival to 1850 and 1860

The sample introduced here makes it possible to compare occupation in the country of origin and occupation in the United States. As in the previous section, we will group occupations into four broad categories (outlined in Appendix E), in order to focus on only the most significant occupational changes. This procedure has the virtue of simplicity, but its simplicity is achieved at a cost: the focus on only four broad occupational categories makes it necessary to overlook subtle changes that immigrants made in occupational status, changes that did not represent movement across the boundaries of these groups but that nonetheless represented genuine improvements in their circumstances. An alternative to using a small number of discrete occupational categories would be to create a continuous measure with which to assess immigrants' performance, based on wages, incomes, or occupational prestige.

The first group is white collar workers. This includes those in professional, commercial, and proprietary pursuits, and corresponds to the high white collar and low white collar designations employed in other studies.[16] The second is skilled, which includes anyone stating that they possessed a skill. These workers correspond to skilled blue collar or skilled manual workers and semi-skilled blue collar or semi-skilled manual workers in other studies. The next group is farmers. The fourth group is the unskilled, which includes those who described themselves simply as laborers and those with unskilled manual jobs. This corresponds to the unskilled blue collar or unskilled manual group in other studies. Those who stated they had no job in the ship lists have been excluded from the analysis.

Table 5-2 presents a comparison of the occupations immigrants stated in the passenger ship lists with the occupations they stated in the 1850 and 1860 censuses. For 1850 and 1860, the category "farmer" includes only farm owners; farm tenants and laborers are grouped with "unskilled" workers. Though the U.S. census was as imprecise as the ship lists in describing the occupations of those employed in agriculture, it is possible to infer whether an individual described as a "farmer" in the 1850 or 1860 census was in fact the owner of a farm. In both years,

16. Thernstrom, *Poverty and Progress*.

Table 5-2. Occupational mobility between arrival and 1850 or 1860
of immigrant arrivals at New York, 1840–50.

Occupation in U.S. Passenger Ship Arrival Records	N	Occupation in U.S. Census			
		White Collar (%)	Skilled (%)	Farmer (%)	Unskilled (%)
1850 Occupation					
White collar	100	38.0	29.0	8.0	25.0
Skilled	429	7.2	58.3	8.4	26.1
Farmer	352	8.2	28.7	19.9	43.2
Unskilled	567	5.6	31.4	7.2	55.7
All	1,448	9.0	38.5	10.7	41.8
1860 Occupation					
White collar	86	20.9	36.0	14.0	29.1
Skilled	347	10.1	46.1	18.4	25.4
Farmer	363	13.8	34.7	23.4	28.1
Unskilled	819	8.2	31.7	12.8	47.3
All	1,615	10.5	35.7	16.5	37.3

Source: Male household heads and unaccompanied males in passenger ship arrival records at port of New York, 1840–1850, linked to 1850 and/or 1860 manuscript census schedules.

Note: A "farmer" in 1850 and 1860 reported his occupation as "farmer" in the census and reported a positive amount of real estate wealth. Occupational categories are defined in Appendix E.

the census recorded the value of any real estate owned by the respondent. Following Bogue, *Prairie to Combelt*, I have classified farmers as those who met two criteria: (1) they were listed in the 1850 or 1860 census as "farmers"; and (2) they were reported in that census to own real estate. Those listed as "farmers" but owning no real estate were classified as "unskilled," as were those listed as "laborers" or "farm laborers" regardless of their real estate holdings.

The results show considerable mobility from occupation in Europe to occupation at the 1850 census. Forty-four percent of those who were described as unskilled in the passenger ship lists had moved up to a higher-status occupation by the time of the 1850 census. A quarter of those in white collar and skilled occupations in the ship lists were found as unskilled workers in 1850. Finally, few immigrants seem to have moved from nonfarm occupations in Europe into farming in the United States. Of the 1,096 immigrants who arrived as white collar, skilled, or unskilled workers, only 8 percent appeared as farmers by 1850. All of this mobility into farming, however, can be accounted for by inaccuracies in the ship lists: Table 5-1 suggests that, in the Dutch ship lists, 16 percent of immigrants who were described as white collar, skilled, or unskilled workers were in fact either farmers or farm tenants before their departure from Europe, so even if the lists used here are twice as accurate as the Dutch lists, all of those moving into farming after entering the United States may have actually been farmers before departure from Europe.

Table 5-3. Specific changes in occupation between arrival and 1850 or 1860 made by immigrant arrivals at New York, 1840–50.

| Change in Occupation | Number at Risk and Percent Making Specified Move | | | | | |
| | British | | Irish | | German | |
	N	%	N	%	N	%
Between Arrival and 1850						
White collar to unskilled	23	21.7	16	37.5	54	22.2
Skilled to unskilled	231	17.1	92	52.2	147	20.4
Farmer or unskilled to white collar, skilled, or farmer	187	63.2	427	35.1	234	58.6
Between Arrival and 1860						
White collar to unskilled	17	23.5	16	62.5	49	22.5
Skilled to unskilled	129	15.5	68	51.5	139	22.3
Farmer or unskilled to white collar, skilled, or farmer	233	76.8	635	41.9	280	81.1

Source: Male household heads and unaccompanied males in passenger ship arrival records at port of New York, 1840–1850, linked to 1850 and/or 1860 manuscript census schedules.

Note: A "farmer" in 1850 and 1860 reported his occupation as "farmer" in the census and reported a positive amount of real estate wealth. Occupational categories are defined in Appendix E.

Table 5-3 presents a breakdown of three types of mobility by country of origin: (1) downward mobility from white collar to unskilled; (2) downward mobility from skilled to unskilled; and (3) upward mobility from farmer or unskilled to any occupation other than unskilled. In the balance of this chapter, those who were described as farmers in the ship lists and those who were described there as unskilled will be grouped together. This is because, as was noted in the previous section, it is not possible to distinguish someone who was the owner or independent operator of a farm from a farm tenant or laborer in the passenger ship lists. In 1850 and 1860, however, farmer and unskilled will remain separate categories.

The Irish clearly had the worst outcomes: the highest percentages moving down and the lowest moving up. The percentages moving down also exceeded the percentage moving up. The British and Germans were quite different from the Irish, but similar to each other, with the percentage moving up for both groups three to four times as great as the percentage moving down. A χ^2 test on the difference across countries of origin in the percentages moving up and down in Table 5-3 was statistically significant at the 5 percent level. These differences across counties of origin could result from several effects. Two that we will consider in the next sections are how long different immigrant groups have been in the United States and how likely the average immigrant from a particular country was to possess specific characteristics associated with moving up from unskilled worker. If the amount of time immigrants have spent in the United States is correlated with the possession of U.S.-specific human capital, or if age and literacy

Table 5-4. Specific changes in occupation between arrival and 1850 or 1860 made by immigrant arrivals at New York, 1840–50, adjusted for misreporting in passenger ship lists.

| | Number at Risk and Percent Making Specified Move | | |
Change in Occupation	British (%)	Irish (%)	German (%)
Between Arrival and 1850			
White collar to unskilled	16.0	32.0	16.0
Skilled to unskilled	4.0	39.0	7.0
Farmer or unskilled to white collar, skilled, or farmer	3.0	−25.0	−1.0
Between Arrival and 1860			
White collar to unskilled	18.0	57.0	17.0
Skilled to unskilled	3.0	39.0	9.0
Farmer or unskilled to white collar, skilled, or farmer	17.0	−18.0	21.0

Source: Male household heads and unaccompanied males in passenger ship arrival records at port of New York, 1840–1850, linked to 1850 and/or 1860 manuscript census schedules; sample of Dutch Immigrants to the United States, 1841–1850, linked from Dutch municipal emigration records to U.S. passenger ship arrival records, provided by Robert Swierenga.

Note: Each entry assumes that the U.S. passenger ship lists used to construct Table 5-3 were just as inaccurate as the Dutch lists used to construct Table 5-1. Negative entries indicate that the mobility in Table 5-3 can be more than accounted for by misreporting in the U.S. ship lists. A "farmer" in 1850 and 1860 reported his occupation as "farmer" in the census and reported a positive amount of real estate wealth. Occupational categories are defined in Appendix E.

are correlated with general human capital, and these types of human capital made it easier for immigrants to move into white collar and skilled jobs after arrival, then the superior performance of the British and Germans might reflect greater average duration in the United States or their possession of greater amounts of human capital.

As was noted earlier, some of the mobility between premigration and postmigration occupation might be the result of inaccuracies in the ship lists. If we assume that the lists used here are as accurate as the Dutch lists for 1841–50, it is possible to calculate how much of the observed occupational mobility in Table 5-3 remains after accounting for inaccuracies. In the Dutch lists described in Table 5-1, 6 percent of white collar workers were actually unskilled, 13 percent of skilled workers were actually unskilled, and 60 percent of farmers and unskilled workers were actually white collar workers, skilled workers, or farmers. Subtracting these percentages from the entries in Table 5-3 produces the adjusted occupational mobility rates in Table 5-4.

These adjustments imply, for example, that if the accuracy of the lists used here was the same as the accuracy of the Dutch lists, the 63.2 percent rate of upward mobility between arrival and 1850 for British immigrants who said they were farmers or unskilled workers in the ship lists consisted of upward mobility of 3 percentage points and mismeasurement of 60 percentage points. Note, however, that substantial differences in mobility by country of origin remain even after these adjustments. As we will see later, differences in mobility by years in the United States are also apparent. Neither of these patterns is likely to have resulted from the misclassification of occupations in the ship lists.

How quickly were gains in occupational status from European occupation to U.S. occupation made and losses in status recouped after arrival? Did occupational mobility occur only at arrival—was entry into the U.S. economy a permanent, one-time shock to an immigrant's career—or was there scope for ongoing change and adjustment in the years after arrival? What were the factors that made occupational mobility more likely? We saw in Table 5-3 how much worse the Irish seem to have done compared to the British and Germans. How can we account for their relatively poor performance? In order to get a better understanding of both the temporal pattern of occupational mobility and what it was about particular individuals and particular places that promoted occupational mobility, we now turn to an analysis of the influence of these factors on occupational mobility in the years after immigrants' arrival in the United States.

The Timing of Occupational Mobility

Two difficulties arise in attempting to determine the extent, timing, and correlates of the occupational change experienced by immigrants between their European and U.S. occupations. The first and most serious is that although the sample tells us each immigrant's European occupation, date of arrival, and 1850 and 1860 occupations, we do not know the date at which occupational changes occurred. We may know, for example, that an immigrant who arrived as a laborer in 1843 had become a carpenter by 1850, but we do not know when during the immigrant's seven years in the United States that transition occurred; all we know is how long the immigrant was at risk to make such a transition and whether it occurred during that period. The second problem is that we do not know the date at which immigrants who had not yet changed occupations by 1850 or 1860 would do so. These observations are right-censored. These are similar to the problems encountered in the previous chapter in assessing the pattern of departure from New York or entry into the West.

A continuous-time duration model with discrete observations can again address both of these problems. This method consists of estimating the following probability for each individual:

$$P_{jk}(t;X) = Prob[in\ occupation\ k\ at\ time\ t\ |\ in\ occupation\ j\ at\ time\ 0;X] \quad (1)$$

The date of arrival is time 0 and the time since arrival is t; the vector X contains both personal characteristics and the characteristics of the immigrant's location.

Estimation of such a model will allow us to calculate the probability that an immigrant had changed occupation at various times after arrival, which in turn will allow us to infer a distribution and mean for the time between arrival and occupational change. This technique compensates for the lack of information on each individual immigrant's date of occupational change. Since the model utilizes information on both those who have changed occupations and those who have not by time t, it also surmounts the right-censoring problem.

The hazard function is motivated, as it was in chapter 4, with a simple analysis of the decision problem faced by an immigrant in the years after arrival. The immigrant can either devote all his time to an unskilled job or use some of his time to work as an unskilled worker and some to prepare for and seek a better job in the "other" category (as a white collar or skilled worker, or as a farmer). If the immigrant determines the intensity with which to seek a new job based on the costs and benefits of changing occupations (where costs include search and training costs, and benefits include higher wages and greater employment security), this results in a function $\theta(t;X)dt$ that describes the probability at each date since arrival in the United States that the immigrant will be offered a new job in the interval $(t, t + dt)$. If $\gamma(t;X)$ represents the probability that such a job offer is worth accepting—that accepting such a job would allow the immigrant to move out of the unskilled category and result in a higher present value of lifetime utility—then the probability that the immigrant will change from unskilled to "other" in the interval $(t, t + dt)$ is the hazard function, $\lambda_{12}(t;X)dt = [\theta(t;X)][\gamma(t;X)]dt$, where the subscripts refer to the transition from occupation 1 (unskilled worker) to occupation 2 ("other": white collar, skilled, or farmer).

As Appendix B demonstrates, the hazard function for a sample of individuals is related to $P_{12}(t;X)$, the probability that the immigrant had left the unskilled category after t years in the United States, by the relationship

$$P_{12}(t;X) = 1 - \exp\left(\int_0^t -\lambda_{12}(u;X'\beta) \ du\right) \qquad (2)$$

where β is a vector of parameters to be estimated. Appendix B describes the likelihood function that is used to estimate these parameters. We will again assume that the hazard function follows either a *Weibull* distribution or a *log-logistic* distribution.

The probability that an immigrant has moved up from unskilled worker at each date since arrival should reflect the skills he possesses at arrival: those described as white collar or skilled workers in the ship lists, for example, should have less difficulty moving quickly into such occupations after arrival than workers who were unskilled when they left Europe. Separate analyses are thus performed for two groups, based on the occupations they stated in the passenger ship lists: (1) immigrants who were described as farmers or unskilled workers; and (2) immigrants who were described as white collar or skilled workers. An immigrant will be said to have entered an occupation other than unskilled worker if either of two conditions is true: (1) he was described as working in a white collar or skilled occupation in the U.S. census; or (2) he was described as a farmer in the census and his recorded real estate wealth was greater than zero.

Before we proceed to estimate the rate at which immigrants were able to move up from unskilled worker to a better occupation, we need to consider the possibility that a correlation between occupational status and duration in the United States might be the result of differences in the propensities of successive cohorts of arrivals to move up at all, irrespective of their propensities to move up or down as their time in the United States increased. For example, in a single cross section, if earlier arrivals are more likely to have moved up at any time since arrival than more recent arrivals (either because they are of higher quality or because they faced a better job market at their arrival), we might mistakenly attribute the higher occupational status of earlier arrivals to the fact that their duration in the United States is greater, when in fact their status would be higher even if they were observed at the same duration in the United States as more recent arrivals.[17]

In order to get around this problem, we will again exploit the fact that some immigrants in the sample are observed in 1850, some are observed in 1860, and some are observed in both years. This will allow us to control for both duration in the United States and year of arrival. Each immigrant in the sample contributes one observation to the analysis. This means that a group of immigrants with the same year of arrival will contain some immigrants who have been in the United States t years and some who have been in the United States $t + 10$ years.[18] To determine the impact of duration in the United States, we estimate the hazard function using dummy variables for year of arrival as the only covariates in the X vector and years since arrival in the United States for t.

Since each immigrant is assumed to have been able to find work as an unskilled worker at arrival, an observation is considered to have made a move out of the unskilled category only if one of the following conditions is true: (1) the individual was observed only in 1850 and had moved out of the unskilled category by that date (so t is the time from arrival to 1850); (2) the individual was observed only in 1860 and had moved out of the unskilled category by that date (so t is the time from arrival to 1860); (3) the individual was observed in both 1850 and 1860 and had moved out of the unskilled category by 1850 (so t is again the time from arrival to 1850); or (4) the individual was observed in both 1850 and 1860, was still an unskilled worker in 1850, but had moved out of the unskilled category by 1860 (so t is again the time from arrival to 1860). Individuals who were observed only in 1850 and were unskilled workers in that year were considered not to have made an occupational change, and the time from arrival to 1850 was used for t.

17. See Heckman and Robb, "Using Longitudinal Data," for a discussion of these effects. Borjas, "Self-Employment," finds such effects in his work on immigrant entry into self-employment, though they are not strong enough to eliminate his finding that immigrants were more likely to be self-employed the longer they had been in the United States.

18. For example, if two immigrants arrived in 1845, and one rose to a skilled occupation by 1850 but the other was not observed as a skilled worker until 1860, the sample would contain two 1845 arrivals, but the years since their arrival that would be used in the analysis would be 5 and 15, respectively.

Individuals who were observed only in 1860 and were unskilled workers in that year were considered not to have made an occupational change, and the time from arrival to 1860 was used for t. Individuals who were observed in both 1850 and 1860 but were unskilled workers in both years are considered not to have made an occupational change, and the time from arrival to 1860 was used as the value for t.

The coefficients on the dummy variables for year of arrival will embody two effects: differences in the state of the labor market faced by cohorts at their arrival and differences in the overall quality of successive cohorts. If labor market conditions were deteriorating over the 1840s and an immigrant's first occupation in the United States is an important determinant of his entire occupational trajectory, the estimated effect of duration would overstate the effect of time since arrival in the absence of controls for the immigrant's specific arrival cohort. The magnitude of this effect is probably slight: real wages for both laborers and artisans rose from 1840 to 1843, fell gradually through 1846, fell precipitously in 1847, and recovered thereafter to stand in 1850 at about the same level as in 1840.[19] There was thus no obvious trend in the wages immigrants faced at arrival that would indicate that declining initial labor market conditions were biasing the effect of duration upward. Since the impact of aggregate labor market conditions at the time of entry should not vary substantially by country of origin, comparing the year of arrival effect across origins for a particular year of arrival will make it possible to isolate the impact of changes over the 1840s in the overall quality of successive cohorts.

Events in several countries over the 1840s may have made immigrants from those countries either more or less likely to move up in occupation after arrival in the United States, irrespective of their time in the United States, by influencing the average quality of emigrants sent out in particular years. For example, the Germans who arrived in the late 1840s may have been quite different from those who had arrived earlier from Germany as a result of the revolutions that swept continental Europe, including large parts of Germany, in 1848. The Irish also experienced an event that could have been expected to produce a change in the quality of the migrants leaving Ireland—the potato famine of the late 1840s. It will be possible to test whether these events had an impact on the propensity of immigrants to improve their occupational status by examining the coefficients on the dummy variables for specific years of arrival after controlling for time since arrival.

The impact of duration will likewise embody two effects: the impact of an additional year in the United States and the impact of particular years in the United States. The second effect will be important if the 1850s differed significantly from the 1840s in the state of the labor market and its impact on occupational mobility. For example, immigrants who arrived in 1845 and were observed in 1860 may be different from immigrants who arrived in 1845 and were observed in 1850 in two respects: the former have been in the United States ten years longer when

19. Margo, "Wages and Prices," p. 184.
20. Ibid.

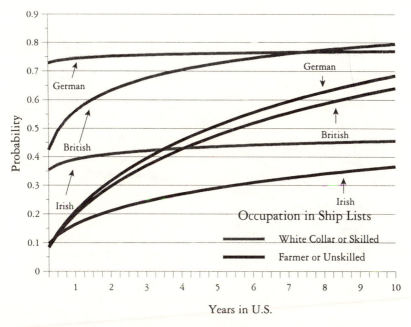

Figure 5-1. Probability of becoming a white collar or skilled worker or farmer by years in the United States. *Note:* Assuming a Weibull hazard function. *Source:* Male household heads and unaccompanied males in passenger ship arrival records at port of New York, 1840–1850, linked to 1850 and/or 1860 manuscript census schedules.

they are observed, and are observed after having passed through a particular period (the 1850s), which contained the Panic of 1857 that may have made labor market conditions more difficult than they had been in the 1840s.

The evidence suggests, however, that the 1850s were much like the 1840s: there was a slight rise in real wages early in the 1850s, a gradual decline after 1852–53, a more precipitous decline through the Panic of 1857, and some recovery later in the decade.[20] The hazard function adopted here, which allows the impact of duration in the United States to change as time in the United States changes, will make it possible to capture the impact of a change between the 1840s and the 1850s in the effect of a year of time spent after arrival in the United States.

Figures 5-1 and 5-2 present plots of the maximum-likelihood estimates of the effect of time since arrival in the United States on the probability that immigrants would be observed as white collar or skilled workers or farmers rather than as unskilled workers at each date since arrival, controlling for the specific year of arrival.[21] The log-likelihood functions estimated are equation B10 in Appendix B (the Weibull hazard) for Figure 5-1, and the corresponding log-likelihood using the log-logistic hazard for Figure 5-2. These plots show the value of $P_{12}(t;X)$ at

21. The sample sizes used to construct Figures 5-1 and 5-2 are as follows. For white collar and skilled workers at arrival: British, 283; Irish, 169; German, 330. For farmers and unskilled workers at arrival: British, 375; Irish, 903; German, 431.

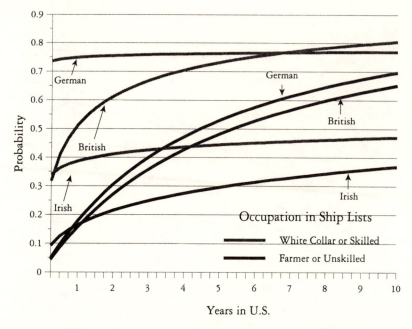

Figure 5-2. Probability of becoming a white collar or skilled worker or farmer by years in the United States. *Note:* Assuming a log-logistic hazard function. *Source:* Male household heads and unaccompanied males in passenger ship arrival records at port of New York, 1840–1850, linked to 1850 and/or 1860 manuscript census schedules.

each date since arrival, with two separate plots for those who arrived as white collar or skilled workers, and farmers or unskilled workers, using the average year of arrival effect in the sample.[22] They reflect the experience of an average immigrant who arrived between 1840 and 1850. For both those who arrived as farmers and unskilled workers and those who arrived as white collar and skilled workers, and for all countries of origin, the marginal effect of an additional year in the United States on the probability of moving up from work as an unskilled worker was greatest for those who had been in the United States the least time. When the log-logistic hazard function—which allows a nonmonotonic hazard—is used in Figure 5-2, the results are identical to those in Figure 5-1 using the monotonic Weibull hazard, suggesting that in this case the assumption of a monotonic hazard function is reasonable.

Immigrants who were reported in the passenger ship lists to have white collar or skilled jobs were considerably more likely than their countrymen who were reported to be farmers or unskilled workers to leave the unskilled category soon after arrival. For the British and Germans, for example, more than 55 percent of white collar and skilled arrivals had returned to these jobs or entered farming

22. In creating Figures 5-1 and 5-2, a small positive value (0.001) was substituted for zero years since arrival, because the natural log of zero is undefined.

within a year of entering the United States; only about 20 percent of British and German immigrants who were described as farmers or unskilled had moved into white collar or skilled jobs or entered farming. The same differences based on occupation in the ship lists can be seen for the Irish, but at a lower level: after a year in the United States, 40 percent of white collar and skilled arrivals had moved up from unskilled work, as opposed to only 15 percent arrivals who were farmers or unskilled. For German and Irish immigrants, the impact of an additional year in the United States on the probability of moving up from unskilled work was greater for those reporting unskilled or farm jobs at arrival than for those reporting white collar or skilled jobs at arrival. For the British, the opposite was true.

Because more mobility in each origin or occupation-at-arrival group occurs earlier than later in the years after arrival, estimates of occupational mobility that exclude the most recent arrivals will clearly understate the actual amount of mobility that occurs among immigrants. This can be seen most clearly in the case of British immigrants who arrived as white collar or skilled workers. If we assume that immigrants appear in the census only after two years in the United States, the rate of upward occupational mobility in a single cohort of immigrants observed in, say, both the 1850 and 1860 U.S. censuses will be 43 percent: at two years, 35 out of 100 arrivals will still be unskilled workers when they are observed in the 1850 census; at twelve years, 20 out of the original 100 arrivals will still be unskilled workers, yielding an upward mobility rate over ten years of 15/35 (43 percent). If we could observe immigrants from immediately after their arrival, though, the ten-year upward mobility rate would be 65 percent instead: immediately after arrival, 57 out of 100 arrivals would be unskilled workers; after ten years, 20 out of the original 100 arrivals in that cohort would still be unskilled workers, producing an upward mobility rate of 37/57 (65 percent). These calculations suggest that previous studies of nineteenth-century occupational mobility may have substantially understated the mobility experienced by immigrants if recently arrived immigrants were less likely than immigrants who had been in the United States longer to be enumerated in the census, city directories, or tax records.

The mobility patterns for white collar and skilled arrivals in Figures 5-1 and 5-2 suggest that the occupations reported by immigrants in the ship lists represent a reasonable measure of the value of the human capital transferred to the United States by the arrival of British and German immigrants: within just four years of arrival, more than 70 percent of these immigrants were able to employ the skills they had brought with them. For the Irish, however, the fraction of white collar and skilled arrivals who left the unskilled category never reached 50 percent, suggesting that for this group, the distribution of occupational titles in the ship lists provides an overstatement of the human capital transfer occasioned by their immigration to the United States. This assumes that Irish white collar and skilled workers were unable to return to these jobs because their training in these areas was a poor match for the skills needed in the U.S. labor market. If their poor performance resulted instead from outright discrimination in hiring and promotion, then Irish arrivals did indeed transfer human capital with them, but the United

States simply chose not to utilize that capital. Irish immigrants, like other immigrants, contributed to an outward expansion of the production possibility frontier, but the economy chose to operate at a point inside the frontier. The foregone production was the "price" paid to purchase the observed level of discrimination.

The gradual improvement in the position of immigrants who arrived as farmers or unskilled workers does not support the view that the distribution of occupational titles in the ship lists understates the value of human capital embodied in immigrants because of rigidities in the labor and land markets they left. If such rigidities had been an important impediment to occupational mobility and the United States had fewer of these structural impediments to occupational improvement, the curves for arriving farmers and unskilled workers in Figures 5-1 and 5-2 either would have had a higher intercept or would have been much steeper in the early years after arrival than later.

In order to assess the impact of arrival in a particular year, and the impact of arrival after the start of the Irish famine or after the German revolutions of 1848, the Weibull hazard used to generate Figure 5-1 was reestimated, for each country of origin, with the inclusion of two additional variables: a dummy variable for either arrival in the period from the fall of 1846 through the summer of 1850 (post-famine Irish immigrants) or arrival in the period from the fall of 1848 through the summer of 1850 (post-Revolution German immigrants), and interactions between these dummies and years since arrival in the United States. Attention is restricted to Irish and German immigrants here since, in generating Figures 5-1 and 5-2, there were no apparently significant differences in the effect of year of arrival for British immigrants; for Irish and German arrivals, though, there was an apparent change in the performance of those who arrived late in the 1840s. The specification used here allows both the probability of moving up from unskilled work immediately after arrival and the change in that probability as time in the United States increases to differ between arrivals from the early 1840s and those from the late 1840s. Recall that year-of-arrival effects will capture two influences: the impact of aggregate labor market conditions in the United States at arrival, and the impact of changes over the 1840s in the average propensity to move up from unskilled work for arrivals from each country of origin. Comparing the year-of-arrival effects for the Irish and Germans (within either occupation-at-arrival group) will allow us to infer the impact of the second of these influences.

The results shown in Table 5-5 for white collar and skilled immigrants provide some evidence for a widening gap between the performance of German and Irish immigrants at the end of the 1840s. For Germans who arrived after the revolutions of 1848, the probability of moving up from unskilled work immediately after arrival was 34 percentage points higher than the probability of making such a move for 1840 arrivals. At the same time, the Irish show very little net change in the probability of moving up immediately after arrival. For Germans who arrived as farmers or unskilled workers, there was a slight increase in the probability of immediate upward mobility among those who arrived in the years after 1847, compared to the probability for 1840 arrivals, but this pattern mirrors the pattern for the Irish in this occupation group (though the changes relative to 1840 for the

Table 5-5. Effect of specific year of arrival on the probability of entering a white collar or skilled occupation or farming, controlling for years in the United States, for immigrant arrivals at New York, 1840–50.

	White Collar or Skilled at Arrival		Farmer or Unskilled at Arrival	
Year of Arrival	Irish $\delta P_{12}/\delta X$	German $\delta P_{12}/\delta X$	Irish $\delta P_{12}/\delta X$	German $\delta P_{12}/\delta X$
1841	0.085	−0.119	0.040	0.055
1842	0.158	0.046	0.152**	0.045
1843	0.156	−0.009	0.292***	0.053
1844	0.254	0.039	0.061	0.170*
1845	0.219	0.022	0.171*	0.096
1846	0.021	—	0.183**	—
1847	−0.407	—	0.275	—
1848	−0.287	0.196**	0.322	0.279***
1849	0.061	0.214	0.303	0.336*
1850	−0.301	0.144	0.332	0.425**
Irish Famine	0.385		−0.035	
German Revolution		0.335**		0.093
$\bar{P}_{12}$	0.468	0.737	0.353	0.674
No. of obs.	169	330	903	431

Source: Male household heads and unaccompanied males in passenger ship arrival records at port of New York, 1840–1850, linked to 1850 and/or 1860 manuscript census schedules.

Note: "$\delta P_{12}/\delta X$" is the difference between (1) the probability that an individual who arrived in the indicated year was employed in a job other than "unskilled worker" after arrival; and (2) the probability that an individual who arrived in 1840 was employed in a job other than "unskilled worker" the same number of years after arrival ($\bar{P}_{12}$). It is calculated as $\delta P_{12}/\delta X = (\beta\alpha)(-\bar{P}_{11})(\log(\bar{P}_{11}))$, where each β is an estimate of the coefficient on a dummy variables for a year of arrival and α is an estimate of the parameter from the Weibull hazard function (equation B8 in Appendix B) obtained by maximum likelihood,

$$\bar{P}_{11} = \sum_{i=1}^{N} [\exp(-\exp(X_i'\beta)t_i)^{\alpha}]/N$$

is the average probability in the sample that an individual had not moved up from unskilled worker, and $\bar{P}_{12} = 1 - \bar{P}_{11}$. The regression included two other variables (not shown): years since arrival in the United States and interactions between years since arrival in the United States and either arrival after the start of the Irish Famine (Fall 1846–1850) or arrival after the German Revolutions of 1848 (Fall 1848–1850). Probability that the true $\delta P_{12}/\delta X$ is equal to zero: *<10%; **<5%; ***<1%.

Irish are not statistically significant). The increasing difference in performance at arrival seen for white collar and skilled workers could result from (1) higher average quality German arrivals after the revolutions; (2) lower average quality Irish arrivals after the start of the famine; (3) increased anti-immigrant prejudice in the late 1840s that was directed particularly toward Irish immigrants; or (4) a combination of these.[23] The weight of the available evidence suggests the widening gap in performance between Irish and German white collar and skilled workers was produced by developments in Germany and not by those in Ireland.

There is some circumstantial evidence suggesting that the revolutions of 1848 produced an improvement in the average quality of German arrivals in white collar and skilled jobs at the end of the 1840s. Levine notes the prominent role played in the uprisings by urban artisans, who accounted for two-thirds of the deaths on the barricades erected by the revolutionaries in the streets of Berlin in the spring of 1848.[24] Chapter 6 suggests that Germans who arrived in the wake of the revolutions held less real estate on average than other German immigrants after controlling for years since arrival. Finally, Wittke describes the importance of Germans who arrived in 1848 and after as leaders in the political and economic life of the German community in America.[25] These observations are consistent with the need for some otherwise successful urban white collar and skilled workers to leave Germany to escape the postrevolutionary reaction, their departure with little financial capital, and their ability to employ their human capital after arrival and rise to positions of prominence in their communities.

There is little evidence of a decline in the average quality of Irish arrivals after the start of the famine that would have decreased the ability of the Irish to leave unskilled work shortly after arrival. Though Mokyr and Ó Gráda show decreasing numeracy among Irish immigrants to the United States over this decade, the trend they observe begins before the start of the famine.[26] Most other research on the characteristics of pre-1846 and post-1846 Irish emigrants has found no marked differences between these groups. Most came from the regions that had traditionally sent large numbers abroad, and similar proportions were independent farmers and skilled workers. At least initially, the best that the most impoverished could do was to reach Britain. They lacked the resources for a transatlantic voyage, and hoped to earn or beg their fare in Britain's port cities, or wait there for remittances from America. It was not until 1851, as emigrants received those resources, that differences in the characteristics of immigrants became apparent.[27]

The ability to observe immigrants at several points after their arrival makes it possible here to distinguish the effect of time in the United States (the duration effect) from the effect of changes over time in the average performance at arrival of successive groups of immigrants (the cohort effect). Much of the debate over the performance of contemporary immigrants to the United States has centered on the relative magnitudes of these duration and cohort effects. Borjas suggests that cohort effects account for a substantial portion of the impact of years since arrival in cross-sectional data; a number of other studies have disputed this

---

23. The impact of differences in the degree of discrimination faced by the British, Irish, and Germans on their relative performance will be considered in greater detail below.

24. Levine, *Spirit of 1848*, pp. 36–37.

25. Wittke, *Refugees of Revolution*.

26. Mokyr and Ó Gráda, "Emigration and Poverty."

27. Miller, *Emigrants and Exiles*, pp. 293–295.

Table 5-6. Effect of years in the United States on the probability of immigrant arrivals at New York, 1840–50, entering white collar or skilled occupations or farming after arrival, with and without controls for specific year of arrival.

Occupation in U.S. Passenger Ship Arrival Records	Without Year of Arrival Effects $\delta P_{12}/\delta X$	With Year of Arrival Effects $\delta P_{12}/\delta X$
White collar and skilled		
British	0.087**	0.093**
Irish	0.089**	0.030
German	0.007	0.011
Farmer and unskilled		
British	0.229***	0.244***
Irish	0.098***	0.114***
German	0.214***	0.253***

Source: Male household heads and unaccompanied males in passenger ship arrival records at port of New York, 1840–1850, linked to 1850 and/or 1860 manuscript census schedules.

Note: "$\delta P_{12}/\delta X$" is the effect of an additional year in the United States on the probability that an individual was employed in a job other than "unskilled worker" after arrival. It is calculated as $\delta P_{12}/\delta X = (\beta\alpha)(-\overline{P}_{11})(\log(\overline{P}_{11}))$, where α is an estimate of the coefficient on "ln(Years in U.S.)," with or without controls included for specific years of arrival, from the Weibull hazard function (equation B8 in Appendix B) obtained by maximum likelihood,

$$\overline{P}_{11} = \sum_{i=1}^{N} [\exp(-\exp(X_i'\beta)t_i)^{\alpha}]/N$$

is the average probability in the sample that an individual had not moved up from unskilled worker, and $\overline{P}_{12} = 1 - \overline{P}_{11}$. The regression included two other variables (not shown): years since arrival in the United States and interactions between years since arrival in the United States and either arrival after the start of the Irish Famine (fall 1846–1850) or arrival after the German Revolutions of 1848 (fall 1848–1850). Probability that the that the true $\delta P_{12}/\delta X$ is equal to zero: *<10%; **<5%; ***<1%.

claim.[28] It is possible to use the present sample to see how much of the effect of time since arrival represents duration and cohort effects by comparing the coefficients on log(*Years in the U.S.*) controlling for year of arrival effects (the coefficients used to construct Figures 5-1 and 5-2) with the coefficients on log(*Years in the U.S.*) without controls for year of arrival.

The only group for which the introduction of year of arrival effects makes a substantial change in the effect of time since arrival is the Irish who arrived in white collar and skilled jobs. Without controls for year of arrival, their coefficient on log(*Years in the U.S.*) is 0.089 (significant at the 5 percent level)—an effect identical to that for the British. With the introduction of controls for year of arrival, the coefficient falls in magnitude to 0.030 and is reduced to statistical insignificance. The coefficients on log(*Years in the U.S.*) without controls for year

28. Borjas, "Economics of Immigration"; Chiswick, "Performance of Immigrants," p. 108.

of arrival and with such controls are shown in Table 5-6 for each occupation at arrival and country of origin group. This difference is consistent with the decline over the 1840s in the numeracy of Irish immigrants to the United States observed by Mokyr and Ó Gráda.[29]

The Role of Personal and Locational Characteristics

The clear differences by European occupation and ethnicity in postarrival occupational mobility after accounting for year of arrival effects deserve further attention. The success of Germans who entered the United States with the handicap of not speaking English and the failure of Irish who arrived without such a handicap are somewhat puzzling. Such differences in performance could be the result of differences across groups in the possession of observed characteristics associated with rapid occupational mobility or the result of unobserved origin-specific differences in such characteristics. We thus now turn to a more detailed examination of the characteristics that influenced an immigrant's chances of moving up in occupational status in the years after arrival. The independent variables employed are the immigrant's age at arrival, literacy, and country of origin, controls for region and urban residence, and the 1850 foreign-born population and 1850–60 population growth rate of the county where the immigrant was found. Interactions between residence in the West and the fraction foreign born and population growth rate were also included.

The immigrant's age was included to capture the impact of the length of the time horizon faced by immigrants and of their resources at arrival in deciding whether to change occupation. Older immigrants who arrived as unskilled workers may have been more reluctant than younger immigrants to make the investments that would have allowed them to change occupations, since they had fewer remaining years over which to reap the net benefits of making a change.[30] To see this, suppose an immigrant faces the choice of remaining in occupation 1 or switching to occupation 2, but must incur a fixed cost C to pay for retraining if he switches. The probability that he will switch will be an increasing function of the net income gain, discounted by his rate of time preference (r) over his remaining work life (T):

$$Prob(switch) = h\left[\int_0^T (Y_2 - Y_1)e^{-rt}dt - C\right] \qquad (5)$$

$$h[\ ]' > 0, \quad h[0] = 0, \quad Y_2 > Y_1$$

29. Mokyr and Ó Gráda, "Emigration and Poverty."

30. Chiswick, "Performance of Immigrants," p. 102, describes another mechanism through which greater age at arrival will have a negative influence on the extent of postmigration occupational mobility: immigrants who were older at arrival had also probably received more of their occupational experience in their country of origin. If we had a measure of labor market experience distinct from the immigrant's age, it would be possible to assess the independent influence of this effect.

This probability is higher for immigrants who have a longer remaining work life:

$$\frac{\delta Prob}{\delta T} = h'[\ ]\ (Y_2 - Y_1)e^{-rt} > 0 \qquad (6)$$

Older immigrants, however, may have been better able to reestablish themselves in their original occupations after arrival, or been better able to move up from un-skilled work, if their age was correlated with their possession of greater human or fi-nancial capital. To see this, write the cost of changing occupations above as

$$C = g(T^* - T) \qquad g'(\ ) < 0 \qquad (7)$$

where T^* is the anticipated age at death. Now the impact of age on the probabil-ity of switching occupations is ambiguous and depends on the relative magnitudes of the effect of age on the length of the benefit stream and the effect of age on the cost of changing occupations. Literacy was included as a direct measure of the im-migrant's human capital; literate immigrants should have been more likely to move up from unskilled work.

The characteristics of an immigrant's location were included to see whether particular sorts of places were more conducive to occupational mobility. Strictly speaking, these variables may not be exogenous if immigrants choose where to lo-cate on the basis of how readily a location's characteristics will help him move up in occupation. Given the difficulty of finding suitable instrumental variables for these community characteristics and the difficulty of incorporating a location-choice equation into the hazard analysis, this complication will be ignored here. The differences in occupational mobility experienced by those in different loca-tions may have resulted from either the characteristics of the locations them-selves, or some unobserved individual-specific characteristic (such as wealth at ar-rival) that influenced both the choice of location and occupational mobility. The studies of Kamphoefner and Swierenga suggest a possible link between where an immigrant settled and the extent of occupational mobility.[31] To account for the possibility that the probability of occupational improvement is influenced by the size of the local labor market, the availability of land, and the nature of the out-put produced locally, dummy variables for the region in which the immigrant was located and for whether the immigrant was located in an urban (population greater than 2,500) or rural census subdivision (city, township, or town) were in-cluded.[32] The 1850–60 population growth rate and 1850 size of the foreign- born population for the immigrant's location were included as well.

The effect of the population growth rate could work in either direction.

31. Kamphoefner, *Westphalians*; Swierenga, "Dutch International Migration and Occupational Change."

32. The regions are Northeast (the New England and Middle Atlantic states), which is the ex-cluded category, the North Central states (Ohio, Indiana, Michigan, Illinois, Wisconsin, and Missouri), the Northwest states (Minnesota, Iowa, the Dakotas, Nebraska, Kansas, California, Oregon, and Washington), and the South (everywhere else).

Workers may have moved up more often and down less often where a county's population was growing rapidly if that growth increased the demand for labor and drew workers up into the ranks of the skilled or allowed workers who would have fallen elsewhere to find work in their original occupation.[33] But some places that grew rapidly—such as New York—did so not because of unusually favorable occupational opportunities there. They grew instead because enormous numbers of immigrants passed through them on their way elsewhere. Immigrants' prospects may have been poorer if they settled in eastern cities like New York, Boston, or Philadelphia, with populations inflated by the arrival of other immigrants and wages depressed by glutted labor markets, than if they settled in western cities like Chicago, Cincinnati, or St. Louis, which had both growing populations and booming labor markets. To account for this possibility, an interaction between the population growth rate and whether a place was located in the West (the North Central or Northwest states) was included as an explanatory variable.

Places with large foreign-born populations may have presented more opportunities for advancement than similar locations with smaller foreign-born populations. This would be true if, for example, immigrants found it easier to get jobs from their countrymen or were able to rely on formal or informal support networks among other immigrants.[34] The relationship between occupational mobility and the size of a county's foreign-born community could run in the other direction, though. Those who had fallen in status or failed to rise from the unskilled ranks may have been more often drawn to the support networks available in places with large numbers of foreign born. Competition for jobs may have also been more intense in places with large foreign-born populations, such as New York, Boston, and Philadelphia.[35]

The mean values for the variables used in the analysis and the parameter estimates are presented in Table 5-7. The differences between the sample sizes used here and the full sample of 2,557 immigrants located in either 1850 or 1860 (on whom Tables 5-2 and 5-3 were based) is the exclusion of 25 white collar and skilled arrivals, and 71 farmers and unskilled workers at arrival, for whom it was not possible to calculate a county population growth rate because their 1860 county did not exist in 1850. The results in the first three columns of Table 5-7 are for immigrants who were white collar or skilled workers at arrival, with all nationalities pooled. The estimated parameters suggest that both the characteristics of individual immigrants and the characteristics of their locations exerted a strong influence

33. Galenson, "Economic Opportunity," suggests that the success of immigrants in accumulating wealth in Chicago in the 1850s may have resulted from the opportunities that opened up in a rapidly growing economy. Similarly, chapter 6 shows that wealth accumulation among immigrants was most rapid for those who were located in rapidly growing places over the 1850s.

34. For contemporary immigrants, Borjas, "Self-Employment," pp. 502–505, found that immigrants were more likely to enter self-employment if they were located in places with large foreign-born populations.

35. The 1850 Census of Population records only the total foreign-born population of each county; breakdowns by country of origin are given only at the state level. The foreign born population figure used in the following analysis is thus not the best suited to answer these questions, but it seemed a better choice than the alternative (the state-level figure for a state's ethnic composition), since so many of the immigrants in the sample went to only three states.

Table 5-7. Estimates of the parameters of the hazard function for entering white collar or skilled occupations or farming among immigrant arrivals at New York, 1840–50.

Variable	White Collar or Skilled at Arrival			Farmer or Unskilled at Arrival		
	Mean	$\delta P_{12}/\delta X$	Prob.	Mean	$\delta P_{12}/\delta X$	Prob.
Personal Characteristics						
Age	27.179	0.029	0.012	22.947	0.015	0.001
Age$^2 \times 10^{-2}$	7.986	−0.042	0.015	6.182	−0.017	0.014
Origin						
Irish	0.210	−0.276	0.000	0.514	−0.294	0.001
German	0.410	−0.012	0.792	0.245	0.000	0.990
Other	0.026	−0.039	0.733	0.025	−0.068	0.370
Literate	0.960	0.321	0.006	0.912	0.296	0.001
Year of arrival						
1841	0.085	−0.146	0.081	0.079	0.080	0.169
1842	0.175	−0.053	0.472	0.147	0.097	0.051
1843	0.078	−0.027	0.756	0.101	0.142	0.007
1844	0.107	−0.047	0.559	0.091	0.079	0.164
1845	0.085	−0.089	0.293	0.080	0.059	0.327
1846	0.021	−0.050	0.730	0.046	0.179	0.018
1847	0.046	−0.282	0.014	0.035	0.151	0.071
1848	0.129	−0.097	0.244	0.091	0.140	0.021
1849	0.120	−0.089	0.292	0.118	0.147	0.011
1850	0.062	−0.085	0.439	0.099	0.180	0.003
ln(Years in U.S.)	2.073	0.042	0.086	2.207	0.203	0.001
Location Characteristics						
Region						
North Central	0.333	0.047	0.466	0.326	0.115	0.015
Northwest	0.037	0.095	0.406	0.023	0.272	0.002
South and Far West	0.082	0.034	0.644	0.070	−0.034	0.580
Urban	0.640	0.038	0.553	0.595	0.060	0.214
Urban × Northwest	0.154	0.027	0.785	0.112	−0.107	0.170
%Δ Population	0.302	0.178	0.071	0.280	0.015	0.805
%Δ Population × Northwest	0.102	−0.189	0.108	0.078	−0.054	0.524
%Δ Foreign Born	0.283	0.168	0.270	0.267	0.212	0.044
$\bar{P}_{12}$		0.713			0.499	
Log-Likelihood		−412.804			−999.464	
No. of obs.		778			1,683	

Source: Male household heads and unaccompanied males in passenger ship arrival records at port of New York, 1840–1850, linked to 1850 and/or 1860 manuscript census schedules.

Notes. "$\delta P_{12}/\delta X$" is the impact of a one unit change in a variable on the probability that the individual was in an occupation other than unskilled, evaluated at the mean probability in the sample. It is calculated as $\delta P_{12}/\delta X = (\beta\alpha)(-\bar{P}_{11})(\log(\bar{P}_{11}))$ where β and α are estimates of the parameters from the Weibull hazard function (equation B8 in Appendix B) obtained by maximum likelihood,

$$\bar{P}_{11} = \sum_{i=1}^{N} [\exp(-\exp(X_i'\beta)t_i)^\alpha]/N$$

is the average probability in the sample that an individual was still unskilled, and $\bar{P}_{12} = 1 - \bar{P}_{11}$. For "ln(Years in the U.S.)" $\beta = 1$. "Prob." is the probability that the true $\delta P_{12}/\delta X$ is equal to zero. All characteristics are as reported in the passenger ship lists, except "Years in U.S.," "Literate," and the location characteristics which are measured in 1850 or 1860 (see text). The omitted categories are "British," "Illiterate," "1840 arrival," "Northeast," and "Rural."

on their ability to rise from unskilled work into other occupations. The impact of age on the probability of leaving unskilled work was nonlinear: it was positive at younger ages, achieved a maximum at age 34.5, and became negative at older ages. This suggests that the impact of age on immigrants' ability to change occupations (through the positive correlation between age and human capital) was more important at younger ages than the impact of age on immigrants' valuation of the benefits of changing occupations. After age 34.5, the effect of the time horizon dominated the effect of the ability to change occupations. Since the average age at arrival for this group was 27 years, many immigrants in this group reached ages where an additional year of age reduced the probability that they would move up from unskilled work. Immigrants who were able to read or write were 32 percentage points more likely to move up at each date since arrival than those who could not.

Finally, immigrants who were located in more rapidly growing counties were also more likely to move up, though this effect was absent in the western states. In the Northeast and South, an increase of 10 percentage points in a county's population growth rate was associated with a 1.8 percentage point increase in the probability of moving up from unskilled work. The only arrival cohorts with statistically significant coefficients for year of arrival were 1841 and 1847; in both cohorts, immigrants were considerably less likely to move out of unskilled work than 1840 arrivals. The 1847 arrivals may have faced a particularly unfavorable labor market at their arrival, as indicated by the real wage data cited above.[36]

Results for immigrants who arrived as farmers or unskilled workers are shown in the last three columns of Table 5-7. The impact of age on movement out of unskilled work at each time since arrival was again nonlinear: age increased this probability through age 44.1, and decreased it thereafter. Since the average age at arrival for this group was only 22 years, most immigrants who arrived as farmers or unskilled workers were still at ages when an additional year of age increased the probability of upward occupational mobility. Literacy increased upward mobility here as well: immigrants who arrived as farmers or unskilled workers and who could read or write were 30 percentage points more likely to move up after arrival than those who could not. Immigrants who went to the West did better than those in the Northeast and South, while immigrants who went to places with large foreign-born populations did better than those who went elsewhere. The population growth rate of an immigrant's location had no impact on his chances of changing occupation. The only difference by year of arrival in the probability of moving up from unskilled work into skilled or white collar employment was the apparently easier transition experienced by those who arrived after 1845.

The coefficients on country of origin for both white collar and skilled workers and farmers and unskilled workers at arrival suggest that the Irish did worst at moving up from unskilled jobs not just because they possessed fewer of the characteristics that were associated with easy occupational mobility—such as literacy—but also because unobserved origin-specific differences made them less successful at making these moves than otherwise identical immigrants from Britain and Germany.

36. Margo, "Wages and Prices," p. 184, reports that real wages fell sharply in 1847.

For Irish white collar and skilled workers, such unobservable characteristics could consist of several factors. One is the specific occupational skills with which the Irish arrived: their poor performance may have been the result of arriving more often than the British and Germans in the sorts of occupations that made a poor fit with the U.S. economy—for example, crafts such as weaving that were increasingly mechanized in the United States.[37] This does not appear to have been the case, however. If skilled occupations are grouped into those seen by contemporaries as offering good and poor prospects in the United States, the Irish who arrived as skilled workers arrived far more often than British skilled workers with "good" skills: 90 percent of Irish skilled workers were in these specific crafts, as opposed to only two-thirds of the British.[38] The Germans were just as likely as the British to be in good craft occupations.

The poor performance of Irish white collar and skilled workers is also consistent with Chiswick's findings for more recent immigrants.[39] Because of the imperfect international transferability of skills, there is a clear pattern of downward movement in status with arrival in the United States among contemporary immigrants, with the extent of the downward move a function of the similarity of the sending and U.S. economies. Immigrants from countries markedly less developed than the United States experience a larger drop in status (but also a more rapid rise in status) after arrival than immigrants from economies at a similar stage of development. Britain probably had more places that were at a stage of development similar to that of the United States than did Germany, and Ireland probably had less than either of these.[40] Thus many British immigrants may have arrived familiar with life in a sophisticated market system; fewer Germans and still fewer Irish may have arrived with backgrounds that would have allowed them to become easily integrated into the U.S. economy.

This explanation fits the poor initial performance of the Irish. It does not, however, account for the continued poor performance of the Irish after their arrival.

---

37. Potential immigrants were advised by guidebooks and letters from America before their departure that some occupations and skills could be readily transferred to the U.S. economy, but that others could not; Thompson, *Hints to Emigrants*. The skills thought to be of little use in the United States were those being displaced by industrial production methods. For example, one prominent guidebook suggested that needle makers, bookbinders, tinsmiths, horn turners, dyers, nail smiths, and rope makers would all have difficulty securing employment in their trades in the United States. Lawyers were similarly advised to expect difficulty, because of differences between the German and U.S. legal systems. Doctors and surgeons, however, were expected to do well in the United States; Ficker, "Friendly Adviser," pp. 473–474.

38. The bad crafts were carder, dresser, dyer, warper, weaver, cordwainer, bookbinder, and turner. The good crafts were carpenter, engineer, founder, machinist, mason, plasterer, plumber, tailor, and wheelwright. These were described as good and bad occupations by two contemporary observers, Ficker, "Friendly Adviser"; and Thompson, *Hints to Emigrants*.

39. Chiswick, "Occupational Mobility of Immigrants."

40. In 1851, 27.7 percent of the population of Great Britain lived in cities of more than 50,000 inhabitants. The 1855 population of cities with more than 50,000 inhabitants in Saxony was 9.0 percent of Saxony's total population in 1852. In Ireland, 7.6 percent of the 1851 population lived in cities of more than 50,000 inhabitants. These figures were calculated from U.S. Census Office, *Seventh Census*, pp. xxxiv, and U.S. Census Office, *Compendium of the Eighth Census*, pp. lii–liii.

Among contemporary immigrants, those from places least like the United States make the most investment in acquiring U.S.-specific skills after arrival, leading to a rapid rise in occupational status. This does not appear the case among the Irish. They moved out of unskilled work more slowly than the British or Germans. To explain the slow departure from unskilled work among the Irish we need to look elsewhere. Differences-in-development as a cause of differences in performance in the United States must be no more than part of the residual left after accounting for other observed factors influencing performance.

Irish immigrants who were farmers or unskilled workers before arrival also fared worse after arrival than British and German arrivals in these jobs. The fact that the Irish experienced difficulties regardless of their occupation at arrival suggests another explanation for their slow upward mobility. Their slow escape from unskilled jobs may also represent the effect of barriers to entry in U.S. skilled labor markets, barriers that had a greater impact on the Irish than on the British or Germans. If the Irish were barred from entering some pursuits after arrival, and had to spend more time proving themselves as unskilled assistants or apprentices than the British or Germans, the result may have been to slow the departure of the Irish from unskilled work in the years after arrival.[41]

The coefficients on country of origin in Table 5-7 are insufficient for assessing the impact of discrimination, since they constrain the "prices" paid for each characteristic to be the same for all origins. Discrimination may have occurred through unequal payments for identical characteristics. If the equations in Table 5-7 are reestimated with the addition of interactions between Irish origin and the characteristic that had the largest impact on the probability of moving up from unskilled work—literacy—there are in fact differences in the return to literacy by origin, but the differences do not go in the expected direction. For both white collar and skilled workers and farmers and unskilled workers, the impact of literacy was greater for the Irish than for the British and Germans. The dummy variable for Irish origin, however, remains negative, substantial in magnitude, and statistically significant. The magnitude of the positive literacy effect for the Irish, however, was dwarfed by the remaining negative effect of Irish origin. Even though they earned a greater return on their literacy than the British or Germans, they still were less likely to move out of unskilled work. These results suggest that the slow occupational mobility of the Irish is probably the product of both the differences between their Irish origins and the circumstances they faced in the United States and the burden of discrimination they bore in greater measure than other groups of immigrants.

Conclusion

European immigrants to the United States in the antebellum period, like immigrants a century later, experienced considerable occupational mobility. In the

41. Other personal characteristics correlated with country of origin that are not observed, such as wealth at arrival, for which we have only imperfect proxies, may also be important here.

years after their arrival, many who arrived as white collar and skilled workers were able to regain that occupational status or enter farming. The most successful at making these transitions were immigrants who were literate and those who located in rapidly growing places in the Northeast and South. Age was associated with more rapid movement out of unskilled work at young ages, but with less mobility at older ages. Among those who arrived as farmers or unskilled workers, mobility was again more rapid among the literate. The impact of population growth was absent for this group, however. Instead, these immigrants did better if they moved to the North Central and Northwest states and settled in places with large concentrations of foreign born. The only group in which the introduction of controls for the specific year of arrival produced a change in the effect of duration in the United States was the Irish who arrived as white collar and skilled workers. For them, it appears that declining average quality over the 1840s would produce an overstatement of the effect of duration in the absence of controls for year of arrival. The clearest pattern to emerge from the year of arrival effects themselves is an apparent rise in the average quality of German white collar and skilled workers who arrived in the years following the revolutions of 1848.

All immigrants experienced more occupational mobility earlier in their time in the United States than they experienced later, suggesting that previous studies concentrating on immigrants only after they have spent some time in the United States have understated the occupational mobility experienced by antebellum immigrants. The escape from unskilled work by the British, Irish, and Germans who were farmers and unskilled workers in Europe is more consistent with their accumulation of financial and U.S.-specific human capital than with the opportunity after arrival to utilize talents that had been underutilized at their place of origin. The human capital transfer produced by immigration thus does not appear to have been underestimated for those who arrived as farmers and unskilled workers. The relatively rapid escape from unskilled work by the British and Germans who were in white collar or skilled jobs before leaving Europe suggests that for these immigrants the distribution of occupations in the ship lists represents only a slight overstatement of the human capital transferred to the United States by their arrival. This pattern is also consistent with the distribution of occupations in the ship lists representing an overstatement of the human capital brought by British and German white collar and skilled workers, and substantial labor market discrimination *in favor of* these workers in the U.S. labor market. The weight of the evidence argues against such an interpretation, however. The human capital brought to the United States by the Irish white collar and skilled workers, who had such difficulty escaping unskilled work after arrival, is overstated if their difficulty resulted from differences between the Irish and U.S. economies. If their difficulties resulted instead from discrimination, it is unclear whether the transfer is overstated or understated by the distribution of ship list occupations.

Finally, the results suggest some of the impediments faced by immigrants as they entered the U.S. labor market. The Irish fared particularly poorly regardless of their premigration occupations. The available evidence suggests that this poor performance may have been the result of a combination of a lack of readily transferable general labor market skills — controlling for the specific skills they possessed at arrival — and labor market discrimination. Together with the results for British and German immigrants, these findings show the importance of both premigration experience and postmigration labor market conditions in shaping the outcome of the migration process.

6

Wealth Accumulation, 1840–1860

Antebellum immigrants to the United States clearly experienced a great deal of geographic and occupational mobility in the years after their arrival. But what was the value of this mobility? How did the material circumstances in which antebellum immigrants lived change as their time in the United States increased? And how did their material circumstances compare to those of the native born as their time in the United States increased? Up to now, we have considered where immigrants went and what they did when they got there. But the sample allows us to say more. It allows us to say how immigrants fared in financial terms as a result of these experiences. The U.S. censuses of 1850 and 1860 provide a unique measure of the economic progress of immigrants and natives: individuals were asked the value of their wealth. The linked immigrant and native data thus makes it possible to examine immigrants' and natives' accumulation of property.

Three questions can be addressed: (1) How did immigrants' wealth change with greater duration of residence in the United States; (2) What were the causes of changes in wealth with increased duration of residence; (3) And how did immigrants' wealth compare to that of natives? Although a number of studies have examined the level of wealth and its correlates for both immigrants and natives in the nineteenth century, this is the first study in which it has been possible to use a national sample of immigrants that measures the effect of an immigrant's length of residence in the United States and characteristics at arrival on his level of wealth.[1] This sample makes it possible to examine the magnitude of the differ-

1. Previous studies of the wealth accumulation of both immigrants and natives include Curti, *Making*; Bogue, *From Prairie to Cornbelt*; Soltow, *Men and Wealth*; Atack and Bateman, "Egalitarianism"; Galenson and Pope, "Economic and Geographic Mobility"; Galenson, "Economic Opportunity"; Pope, "Households" and "Coming to Zion"; and Steckel, "Poverty and Prosperity" (1990).

ences in wealth among immigrants and between immigrants and natives, as well as whether and how rapidly those differences narrowed as immigrants' duration of residence increased. Acquiring material wealth was surely not the immigrant's only objective. Many no doubt looked forward to enhanced job security, greater political freedom, a better chance for their children, or any of several improvements that migration might bring. Wealth is merely a convenient yardstick with which to measure the experience of immigrants.

To see what light such an analysis might shed on the economic performance of antebellum immigrants, consider an individual from the sample who was introduced in chapter 1. Late on a spring afternoon in 1840, an Irish immigrant named John Claxton arrived in New York after a five-week journey under sail from Liverpool. When he disembarked on the docks of lower Manhattan, he was thoroughly unremarkable: a 36-year-old domestic servant in a year when nearly half of all immigrants arrived from Ireland, two-thirds of immigrants were between the ages of 15 and 40, and nearly a quarter of all immigrants were unskilled workers or servants.[2] In the summer of 1850, Claxton was working as a miller in Whitestown, New York. Although he had been in the United States for a full decade, like the majority of American men in 1850, he owned no real estate.[3] In the autumn of 1860, he was a farmer in a small town in McHenry County, Illinois. His fortunes had improved over the 1850s; after 20 years in the United States, his real estate and personal wealth together were valued at $2,150, about 80 percent of the national average total wealth of individuals in 1860.[4]

We thus know many of the details of Claxton's experience during his first two decades in the United States: where he moved after arriving at New York, what occupations he pursued, and how his wealth rose as he moved from the East to the West, as he rose from servant, to miller, to farmer, and as his age and length of residence in the United States increased. Although his origins were quite common, it is worth asking how common were his experiences after arrival? How rapidly were antebellum immigrants able to acquire property after they entered the United States? How widespread was property ownership among immigrants? If some were more likely than others to own property, what characteristics were associated with a greater likelihood of owning property? How did ownership patterns of immigrants compare to those of natives? What do the answers to these questions tell us about the transformation of immigrants as their time in the United States increased?

Correlates of Wealth Ownership in 1850 and 1860

The 1850 census asked respondents only the value of their real estate wealth (land and buildings). Personal wealth (movable property) was not recorded until 1860. Although real estate wealth was the only wealth recorded in 1850, real estate

2. U.S. Department of the Treasury, *Immigration*.
3. Soltow, *Men and Wealth*, p. 41.
4. Ibid., p. 77.

wealth was clearly the major component of total wealth across regions and occupations. In the Northeast in 1860, the average male held 65 percent of his total wealth as real estate. In the more rural Midwest, 71 percent of the average male's total wealth was real estate. Real estate comprised 60 percent of the total wealth of the average farmer in 1860 and 54 percent of the total wealth of the average nonfarmer.[5]

Census marshals were instructed to record only gross wealth and to ignore any liens or encumbrances on property. This is unlikely to present a problem, since antebellum mortgages usually required substantial down payments. Where mortgages were granted, down payments were generally more than half the value of the property.[6] The wealth each individual reported was apparently close to his true net wealth: there was a close correspondence between wealth reported to census marshals and wealth reported to tax authorities, with the anticipated bias: as there was no federal tax on real estate, individuals reported more wealth in the census than in local tax records.[7]

The most comprehensive study of nineteenth-century native and immigrant wealth-holding patterns is Lee Soltow's examination of more than 30,000 males drawn from the 1850, 1860, and 1870 U.S. federal census manuscripts.[8] Soltow found a clearly concave relationship between age and wealth in his sample. This is not surprising. A large literature has evolved that describes a variety of mechanisms to account for this relationship between age and wealth. For example, if individuals must save some of their current income to finance a period of retirement or if they want to make *inter vivos* bequests to their children, wealth would grow at a decreasing rate with age, achieve a maximum, and then decrease.[9]

But Soltow also discovered marked differences in wealth between the native born and foreign born, as well as differences by country of origin among the foreign born. He suggested that these differences might have resulted from differences in immigrants' length of residence in the United States and in their ability in the years since arrival to overcome the barriers of language, prejudice, and a lack of marketable skills. But because the 1850, 1860, and 1870 censuses collected no information on immigrants at arrival, he was unable to assess the importance of these factors. Because the sample used here contains information on immigrants' duration of residence in the United States as well as on their characteristics at arrival, we can explore some of the issues raised by Soltow. Before doing so, however, it will be useful to outline the patterns of wealth holding in the sample by age, origin, occupation, and location.

Figure 6-1 shows estimated age-wealth profiles for the native and ship list samples in 1850 and 1860. These curves were produced by regressing the natural log of real estate wealth (plus $1.00) on age, age squared, and age cubed for each group in each year, then using the resulting coefficients to estimate wealth by age and

5. Soltow, *Men and Wealth*, pp. 77–81.
6. See Steckel, "Poverty and Prosperity" (1988), for references.
7. Pope, "Households"; and Knights, *Yankee Destinies*.
8. Soltow, *Men and Wealth*.
9. References to this literature can be found in Pope, "Households."

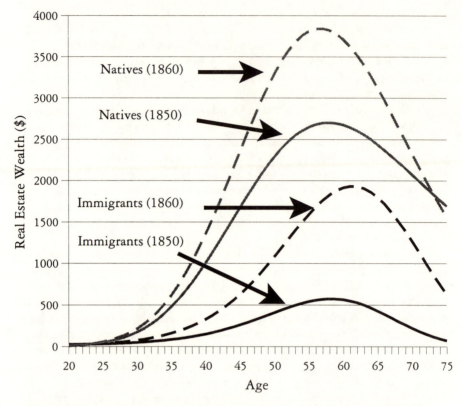

Figure 6-1. Estimated real estate wealth by age for natives and immigrants, 1850 and 1860. *Source:* Males fifteen years and older in 1850 Public Use Microdata Series linked to the 1860 manuscript census schedules; male household heads and unaccompanied males in passenger ship arrival records at port of New York, 1840–1850, linked to 1850 and/or 1860 manuscript census schedules.

forcing the resulting profile to pass through the reported average wealth between ages 50 and 59.[10] All four real estate wealth profiles display the concavity noted by Soltow. For 1850 and 1860, for example, natives' real estate wealth rises with age, reaching a peak at age 57. Immigrants' real wealth peaked at age 58 in 1850 and at age 61 in 1860. There was also a positive, concave relationship between age and the probability of owning any property for both immigrants and natives. For both groups, the probability of owning real or personal property peaked be-

10. Using the formula

$$W_{Age} = (W_o) (\exp[\alpha + \beta_1 Age + \beta_2 Age^2 + \beta_3 Age^3])$$

with *Age* set equal to 55 and W_{Age} set equal to the average wealth for the 50–59 age group and solving for W_0 produced a profile that passed through average wealth between ages 50 and 59.

Table 6-1. Wealth of natives and immigrant arrivals at New York, 1840–50, by origin, 1850 and 1860.

	All		Country of Origin		
	Natives	Immigrants	British	Irish	German
1850 Real wealth					
Percent > 0	46.4	23.3	34.8	10.4	26.5
Mean ($)	1,123.63	262.07	388.14	106.93	283.04
Median ($)	0.00	0.00	0.00	0.00	0.00
N	2,913	1,416	428	531	483
1860 Real wealth					
Percent > 0	55.3	38.0	49.3	24.8	48.6
Mean ($)	2,231.58	921.26	1,228.72	607.02	1,124.95
Median ($)	322.50	0.00	0.00	0.00	0.00
N	4,222	1,647	381	733	484
1860 Personal wealth					
Percent > 0	76.6	60.2	69.3	47.2	71.9
Mean ($)	1,549.28	406.95	424.38	268.23	576.18
Median ($)	260	75.00	150.00	0.00	150.00
N	4,222	1,647	681	733	484

Source: Males fifteen years and older in 1850 Public Use Microdata Series linked to the 1860 manuscript census schedules; male household heads and unaccompanied males in passenger ship arrival records at port of New York, 1840–1850, linked to 1850 and/or 1860 manuscript census schedules.

Note: Natives are males age 15 and over in 1850 who were linked from the 1850 Public Use Microdata Series sample to the 1860 manuscript census schedules. Immigrants were male family heads and unaccompanied males who arrived at port of New York, 1840–50, and were linked from U.S. passenger ship arrival records to the manuscript schedules of the 1850 and/or 1860 census. "Real wealth" is buildings and land; "Personal wealth" is moveable property.

tween ages 60 and 69 in both 1850 and 1860. The age-wealth profile thus resulted from two effects: an increasing propensity to own any property as age increased, and increases in the amount of property owned with age among those who owned positive amounts. But there are striking differences among the profiles as well: for both natives and immigrants, the real estate wealth profile is considerably steeper for 1860 than it is for 1850. That is, wealth increased by a larger increment with each additional year of age in 1860 than it did in 1850. Both groups also owned more wealth at each age in 1860 than in 1850. We will return later to the differences between the 1850 and 1860 age-wealth profiles.

There were other differences in wealth holdings between natives and immigrants, as Soltow observed. Table 6-1 shows these differences by country of origin. In 1850, immigrants were half as likely as natives to own any real estate, and owned only a fifth as much real estate as natives on average. Like natives, more than half of all immigrants did not own any real estate in 1850. By 1860, the position of immigrants relative to natives had improved somewhat: the difference in the proportion owning wealth fell, and the ratio of natives' average real wealth to immigrants' average real wealth fell from five in 1850 to just over two in 1860. There was a great deal of heterogeneity among immigrants, however. British immigrants were most likely to own real estate and owned the greatest average amounts. The Germans were less likely to own any real property in 1850 and they owned a smaller average amount than the British. These differences narrowed by 1860, however, with the Germans even surpassing the British in their average holdings of personal property. In each year and for each kind of property, the Irish were least likely to own any property and owned smaller average amounts than the British or Germans, though these differences also narrowed between 1850 and 1860.

Soltow also noted large differences in wealth by occupation and emphasized the differences between farmers and nonfarmers. These differences are apparent among both immigrants and natives. Table 6-2 shows that farmers indeed owned the most real estate in 1850 and 1860. But white collar workers also owned significant amounts of real estate in 1850 and 1860, and they owned more personal property in 1860 on average than farmers, enough that their average total wealth was actually greater than that of farmers. Both skilled workers and unskilled workers held considerably less property in 1850 and 1860 than white collar workers or farmers.

The advantage enjoyed by farmers is clearly more than a mere portfolio effect: farmers also possessed more total wealth than skilled workers and unskilled workers in 1860. In 1860, real estate wealth was 69 percent of total wealth for foreign-born farmers and 61 percent of total wealth for foreign-born nonfarmers.[11] The greater total wealth of farmers reported here no doubt reflects the fact that farmers were by definition those who owned farms. Agricultural workers who had not achieved independent ownership of their own farms were most often described simply as laborers. The correspondence between designation as a farmer and ownership of a farm, however, was not perfect.[12] The difference in wealth between those in white collar and skilled occupations and those described as unskilled workers corresponds to the advantage enjoyed by white collar workers and skilled workers in earnings. The national average daily wage paid to carpenters in 1850 was almost twice the daily wage of day laborers.[13]

The rates of increase in real estate wealth over the 1850s were greater among immigrants than among natives. Natives' real estate wealth grew at an annual rate of 6.9 percent between 1850 and 1860, but immigrants saw their wealth grow 12.6 percent per year over the same period. Among the immigrants, the increase was more remarkable for skilled workers and unskilled workers, particularly skilled workers, than for farmers and white collar workers. Though skilled workers held an average of only $200 in real estate in 1850, their holdings grew five times by 1860, and the fraction owning at least some property nearly doubled. Only 8 percent of unskilled workers owned real estate in 1850, but this percentage also nearly

11. Soltow, Men and Wealth, pp. 76–77.

12. Curti, Making; Bogue, From Prairie to Cornbelt; Atack and Bateman, To Their Own Soil, pp. 44–45.

13. U.S. Census Office, Compendium of the Seventh Census, p. 231.

Table 6-2. Wealth of natives and immigrant arrivals at New York, 1840–50, by occupation, 1850 and 1860.

	White Collar	Skilled	Farmer	Unskilled
Natives				
1850 Real wealth				
Percent > 0	38.0	37.1	100.0	6.2
Mean ($)	1,858.85	539.07	2,432.25	76.36
Median ($)	0.00	0.00	1,500.00	0.00
N	271	688	906	868
1860 Real wealth				
Percent > 0	50.9	40.3	100.0	10.9
Mean ($)	3,444.26	891.39	4,087.08	193.28
Median ($)	300.00	0.00	2,000.00	0.00
N	483	853	1,549	1,044
1860 Personal wealth				
Percent > 0	77.6	70.9	98.2	58.2
Mean ($)	3,380.20	546.51	2,570.48	270.11
Median ($)	500.00	150.00	600.00	50.00
N	483	853	1,549	1,044
Immigrants				
1850 Real wealth				
Percent > 0	22.3	18.7	100.0	7.6
Mean ($)	802.25	193.49	967.38	36.05
Median ($)	0.00	0.00	700.00	0.00
N	130	562	154	525
1860 Real wealth				
Percent > 0	39.1	33.4	100.0	14.3
Mean ($)	1,611.34	900.16	2,188.79	153.47
Median ($)	0.00	0.00	1,400.00	0.00
N	174	590	269	579
1860 Personal Wealth				
Percent > 0	70.7	63.7	95.9	38.5
Mean ($)	1,163.42	411.58	664.22	73.02
Median ($)	250.00	100.00	400.00	0.00
N	174	590	269	579

Source: Males fifteen years and older in 1850 Public Use Microdata Series linked to the 1860 manuscript census schedules; male household heads and unaccompanied males in passenger ship arrival records at port of New York, 1840–1850, linked to 1850 and/or 1860 manuscript census schedules.

Note: Natives are males age 15 and over in 1850 who were linked from the 1850 Public Use Microdata Series sample to the 1860 manuscript census schedules. Immigrants were male family heads and unaccompanied males who arrived at port of New York, 1840–50, and were linked from U.S. passenger ship arrival records to the manuscript schedules of the 1850 and/or 1860 census. "Real wealth" is buildings and land; "Personal wealth" is moveable property.

doubled by 1860. Nearly 40 percent of all unskilled workers owned some personal property by 1860. For natives, the increase was more uniform across occupations: all saw real estate wealth double between 1850 and 1860, while the proportion owning real estate rose less than one and one-half times.

The extent of wealth-holding by region is shown in Table 6-3. Among immigrants, for both real estate and personal wealth, the Midwest states had higher percentages owning some property and higher average amounts of property owned in both 1850 and 1860. Nearly half of all immigrants in the Midwest owned real estate in 1850, whereas nearly three-quarters of immigrants in the Midwest owned personal property in 1860.

Several factors probably contributed to the real estate wealth of immigrants to the Midwest. Among them were the price of land and rapid appreciation of land values outside the Northeast. Immigrants who settled in the Midwest could both buy larger blocks of land and realize more rapid increases in the value of their land than immigrants who settled in the Northeast. In 1850, the average value of all land in the Midwest was only $1.10 per acre, compared to $17.00 per acre in the Northeast. These figures are calculated from the average amounts of real property reported by state and the total area of each state.[14]

Although there are no comparable figures for the 1840 to 1850 period to test this assertion, land values per acre rose nearly ten times more rapidly over the 1850s in the Midwest than in the Northeast. Stanley Lebergott suggests that an important source of these capital gains was improvements to the inland water transportation system which increased the volume of land sales before 1860.[15] The extension of the railroad system into many western states in this period also no doubt increased property values. The appreciation calculated here includes the value of improvements, so this is more than a pure capital gain.[16]

Immigrants who became wealthy in the Midwest are also, of course, those who chose to forsake the economic and physical safety of locating in a more settled area and who survived the rigors of life on the frontier. Their superior wealth may in part represent a return to risk. They were wealthier than those who settled in Buffalo, for example, but immigrants in Buffalo enjoyed the safety of living in a settled community of their countrymen. The greater wealth of immigrants in the Midwest may also represent a selection effect: those who chose to settle in the west and who survived the trials of frontier life may have been the ablest and most ambitious immigrants. The higher level of real estate wealth observed in the Midwest is clearly more than a mere portfolio effect (immigrants on the frontier holding a greater share of their total wealth in the form of real estate than immigrants outside the Midwest). Men in the Midwest held 71 percent of their total

14. U.S. Census Office, *Compendium of the Eighth Census*, p. 224.

15. Lebergott, "Demand," pp. 194–198.

16. These increases in land values occurred despite the presence of an important force working to depress land values: federal sales of land. If they were unanticipated, these sales would have depressed the value of existing farms by reducing the price of a close substitute, unimproved land from which a new farm could be made.

Table 6-3. Wealth of natives and immigrant arrivals at New York, 1840–50, by region, 1850 and 1860.

	New England	Middle Atlantic	Midwest	Southeast	South Central	FarWest
Natives						
1850 Real wealth						
Percent > 0	47.9	42.4	52.3	44.8	49.1	35.7
Mean ($)	1,027.08	1,391.11	926.90	1,017.57	908.84	152.86
Median ($)	0.00	0.00	137.50	0.00	0.00	0.00
N	666	1,046	572	393	222	14
1860 Real wealth						
Percent > 0	56.7	51.2	61.3	51.5	59.1	29.7
Mean ($)	1,734.40	2,566.63	1,984.35	2,792.78	2,307.06	504.69
Median ($)	400.00	150.00	600.00	87.00	400.00	0.00
N	823	1,344	1,086	555	350	64
1860 Personal wealth						
Percent > 0	70.7	74.5	81.2	78.6	85.7	54.7
Mean ($)	1,008.62	1,087.32	740.96	3,847.80	3,604.41	747.67
Median ($)	200.00	250.00	300.00	210.00	410.00	100.00
N	823	1,344	1,086	555	350	64
Immigrants						
1850 Real wealth						
Percent > 0	7.6	16.6	42.8	17.3	17.2	33.3
Mean ($)	66.95	203.80	456.03	284.89	285.60	70.89
Median ($)	0.00	0.00	0.00	0.00	0.00	0.00
N	197	679	421	52	58	9
1860 Real wealth						
Percent > 0	23.1	27.4	60.2	37.8	27.3	20.8
Mean ($)	365.65	647.60	1,484.59	645.50	1,051.75	393.63
Median ($)	0.00	0.00	400.00	0.00	0.00	0.00
N	216	654	588	37	99	53
1860 Personal wealth						
Percent > 0	43.5	59.0	72.1	73.0	40.4	39.6
Mean ($)	104.53	383.83	464.51	452.46	889.09	396.00
Median ($)	0.00	75.00	150.00	100.00	0.00	0.00
N	216	654	588	37	99	53

Source: Males fifteen years and older in 1850 Public Use Microdata Series linked to the 1860 manuscript census schedules; male household heads and unaccompanied males in passenger ship arrival records at port of New York, 1840–1850, linked to 1850 and/or 1860 manuscript census schedules.

Note: Natives are males age 15 and over in 1850 who were linked from the 1850 Public Use Microdata Series sample to the 1860 manuscript census schedules. Immigrants were male family heads and unaccompanied males who arrived at port of New York, 1840–50, and were linked from U.S. passenger ship arrival records to the manuscript schedules of the 1850 and/or 1860 census. "Real wealth" is buildings and land; "Personal wealth" is moveable property.

wealth in real estate in 1860, but the corresponding figure for the Northeast was 65 percent, only slightly lower.[17]

Of course, all of these reasons for expecting higher average wealth in the Midwest apply to the native born with equal force. It is therefore somewhat puzzling that the average real estate wealth for natives in the Midwest in Table 6-3 is actually well below the average for the Middle Atlantic and Southeast states in both 1850 and 1860, whereas the rate of growth in per capita real estate wealth in the Midwest is no greater than that in the Middle Atlantic states, and somewhat below that in the Southeast. It remains to be seen whether the advantage enjoyed by immigrants in the Midwest compared to natives can be explained by their characteristics (either observed or not observed). If not, an explanation must be sought in characteristics of the region that made it the best region for wealth accumulation among immigrants but only an average region for real estate growth among the native born.

Wealth and Duration in the United States, 1850–1860

The sample contains considerable detail on the characteristics of immigrants and how those characteristics evolved as immigrants' time in the United States increased. One of those characteristics—wealth—provides a convenient summary measure of the economic success of immigrants in the years after their arrival. Other studies have examined the level of wealth and the links between age and wealth, as well as the links between occupation and wealth, among immigrants, but none has examined how their wealth changed as their time in the United States increased. As a result, we know that immigrants held less wealth on average than the native born, even after accounting for age and occupation; but we do not know whether those differences diminished as immigrants' length of residence increased or, if such improvements in immigrants' wealth did occur, how they were brought about.

Age and the Effect of Duration in the United States

The effects of age, country of origin, and duration of residence in the United States on the amount of real estate wealth owned in 1850 and 1860 can be seen in a multivariate regression analysis, the results of which are presented in Table 6-4. Observations from 1850 and 1860 are pooled. The dependent variable is the natural logarithm of real estate wealth, plus one dollar to account for observations with zero wealth.[18] The expected concave age-wealth relationship is evident for

17. Soltow, *Men and Wealth*, p. 81.

18. For a discussion of the choice of this functional form, see Appendix A. When a tobit specification was employed, the same qualitative results were obtained—a concave age-wealth profile, higher wealth for farmers and those in the Northwest, and greater wealth with greater duration in the United States—though the magnitudes of the coefficients were greater than those presented here. In order to enhance comparability with previous studies of the age-wealth relationship, no adjustment

Table 6-4. Ordinary least squares regressions on real wealth of natives and immigrant arrivals at New York, 1840-50, controlling for immigrants' years in the United States, 1850 and 1860.

Variable	Natives		Immigrants		Immigrants	
	β	Probability	β	Probability	β	Probability
Intercept	−7.3016	0.0001	−3.1882	0.0001	−3.1265	0.0001
Age	0.4655	0.0001	0.1882	0.0001	0.1894	0.0001
Age^2	−0.0040	0.0001	−0.0014	0.0002	−0.0014	0.0002
Origin						
Irish			−1.2669	0.0001	−1.3045	0.0001
German			−0.0039	0.9787	−0.0355	0.8182
Other			0.3461	0.3259	0.3748	0.2919
Years in U.S.			0.1559	0.0001	0.1519	0.0001
Years in U.S.^{2}			−0.0039	0.0218	−0.0034	0.0487
Arrival cohort						
1841					−0.0298	0.9025
1842					−0.0736	0.7675
1843					−0.1739	0.5374
1844					0.1510	0.6012
1845					0.0789	0.7625
1846					−0.2798	0.2818
1847					0.1727	0.5155
1848					−0.2076	0.4114
1849					−0.2880	0.2927
1850					−0.2334	0.3844
Adjusted R^2	0.2290		0.1608		0.1602	
F	1060.646	0.0001	84.790	0.0001	35.355	0.0001
N	7,134		3,063		3,063	

Source: Males fifteen years and older in 1850 Public Use Microdata Series linked to the 1860 manuscript census schedules; male household heads and unaccompanied males in passenger ship arrival records at port of New York, 1840–1850, linked to 1850 and/or 1860 manuscript census schedules.

Notes. The dependent variable is ln(*Real Wealth* + $1.00). For continuous variables, β is a *semi-elasticity*: the percentage change in wealth associated with a one-unit change in variable X. For dichotomous variables, the percentage impact of possession of a characteristic is $e^β − 1$, where β is the estimated regression coefficient for the dummy variable for that characteristic. For example, in the second regression, the coefficient on Irish origin of −1.2669 indicates that the Irish possessed 71.8 percent less wealth than the British ($e^{−1.2669} − 1$) after controlling for age and years since arrival. "Probability" is the probability that the true β is zero. The omitted groups are "British" and "1840 arrival."

both natives and immigrants. In column 1, natives' real estate wealth rose with age by 30.6 percent per year at age 20, by 22.6 percent at age 30, and by 14.6 percent at age 40, and achieved a maximum at 58.2 years of age. The profile for immigrants in column 2 was somewhat less steep, rising at 13.2 percent at age 20,

was made for the impact of an individual's birth cohort on the wealth-by-age relationship. See Mirer, "Age-Wealth Relation."

10.4 percent at age 30, and 7.6 percent at age 40, and peaking at 67.2 years of age. The Irish were 72 percent and the Germans 0.4 percent less wealthy than the British, after controlling for age and duration in the United States.

The 1860 census asked respondents the value of their personal property as well as the value of their real estate holdings. A regression analysis similar to that reported in Table 6-4, but with personal wealth as the dependent variable, produced results similar to the results obtained for real estate wealth when attention is confined to 1860: for example, for immigrants, the rate of accumulation with age for personal wealth was 15.7 percent per year at age 20, compared to 19.8 percent per year for real estate wealth at the same age. For immigrants, personal wealth peaked at 57.4 years of age, whereas real estate wealth peaked at 67.2 years of age. This suggests that we are not losing a great deal of information in concentrating on real estate wealth, for which we have information in both 1850 and 1860.

Other researchers have examined the relationship between age and wealth in the nineteenth century for national samples. Atack and Bateman found the total (real and personal) wealth of immigrants in 1860 rising at only 2.8 percent at age 20 and 0.8 percent per year at age 30, whereas wealth was actually falling by 1.2 percent per year at age 40.[19] If we follow Atack and Bateman and confine the sample to those in the rural North and estimate a regression for 1860 total wealth with the controls they used in addition to age (literacy and farm/nonfarm occupation), the immigrants here were clearly accumulating with age at a more rapid rate in percentage terms than the immigrants in their sample. The estimated rates of accumulation with age for this sample are 16.9 percent at age 20, 11.4 percent at age 30, and 5.9 percent at age 40.

Steckel found 1860 real estate wealth for a pooled national sample of natives and immigrants rising at 7.7 percent at age 20, 5.8 percent at age 30, and 3.8 percent at age 40.[20] If we confine the sample to those who were located in both 1850 and 1860, as did Steckel, and estimate a regression for 1860 real estate wealth with the controls he used in addition to age (family size in 1850 and 1860, literacy, country of origin, and occupation and location in 1850 and 1860), the rates of accumulation with age here are again larger. The rates of accumulation are 12.2 percent at age 20, 9.2 percent at age 30, and 6.3 percent at age 40.

In fact, the age-wealth relationship for immigrants here is steeper than the age-wealth profile observed for Chicago in 1860, the most rapid rates of accumulation with age that had been previously observed anywhere in the United States for that year. Galenson found total wealth for a pooled sample of 1860 natives and immigrants in Chicago rising at 27.9 percent per year at age 20, 18.7 percent at age 30, and 9.5 percent at age 40.[21] If we confine the sample to those in urban places outside the Northeast, and estimate a regression for 1860 total wealth using the controls employed by Galenson in addition to age (country of origin), the results sug-

19. Atack and Bateman, "Egalitarianism," p. 87.
20. Steckel, "Poverty and Prosperity" (1988), p. 17.
21. Galenson, "Economic Opportunity," p. 589.

gest that the wealth of immigrants here grew with age by 27.6 percent per year at age 20, 19.6 percent at age 30, and 11.6 percent at age 40.

The age-wealth relationship for immigrants here is clearly steeper than those found for the native born in previous studies. This might simply be because of the functional form employed here and in those studies: the impact of age on wealth was measured in percentage rather than in absolute terms. Large increases in wealth with increases in age might represent only small absolute additions to wealth with each additional year of age. Because the native born had more wealth on average than immigrants, immigrants might exhibit a steeper age-wealth profile than natives, even though they added less in absolute terms to their wealth each year.

A second possible explanation for the finding of a steeper age-wealth profile than those previously observed for both natives and immigrants may lie in the disruption of life-cycle savings patterns caused by migration. If older migrants with families faced a higher cost of migrating than younger, single migrants, migration may have produced a flat age-wealth profile at arrival. If older migrants had greater wealth than younger migrants before their departure from Europe, differences in migration costs might have left old and young immigrants at roughly the same level of wealth at arrival. In order to return to their desired lifetime savings path, older immigrants would have to save more out of their current income than younger immigrants, leading to a steeper age-wealth profile as time in the United States increased. All of the immigrants in this sample had been in the United States ten to twenty years by 1860. The samples used in other studies of 1860 wealth no doubt contained more immigrants who had arrived during the 1850s. These recent arrivals would have had less time to reestablish the age-wealth relationship that prevailed before their departure from Europe than the immigrants observed here.

The comparison between the results for natives and immigrants in Table 6-4, however, does not support this view. Since the savings pattern of the native born had not been interrupted in this way, they would have saved a lower percentage of income at each age than immigrants who sought to reestablish such a pattern, unless natives had a substantially higher target level of wealth they hoped to attain. The rate of wealth accumulation with age is considerably greater for the natives than for the immigrants in Table 6-4. What needs to be explained, then, is why rates of wealth accumulation for both immigrants and natives are greater in the sample used here than in previous studies. The answer may lie in the nature of the sample used here: large numbers of individuals located in two successive census enumerations, even if they had left the community in which they were located in 1850. Previous studies of locations at a single point in time may have missed an important dynamic aspect of the wealth accumulation process: the changes individuals make in their circumstances in response to changes in market signals. The issue of how much economic mobility is obscured by concentrating on those who remain in the same community for a decade or more is taken up in greater detail in chapter 7.

The regression results presented in Table 6-4 improve on previous studies in another way: by incorporating the effect of duration in the United States on the accumulation of real estate wealth. The regressions for immigrants include the immigrant's duration in the United States as a regressor. Duration has a large and statistically significant impact on wealth: among the most recent arrivals, each additional year of time in the United States increases wealth by 16 percent; among immigrants who have been in the United States ten years, the impact of an additional year of duration is 7.8 percent. The impact is positive until 20 years after arrival. The addition of the duration effect raises the rate of accumulation to more than 28 percent per year at age 20, 26 percent at age 30, and 23.2 percent at age 40 for recently arrived immigrants. The practical impact on real estate wealth of the duration effect shown in Table 6-4 and the relatively steep age-wealth profile is that a 20-year-old immigrant who arrived in 1840 with $100 of wealth and kept all his subsequent investments in real estate would have amassed more than $377 by age 25, after only five years in the United States, and nearly $912 by age 30, after ten years in the United States. A duration effect of such magnitude would go a long way toward explaining the differences Soltow observed between immigrants from the same country of origin.

The impact of duration of residence on personal wealth was negligible: when the regressions in Table 6-4 were estimated using personal rather than real estate wealth as the dependent variable, the rise per year in personal wealth was essentially zero. Since our interest here is how and why immigrants' wealth changed as their time in the United States increased, the following discussion will focus on real estate wealth and set aside the question of why additions to wealth with greater length of residence were made in real estate but not in personal property.

It is possible that the large effect of duration in the United States on immigrants' real estate wealth reported in Table 6-4 is an illusion—that the greater wealth of early arrivals resulted from their having greater wealth at arrival than later arrivals, rather than from the accumulation of greater wealth as duration increased. This is an example of a more general econometric problem that is discussed in detail in Appendix A: in a single cross section, it is not possible to separate the impact of duration of residence from the impact of a secular change in the quality of successive cohorts of arrival.

If we could determine how the wealth at arrival of immigrants was changing over the 1840s, we could overcome this difficulty. Unfortunately, this is not possible, due to the imprecision of existing estimates of the wealth possessed by antebellum immigrants at arrival.[22] The data are fragmentary, since systematic statistics on the assets being brought into the country by immigrants were not collected until the last decade of the nineteenth century. Officials of several German principalities recorded the amount of money being taken out by emigrants throughout the 1840s and 1850s, whereas U.S. immigration officials asked immigrants arriving at New York in 1855 and 1856 how much money they were bring-

22. The estimates by German officials are reported in U.S. Census Office, *Compendium of the Eighth Census*, pp. xxiii–xxiv; Kamphoefner, *Westphalians*, p. 48; and Kapp, *Immigration*, p. 142. The estimates by U.S. officials are reported in Wells, *Our Burden*, p. 3.

Table 6-5. Wealth of European immigrants to the United States, 1832–1859.

Years	Origin	Departure or Arrival	Wealth
1832–54	Hanover	Departure	$60.00
1832–58	Hanover	Departure	63.00
1840–49	Baden	Departure	98.00
1842–59	Prussia[a]	Departure	180.00
1844–51	Bavaria[a]	Departure	180.00
1845–51	Bavaria	Departure	93.20
1846–50	Münster	Departure	84.00
1851	Berlin[a]	Departure	64.40
1851–57	Bavaria	Departure	94.40
1853	Brunswick	Departure	96.00
1855	Württemberg	Departure	76.00
1855–56	All Europe	Arrival	68.08
1855–56	All Europe	Arrival	86.00
1856	Württemberg	Departure	134.00

Sources: Wealth figures for Hanover (1832–54), Prussia (1842–59), Bavaria (1844–51), and Berlin (1851) are from U.S. Census Office, *Compendium of the Eighth Census*, pp. xxiii–xxiv. Wealth figures for Hanover (1832–58) and Münster (1846–50) are from Kamphoefner, *Westphalians*, p. 48. Wealth figures for Baden (1840–49), Bavaria (1845–51), Bavaria (1851–57), Brunswick (1853), Württemberg (1855), and Württemberg (1856), and the low wealth figure for All Europe (1855–56) are from Kapp, *Immigration*, p. 142. The high wealth figure for All Europe (1855–56) is from Wells, *Our Burden*, p. 3.

Note: [a] "Officially registered" emigrants only. Figures for Hanover (Osnabrück district), Münster, and Württemberg are net of transportation costs. It is unclear whether the other "Departure" figures are net of transportation costs.

ing into the country. These figures are shown in Table 6-5. There are large differences in estimates for departures from the same ports over roughly the same time. For example, the estimate for Bavarian departures for the period 1844 to 1851 is nearly twice the figure for 1845 to 1851.[23] There is also large variation in year-to-year estimates for the same port, even by the same author: the estimate for Württemberg in 1855 is more than 75 percent less than the figure for departures from the same port only a year later.[24] Because of their wide ranges, these figures on wealth at arrival would not allow us to say with much precision how much of the estimated duration effect represents true accumulation and how much represents the impact of changes in wealth at arrival. According to Friedrich Kapp, one of the Commissioners of Emigration of the State of New York, all of these figures should be treated with a good deal of skepticism, because of immigrants' fear of reporting the full value of the wealth they carried with them.[25]

Instead, the problem must be approached by exploiting the fact that more than

23. U.S. Census Office, *Compendium of the Eighth Census*, p. xxiii; Kapp, *Immigration*, p. 142.
24. Kapp, *Immigration*, p. 142.
25. Ibid., p. 143.

500 immigrants in the sample were observed in both 1850 and 1860.[26] In the regression results reported in the last two columns of Table 6-4, the regressors are the same as previously: age and its square in 1850 or 1860, dummies for country of origin, and years from arrival to 1850 or 1860. The new specification adds dummy variables for year of arrival. Because 508 of these immigrants were observed at two points in time, we can identify both the duration effect and the effect of arrival in a particular year.

The results are similar: the age-wealth profile is concave, the Irish are less wealthy than the British and Germans, duration in the United States increases an immigrant's wealth by 15 percent for every year since arrival among the most recent arrivals, and this effect remains positive for the first twenty years in the United States. The year-of-arrival dummies are in no case statistically significant, but their signs suggest an interesting pattern: immigrants who arrived in 1846 and in the period 1848 to 1850 were poorer than other immigrants, even after taking account of their age and duration in the United States. Although this result is consistent with a change in the quality of arriving immigrants in the wake of the Irish famine and the continental revolutions of 1848 and the crop failures of the late 1840s, this change in quality is not great enough to have produced the effect of duration seen previously: the effect of duration in the United States is still positive, even after isolating it from this cohort effect. When separate regressions were estimated by country of origin, the only statistically significant year-of-arrival dummies were for German arrivals in 1848 (75 percent less wealthy than 1850 arrivals, $p = .1131$) and British arrivals in 1844 (fifty-one times wealthier than 1850 arrivals, $p = .0416$). All the dummies were positive but statistically insignificant for the Irish. The lower wealth at arrival of Germans in 1848 stands in contrast to the finding in chapter 5 that these same immigrants were significantly less likely to suffer a drop in occupational status after their arrival than any other immigrants in the sample. This apparent discrepancy might be the result of their ability to flee Germany with their higher-than-average human capital intact and their inability to liquidate and flee with all of their financial capital.

Heterogeneity and the Effect of Duration in the United States

In Tables 6-2 and 6-3, there were sharp differences in real estate wealth between immigrants in different occupations and locations. To account for the possibility that the return to duration measured in Table 6-4 reflected differences in these characteristics, Table 6-6 presents the results of regressions on 1850 and 1860 real estate wealth that control for literacy, location, occupation, and occupational change since arrival, as well as age and years since arrival. The age-wealth profile is again both concave for immigrants and natives and steeper for natives than for

26. The only characteristic on which those who were linked to both 1850 and 1860 differed from those who were linked to only 1850 or 1860 is age: those linked to both years were younger on average than those linked only to 1850 and older on average than those linked only to 1860. See chapter 2, in this volume.

Table 6-6. Ordinary least squares regressions on real wealth of natives and immigrant arrivals at New York, 1840–50, controlling for personal and locational characteristics and immigrants' years in the United States, 1850 and 1860.

Variable	Natives		Immigrants	
	β	Probability	β	Probability
Intercept	−4.4731	0.0001	−3.3615	0.0001
Age	0.2142	0.0001	0.1353	0.0001
Age^2	−0.0018	0.0001	−0.0012	0.0001
Origin				
Irish			−0.3141	0.0167
German			−0.0751	0.5639
Other			0.2356	0.4187
Years in U.S.			0.1219	0.0001
Years in U.S.^{2}			−0.0027	0.0571
Literate	0.6113	0.0001	0.2643	0.1378
Region				
New England	−0.1070	0.1795	0.0360	0.7938
Midwest	0.0773	0.3207	0.6848	0.0001
Southeast	−0.3968	0.0001	0.3322	0.2236
South Central	−0.2213	0.0523	0.1171	0.5699
Far West	−0.7674	0.0051	−0.3550	0.2759
Urban	−0.2598	0.0004	−0.1159	0.2857
Occupation				
White collar	2.4722	0.0001	1.4628	0.0001
Skilled	1.6340	0.0001	1.3633	0.0001
Farmer	5.8038	0.0001	5.3420	0.0001
Change in occupation since arrival				
Farmer to skilled			−0.3519	0.0765
Farmer to unskilled			0.3682	0.0510
Skilled to unskilled			−0.1133	0.5742
Unskilled to skilled			−0.7010	0.0001
Adjusted R^2	0.6042		0.4423	
F	908.513	0.0001	79.326	0.0001
N	7,134		3,063	

Source: Males fifteen years and older in 1850 Public Use Microdata Series linked to the 1860 manuscript census schedules; male household heads and unaccompanied males in passenger ship arrival records at port of New York, 1840–1850, linked to 1850 and/or 1860 manuscript census schedules.

Note: The dependent variable is ln(Real Wealth + $1.00). Dummy variables for year of arrival were included but are not shown. Omitted groups are "British," "Illiterate," "Middle Atlantic," "Rural," "Unskilled," and "No Change in Occupation/Other Change." "Probability" is the probability that the true β is zero.

immigrants. The profile rises less rapidly than in Table 6-4 where no account is taken of location or occupation. The flatter slope in Table 6-6 suggests that part of the upward trend in wealth by age in Table 6-4 was the result of differences in location or occupation by age. The introduction of controls for personal characteristics reduces the impact of duration in the United States slightly. After controlling for age and other characteristics, duration in the United States increases wealth more then 12 percent per year for the most recent arrivals, a decrease of 3 percentage points from the estimate in Table 6-4 without controls. The effect remains positive for the immigrant's first 20 years in the United States.

The effects of location and occupation are as we would expect in light of Table 6-3: immigrants located in the Midwest states were several times wealthier than those elsewhere, while among natives, the wealthiest were those in the Middle Atlantic states. The results also display a clear hierarchy of wealth by occupation for both immigrants and natives, much like that observed in the other studies of nineteenth-century wealth mentioned earlier. Farmers were clearly the wealthiest: among immigrants, they owned on average twenty times the wealth of unskilled workers, while native farmers owned more than thirty times the real estate wealth of native unskilled workers. For both immigrants and natives, average wealth fell in moving from farmers to white collar workers to skilled workers to unskilled workers.

As chapter 5 showed, many immigrants changed occupation between their arrival and the 1850 census and between 1850 and 1860. The impact of occupational change between arrival and 1850 or 1860 on real estate wealth shows the advantages and handicaps conferred by an immigrant's background. The largest effect of occupation at arrival was the disadvantage in wealth of those who were unskilled workers at arrival and skilled workers in the 1850 or 1860 census relative to skilled workers who did not arrive as unskilled workers. Immigrants who were unskilled workers at arrival and skilled workers in the 1850 or 1860 census were 50 percent less wealthy than skilled workers who stated they were something other than unskilled workers at their arrival. The lower wealth of those who made the transition from unskilled worker to skilled worker could reflect either the fact that unskilled workers arrived with less wealth than skilled workers or the fact that those who arrived as unskilled workers may have risen to skilled occupations only over time, and thus not had the opportunity to earn the higher income associated with skilled occupations for their entire time in the United States.

Though we have controlled for the impact of all of immigrants' observed characteristics in attempting to explain the duration effect, there remains the possibility that the effect reflects unobserved heterogeneity. The results in Table 6-6 controlled for both observed characteristics and unobserved characteristics associated with arrival in a particular year. We can control for all of each immigrant's observed and unobserved characteristics, by again exploiting the fact that 508 immigrants and more than 4,270 natives in the sample were located in both 1850 and 1860. Table 6-7 presents regression results for the unbalanced panel data set created by considering the real estate wealth in 1850 and 1860 of immigrants and natives and estimating a fixed, individual-specific effect for those located in both

Table 6-7. Fixed effects regressions on real wealth of natives and immigrant arrivals at New York, 1840–50, controlling for personal and location characteristics, immigrants' years in the United States, and unobserved heterogeneity, 1850 and 1860.

Variable	Natives β	Natives probability	Immigrants β	Immigrants probability
Age	0.2610	0.0001	−0.1229	0.1356
Age^2	−0.0018	0.0001	0.0024	0.0142
Years in U.S.			0.1710	0.0142
Years in U.S.^{2}			−0.0044	0.0809
Region				
New England	0.9360	0.0258	0.5217	0.3404
Midwest	0.1367	0.5501	0.8781	0.0334
Southeast	0.2297	0.6309	1.4532	0.1426
South Central	0.3924	0.3787	0.2558	0.7525
Far West	−1.0276	0.0729	−1.1021	0.2335
Urban	−0.3483	0.0031	−0.6199	0.0496
Occupation				
White collar	1.6540	0.0001	0.6399	0.2236
Skilled	1.5799	0.0001	1.4921	0.0236
Farmer	5.2403	0.0001	4.8741	0.0001
Change in occupation since arrival				
Farmer to skilled			−0.7210	0.4248
Farmer to unskilled			−0.2162	0.7718
Skilled to unskilled			−0.1080	0.8943
Unskilled to skilled			−1.0407	0.1521
Adjusted R^2	0.7024		0.4816	
F	5.700	0.0001	2.090	0.0001
N	5,826		3,063	

Source: Males fifteen years and older in 1850 Public Use Microdata Series linked to the 1860 manuscript census schedules; male household heads and unaccompanied males in passenger ship arrival records at port of New York, 1840–1850, linked to 1850 and/or 1860 manuscript census schedules.

Note: The dependent variable is *ln(Real Wealth* + $1.00). Regressions control for unobserved, individual-specific fixed effects with an unbalanced panel design. Omitted groups are "British," "Illiterate," "Middle Atlantic," "Rural," "Unskilled," and "No Change in Occupation/Other Change." "Probability" is the probability that the true β is zero.

years. Specification tests indicated that this was preferred to a random effects model or a model without any individual-specific effects.[27] Since any characteris-

27. The specification tests are as follows. For natives: (1) Fixed Effects (H$_1$) vs. No Individual Effects (H$_0$) LR = 6073.665, prob(χ^2_{2912} > H)=0.0001; (2) Fixed Effects (H$_1$) vs. Random Effects (H$_0$) H = 100.410 prob(χ^2_{11}>H) = 0.0001. For immigrants: (1) Fixed Effects (H$_1$) vs. No Individual Effects (H$_0$) LR = 6065.172, prob(χ^2_{2592}>H) = 0.0001; (2) Fixed Effects (H$_1$) vs. Random Effects (H$_0$) H = 26.930, prob(χ^2_{17}>H) = 0.0591.

tics that did not change between 1850 and 1860 are captured in the intercept, this model does not provide separate estimates of the impact of country of origin.[28]

The results are broadly similar to those in Table 6-4. Wealth increases with age for both immigrants and natives. The age-wealth profile is concave for natives, but convex for immigrants, increasing more rapidly at greater ages after age 25. Again, the wealthiest immigrants are those in farming and those located in rural places. We can reject the view that the impact of duration was the result of unobserved individual heterogeneity: the impact of years since arrival on wealth actually increases and remains statistically significant, even after taking account of both observed and unobserved differences among immigrants. The effect is now more than 17 percent per year for recent arrivals.

Language and the Effect of Duration in the United States

Because the effect of duration is apparently genuine rather than an artifact of differences among immigrants in their wealth at arrival or their observed or unobserved characteristics, we are left with the question of how greater duration allowed immigrants to accumulate greater real estate wealth. One possible explanation is that greater duration allowed immigrants who came from non-English-speaking countries to acquire the language skills that would allow them to compete with natives and English-speaking immigrants. If this is the case, Germans should have enjoyed the greatest return to duration. Table 6-8 presents the results of separate regressions on 1850 and 1860 real estate wealth by country of origin. In fact, the Germans do *not* have the largest duration effect. The wealth of British immigrants actually rises more with each year in the United States than does the wealth of the Germans.

The regressions used to produce Table 6-8 also revealed some sharp differences in the shape of age-wealth profiles by origin that are worth noting. Both the British and Germans had clearly concave profiles for real estate wealth. The Irish, however, had a virtually linear and not very steep profile: their wealth rose only 5 percent per year at age 20, and that rate did not fall off appreciably at later ages. The most significant force driving wealth accumulation among the Irish was duration in the United States: duration raised their wealth more than 8 percent per year, whereas the age effect was only 5 percent per year. For both the British and Germans, the age effect was generally greater in magnitude than the duration effect.

The specification used in Table 6-8 to test for the impact of language acquisition on wealth assumes that the importance of the acquisition of language skills is equal across all occupations. In fact, the importance of language skills may have varied considerably by occupation. The disadvantage of a German farmer who was unable to speak English relative to other farmers might have been less severe than the disadvantage of a German clerk or tailor or urban day laborer who was unable to speak English relative to others in the same occupations. The return to dura-

---

28. See Hsiao, *Analysis*, pp. 29–41, for details on the estimation of these models.

Table 6-8. Impact of duration in the United States on real wealth of immigrant arrivals at New York, 1840–50, by origin, occupation and origin, and region, 1850 and 1860.

	N	Years in U.S.		Years in U.S.^{2}	
		β	Probability	β	Probability
Origin					
Britain	808	0.3480	0.0073	−0.0020	0.0384
Ireland	1,263	0.0955	0.0447	−0.0015	0.5019
Germany	906	0.2187	0.0013	−0.0051	0.1214
Occupation & origin					
White collar					
All	303	0.1167	0.4562	−0.0014	0.8430
British	77	0.9241	0.2682	−0.0344	0.3021
Irish	69	0.1358	0.7014	−0.0028	0.8606
German	142	0.0817	0.7031	0.0050	0.6341
Skilled					
All	1,151	0.1400	0.0189	−0.0035	0.2024
British	376	0.3837	0.0378	−0.0128	0.0890
Irish	348	0.1350	0.1458	−0.0035	0.4422
German	398	0.1670	0.0729	−0.0049	0.2851
Farmer					
All	422	0.1119	0.0089	−0.0016	0.3889
British	166	0.1231	0.1609	−0.0016	0.6592
Irish	95	0.0557	0.5649	0.0014	0.7306
German	141	0.1123	0.0977	−0.0010	0.7557
Unskilled					
All	1,103	0.0744	0.0539	−0.0022	0.2304
British	167	0.1615	0.4287	−0.0056	0.5095
Irish	712	0.0092	0.8231	0.0013	0.5268
German	199	0.2836	0.0115	−0.0141	0.0102
Region					
Northeast	1,745	0.1027	0.0212	−0.0025	0.2129
North Central	1,070	0.1693	0.0206	−0.0043	0.1981
South	245	0.1290	0.2735	−0.0033	0.5821

Source: Male household heads and unaccompanied males in passenger ship arrival records at port of New York, 1840–1850, linked to 1850 and/or 1860 manuscript census schedules.

Note: The coefficients on "Years in U.S." and "Years in the U.S.^{2}" are from ordinary least squares regressions of the form $ln(Real\ Wealth + \$1.00) = f(Age, Age^2, Years\ in\ U.S., Years\ in\ U.S.^2, Dummies\ for\ Year\ of\ Arrival)$, with a separate regression for each country of origin, occupation, origin/occupation, and location. Observations from 1850 and 1860 are pooled. "Probability" is the probability that the true β is zero.

tion may therefore have been greater in nonagricultural occupations. The inability to speak English would not have been a handicap for the German tailor or clerk or day laborer who was employed in a German immigrant community like New York's *Kleindeutschland*.[29] To assess the impact of duration by country of origin within occupations, Table 6-8 also shows the duration effect from separate regressions by occupation and country of origin. The results offer weak support for the hypothesis that wealth rose with duration as non-English-speaking immigrants gained language skills that were important in nonagricultural occupations. The impact of duration among the Germans is greatest among skilled workers, smaller among unskilled workers, smaller still among farmers, and smallest among white collar workers (the category that contains proprietors and small shopkeepers). But once again, the duration effect among the British is the largest: British skilled workers saw their wealth rise nearly 40 percent for each year of duration in the United States in the years immediately after arrival. The impact of duration was greatest for the Germans only in the unskilled category.

Origin, Occupation, and Region and the Effect of Duration in the United States

Another possible explanation for the positive association between duration and wealth is that this relationship captures the successes of immigrants in particular subgroups: those who had the easiest adjustment to the U.S. economy (the British), those who entered occupations associated with rapid wealth accumulation in the United States (farmers and white collar workers), and those who went to places where real estate values were growing rapidly (the Midwest). If this explanation is true, we can narrow our search for the causes of the duration effect to those factors that would have had an impact on these subgroups; if not, we must search for a broader explanation.

To assess the importance of the duration effect across these subgroups, Table 6-8 shows the impact of duration in the United States from regressions estimated separately by occupation and location. The only groups for which the impact of duration is not statistically significant are white collar workers and those located in the South. The largest returns to duration by occupation or region are enjoyed by skilled workers, and those located in the Northwest states, but the effect is substantively and statistically significant as well for farmers, unskilled workers, and those in the Northeast.

Capital Gains, Local Economies, and the Effect of Duration in the United States

There was clearly a duration effect that transcended origins, occupations, and locations, especially in the early years of immigrants' experience in the U.S. economy. Several possible explanations for this duration effect remain. One is that the difference in wealth between immigrants who differed only in how long they had been in the United States resulted from differences in the incomes earned by them

---

29. See Nadel, *Little Germany*.

in the recent past. If these immigrants came from a place where they earned a lower income than they earned in the United States, then the earlier arrivals would have had the opportunity to earn a higher income for a longer time than the recent arrivals. If immigrants' marginal propensity to consume out of current income did not rise dramatically with their arrival in the United States, the earlier arrivals would have had greater savings than the recent arrivals simply as a result of this income difference. The data necessary to test this proposition—the incomes earned by immigrants in the sample before and after their arrival in the United States—are not available. Estimates of per capita income in the sending country and the United States would be of little use because of differences in the shapes of the income distributions and the lack of information on the position in those distributions of each immigrant. The sample does, however, contain a proxy for income in the country of origin: occupation in the country of origin. If income differences were an important cause of the impact of duration on wealth, the duration effect for those in a particular occupation in 1850 or 1860 should have been greater for those who were employed in lower-income occupations in Europe. Unfortunately, occupation at arrival was also an important indicator of wealth at arrival; such a test is therefore of little use in the absence of a means to control for wealth at arrival.

Another possibility is that the effect of duration in the United States reflects general growth in the value of real estate over the 1840s. If capital gains accumulated on real assets, we should see greater real estate wealth with duration, even in the absence of the accumulation of additional acreage with greater duration. The census provided no information on the physical quantity of real assets held (for example, acres of land or the number and type of structures) in the population schedules, so it is not possible to distinguish between immigrants' accumulation of additional acres and increases in the value of the land they already held.[30] Although there are no figures on the rate of growth of the value of real estate in the United States between 1840 and 1850, per capita real estate wealth grew at perhaps 5 percent per year between 1850 and 1860.[31] The data on the wealth of natives in Table 6-1 suggests that per capita real estate wealth grew 6.9 percent over the 1850s, but this is clearly an upper bound on the capital gains that immigrants would have realized, since it includes physical additions to natives' real estate stocks for life-cycle motives, as well as the appreciation in the value of assets held at the start of the decade.

The rate of growth in property values was not uniform across localities, however, so residence in particular localities over the 1850s may have exerted greater influence over the growth of immigrants' wealth than the rate of growth in wealth for the country as a whole.[32] For example, the returns to duration for natives and

30. Information on acreage owned was included in the agricultural schedules for farmers, but no attempt was made to locate members of the sample in those schedules.

31. This figure is calculated from the total real estate reported by state in 1850 and 1860 and the population by state in each year; see U.S. Census Office, *Compendium of the Seventh Census*, p. 234; and U.S. Census Office, *Compendium of the Eighth Census*, p. 352.

32. As noted above, land values per acre rose nearly ten times more rapidly in the Northwest than in the Northeast.

immigrants combined in the local economies of Chicago and Utah were 7.1 percent and 6.4 to 6.7 percent per year, respectively.[33] Part of the observed impact of duration in the United States may therefore reflect the effect of duration in specific local economies, rather than duration in the United States generally. The decision to remain in a place that grew rapidly or to escape one where labor market prospects were poor and land value stagnant is just one of a whole range of decisions immigrants and natives made over the course of the 1850s. Part of the return to duration may reflect the particular importance of those decisions to immigrants as they obtained more information about local conditions in the country's thousands of labor markets and farm communities.

Changes in Characteristics Between 1850 and 1860 and Duration in the United States

We have eliminated very little of the return to duration in the United States by introducing additional controls for the observed and unobserved characteristics of immigrants at a single point in time. Since 508 immigrants and 4,270 natives were observed in both 1850 and 1860, it is possible to use another perspective: examining wealth in 1860 as a function of the changes immigrants and natives made in their circumstances between 1850 and 1860. In order to assess the impact of these changes, Table 6-9 introduces a new regression specification.[34] The 1860 real estate wealth of each immigrant or native is a function of age and its square in 1860 and literacy in 1860, as in Table 6-6. But instead of simply using the individual's other characteristics in 1860 as regressors, the regressions in Table 6-9 use the changes in characteristics between 1850 and 1860, as well as the reported 1850 real estate wealth, in an attempt to capture as many of the dimensions of the individual's experience between 1850 and 1860 as can be observed.

The results demonstrate the importance of the changes experienced by immigrants and natives over the 1850s in shaping their 1860 real estate wealth. There is still a clearly concave age-wealth profile for both groups, though the profile for immigrants is now somewhat steeper than the native-born profile. Those who had greater real estate wealth in 1850 also had more in 1860 (the coefficient on the log of 1850 wealth implies that an additional dollar of real estate wealth in 1850 yielded an additional $1.13 in 1860 for immigrants and $1.42 for natives), but there are now observable changes in individuals' circumstances, such as changes in location or occupation, that have a significant impact on wealth as well.

For location, the immigrants who did the best were those who either remained in the West over the entire decade or moved there between 1850 and 1860. It is

---

33. Galenson, "Economic Opportunity," p. 591; and Pope, "Coming to Zion" and "Households," p. 168. Pope, "Coming to Zion," presents separate estimates of the return to duration in Utah for the foreign born by location. The return in 1860 for each year of prior residence in Salt Lake City was 8.7 percent for the British and 0.1 percent for continental-born immigrants. The return in 1860 for each year of residence in a rural county in Utah was 5.9 percent for the British and 7.4 percent for the continental born.

34. This specification was adapted from Steckel, "Poverty and Prosperity" (1988).

not possible solely on the basis of this regression to say whether this was because the West offered greater opportunity for amassing wealth or because the wealthiest immigrants moved there over time as their wealth increased. Chapter 7 suggests, however, that those most likely to make interregional moves were not the wealthiest immigrants, so the explanation is probably that the West offered a greater degree of opportunity. In terms of occupational mobility, those who fared the best in accumulating real estate by 1860 were those who were farmers over the entire decade (the excluded group in the regression) or those who moved into farming between 1850 and 1860, whereas those who did worst were those who fell to the status of unskilled worker or remained as unskilled workers over the decade.

The regression results reported in Table 6-9 take into account whether individuals remained in the same county between 1850 and 1860, as well as age, duration in the United States for immigrants, occupation, region, and country of origin. The magnitude of the return to duration in a local economy may have varied significantly by location, however. A large rate of return to precedence might have been earned by those who had the foresight or good fortune to arrive early and remain in places that were later successful.[35] Early arrivals may have done better than those who later reached the same places because of such factors as the rapid accumulation of capital gains or the ability to recognize emerging business opportunities. To see whether the return to early arrival in a place was indeed greater in places that experienced the most rapid population growth over the 1850s, the regression reported in Table 6-9 included dummy variables for prior residence in the urban East, rural East, urban West, and rural West.

For natives, the largest impact came from persistence in the urban West. The effect of remaining in a place of 2,500 or more in the Midwest, Far West, or Southwest was positive and twice as great as the impact of remaining in the urban Northeast or Southeast. Persistence in the rural West produced a still smaller benefit. For immigrants, the greatest gains in wealth were made among those who persisted in the urban West. The magnitude of this effect is slightly greater than the impact of persistence in the urban West for natives. These results imply that an individual who resided in a western city such as Milwaukee (which grew 101 percent over the 1850s) between 1850 and 1860 was nearly five times wealthier in 1860 than an individual who changed counties between 1850 and 1860.

Although these results are not surprising, they allow us to describe in concrete terms what was happening to these immigrants over the course of the 1850s. Where previously there had been a clear impact from duration in the United States (Tables 6-4, 6-6, and 6-7), there is no significant impact in Table 6-9 (which accounts for the changes in immigrants' circumstances between 1850 and 1860). It appears, then, that the impact on wealth of duration of residence captured in the previous regressions resulted from the specific changes in location and occupation made by many immigrants during the 1850s rather than from adjustment to the U.S. economy experienced by all immigrants, both those who changed their circumstances over the 1850s and those who did not.

35. Galenson, "Economic Opportunity"; Pope, "Households."

Table 6-9. Ordinary least squares regressions on 1860 real wealth of natives and immigrant arrivals at New York, 1840–50, controlling for changes in characteristics 1850–60.

	Natives		Immigrants	
	β	Probability	β	Probability
Intercept	−0.1708	0.7118	−1.0156	0.7981
Age	0.2182	0.0001	0.2428	0.0005
Age^2	−0.0021	0.0001	−0.0020	0.0144
Origin				
Irish			−0.3175	0.3925
German			0.0672	0.8508
Other			0.7712	0.3391
Years in U.S.			−0.0749	0.8744
Years in U.S.^{2}			0.0036	0.8194
Literate	0.5175	0.0141	0.5481	0.3521
Children				
< Age 10 in 1850	−0.2039	0.0001	−0.4635	0.0280
Age 10+ in 1850	−0.0174	0.7070	0.3796	0.0844
< Age 10 in 1860	0.1466	0.0001	0.3882	0.0001
Age 10+ in 1860	0.1461	0.0020	0.1673	0.4017
ln(1850 real wealth)	0.3527	0.0001	0.1308	0.0195
Region, 1850 & 1860				
Northeast, West	−0.0333	0.8588	0.7181	0.1163
South, South	−0.4043	0.0182	1.1546	0.2550
South, West	0.1766	0.5987	0.1113	0.8949
West, West	0.0548	0.7384	0.5382	0.3056
Other	−0.3693	0.1777	−0.2155	0.6947
Size of location, 1850 & 1860				
Rural, urban	−0.9233	0.0001	−0.2877	0.5944
Urban, rural	0.0269	0.8933	0.4568	0.3503
Urban, urban	−0.8180	0.0001	0.3262	0.5139
Occupation, 1850 & 1860				
White collar, white collar	−1.2819	0.0001	−3.6356	0.0001
White collar, skilled	−2.5334	0.0001	−3.7550	0.0004
White collar, farmer	1.9878	0.0001	0.2619	0.8624
Skilled, white collar	−1.3962	0.0001	−3.6648	0.0001
Skilled, skilled	−2.2149	0.0001	−3.4991	0.0001
Skilled, farmer	0.9736	0.0001	0.8654	0.3234
Skilled, unskilled	−3.7647	0.0001	−4.4235	0.0001
Farmer, white collar	−3.0002	0.0001	−3.5608	0.0099
Farmer, skilled	−3.1747	0.0001	−5.3714	0.0028
Farmer, unskilled	−6.7463	0.0001	−6.5285	0.0001
Unskilled, skilled	−1.9581	0.0001	−3.1761	0.0001
Unskilled, farmer	2.2308	0.0001	1.2390	0.1074
Unskilled, unskilled	−3.9515	0.0001	−4.0240	0.0001
Other	−2.1770	0.0001	−3.3558	0.0001

Table 6-9. (*continued*)

	Natives		Immigrants	
	β	Probability	β	Probability
Mobility, 1850–60				
Same County				
Urban East	0.7737	0.0001	0.1134	0.8744
Rural East	0.0103	0.9489	0.4737	0.5334
Urban West	1.4007	0.0001	1.5456	0.0331
Rural West	0.2796	0.0333	0.5409	0.3857
Adjusted R^2	0.5674		0.4341	
F	165.691	0.0001	10.993	0.0001
N	4,270		508	

Source: Males fifteen years and older in 1850 Public Use Microdata Series linked to the 1860 manuscript census schedules; male household heads and unaccompanied males in passenger ship arrival records at port of New York, 1840–1850, linked to 1850 and 1860 manuscript census schedules.

Note: Omitted groups are "British," "Illiterate," "Northeast in both years," "Rural in both years," "Farmer in both years," and "Different County." "Probability" is the probability that the true is zero.

Conclusion

The large returns to changes in occupation and location indicated in Table 6-9 are consistent with the view that immigrants better matched their abilities to both the jobs they worked and the places where they lived as their time in the United States increased. Such a process can also help explain several striking differences between the age-wealth profiles for 1850 and those for 1860 in Figure 6-1: the increases in the steepness of the profiles and in the age at which wealth peaked. For example, the age at which wealth attained a maximum increased from the 1850 cross section to the 1860 cross section for immigrants but not for natives. Also, by 1860, the Irish were no longer statistically different from the British and Germans, after controlling for changes in occupation and location.

These patterns are consistent with immigrants better matching themselves to jobs and places in the years after arrival. For example, if immigrants were essentially distributed randomly across occupations at arrival, regardless of their skills, and sorted themselves into occupations that suited their skills in the following years, differences in wealth by occupation would have been wider in 1860 than in 1850. The reduction in the wealth disadvantage of the Irish between 1850 and 1860, after accounting for all other observed characteristics, is also consistent with more successful matching: having come from Ireland with few skills and little capital may have been less of a handicap after a decade in which one could acquire additional skills or learn where best to put one's existing skills to work.

The later age peak in wealth in 1860 than in 1850 seen in Table 6-3 is also consistent with the view that immigrants over the course of their time in the U.S. economy were able to take better advantage of their comparative advantage in particular pursuits. For example, unskilled workers relied more on simple physical strength than those with greater skill (skilled workers and those in white collar occupations) or those whose income was earned through the use of inputs complementary to physical strength (farmers who used land, animals, and farm machinery). The peak of the age-earnings profile for unskilled workers would have occurred earlier than for workers with greater skill or other inputs to employ, and their age-wealth profile would have occurred earlier as a result. If immigrants were able to move into occupations that made less use of physical strength over the 1850s, this would have allowed them to postpone the age at which their earnings and wealth peaked.

Several of the same trends in the relationship between the age-wealth profile and duration in the economy uncovered here have been observed in the development of the Utah economy and the economies of several western states and counties.[36] Where age-wealth profiles can be traced over a period of decades for an entire economy, an increasingly mature economy consistently displays a higher and later-peaking profile than the same economy earlier in its development. The explanation offered for those changes—that in an increasingly mature economy, individuals may have more opportunities to take advantage of their skills and thereby change the shape and peak of the age-earnings and age-wealth profiles— might account for much of the difference between the profiles in 1850 and 1860. Immigrants who had spent a longer time in the United States (those observed in 1860) might have been like individuals in an economy at a more mature stage of development, whereas recent arrivals (those observed in 1850), like individuals in a newly formed frontier economy, had yet to sort themselves into the occupations and locations in which their skills could earn the greatest return.

The plausibility of this matching process as an explanation for the duration effect is enhanced by the reduced substantive and statistical significance of the duration effect in the regression results presented in Table 6-9, when account is taken of immigrant's ability to make these adjustments in their circumstances. These results suggest that most of the increase in immigrants' wealth as their time in the United States increased may have resulted from their ability to improve the match between the resources they brought with them from Europe and how those resources were employed in the United States.

As a result of these changes in their circumstances, European immigrants to the United States in the 1840s were able to accumulate impressive amounts of wealth in the years after their arrival. In 1850, immigrants who had arrived over the previous decade owned an average of $262 in real estate, only a fifth as much as natives. By 1860, that figure had risen to more than $920, just under half of the wealth held by natives. When personal wealth is included, immigrants possessed an average of $1,327 in 1860 after an average of 15 years in the United States. Like the native born, immigrants' wealth increased with age, though theirs did so more rapidly in percentage terms once changes in characteristics are controlled for.

36. Pope, "Households," p. 168; Soltow, *Men and Wealth*, p. 82.

Although many of the findings presented here have been observed in other studies of nineteenth-century wealth accumulation—a concave age-wealth profile, greater wealth for farmers and white collar workers, higher levels of wealth in the West, and a significant return to early arrival and continued residence in places that grew rapidly—this study has been the first to show how these effects combined to cause immigrants' wealth to increase with the length of residence in the United States. These findings support the view that the ability of immigrants to adapt to the new circumstances they faced after arrival led to the rise in their wealth with duration of residence. Along with other recent research on the entry of immigrants into the United States, these findings indicate both the flexibility of the antebellum U.S. economy and the adaptability of the immigrants it embraced.

7

Economic Mobility and Geographic Persistence, 1850–1860

The process of transformation undergone by the immigrants described in the preceding chapters did not end in 1850. Though we have focused on the changes they experienced between arrival and 1850, making use of data from 1860 only where it was necessary to separate the effects of duration in the United States from changes in cohorts over time, a great deal more mobility occurred among these new Americans between 1850 and 1860. In this chapter, we follow their progress over this decade, considering their geographic, occupational, and financial mobility, and the links among these dimensions of their experience. In doing so, we offer a new contribution to an older literature on the economic mobility of not just immigrants but also natives, and the role of geographic mobility in that process.

It has now been more than thirty years since the publication of Stephan Thernstrom's *Poverty and Progress: Social Mobility in a Nineteenth Century City*, and more than twenty years since the appearance of his other ground-breaking work on mobility in the United States, *The Other Bostonians: Poverty and Progress in the American Metropolis, 1880–1970*. Like the work of Frederick Jackson Turner on the importance of the frontier, these studies defined an agenda for research in quantitative economic and social history that guided the work of a generation.[1] Like the work of Turner and his disciples, the "new urban history" has been a source of persistent controversy.

While the research of the "frontier school" was challenged on the question of the prevalence of common unskilled workers in the movement west, studies of social mobility have been bedeviled by a lack of information on the mobility of non-

1. Recent research in this area includes Griffen and Griffen, *Natives and Newcomers*; Katz, *People of Hamilton West*; and Winkle, *Politics of Community*.

persisters—the 60 percent or more of Americans who did not remain in a place long enough to be observed more than fleetingly in studies of social mobility based on individuals located in successive documentary sources in a single city, town, or county.[2] Carter Goodrich and Sol Davidson were among the first to subject Turner's view to empirical scrutiny.[3] They examined newspaper accounts and other local records for Fall River, Massachusetts, and several other New England urban centers, seeking evidence of the exodus of urban unskilled workers to the West that Turner predicted. Their findings were quite different from Turner's suggestion: "This cumulation of evidence thus points to the conclusion that the movement of eastern wage-earners to western lands was surprisingly small. Too few industrial workers reached the frontier to attract notice in the accounts of settlement."[4] They adopted their largely anecdotal approach after noting the then insurmountable difficulties inherent in using the federal census manuscripts for the purpose of determining who was moving to the frontier: "The Census and the records of the General Land Office throw little light upon the precise question at issue . . . at least short of the task of taking the names of individual wage-earners in a given census and then searching for them in the haystacks of succeeding enumerations."[5] Thernstrom was also aware of the usefulness of data linking movers across censuses, but, like Goodrich and Davidson, lacked the resources to create such data.[6]

This chapter focuses new attention on the link between geographic mobility and occupational and financial mobility. Although it accepts both the questions posed in previous studies of social mobility—how much occupational and financial mobility were exhibited by nineteenth-century Americans, particularly unskilled workers?—and the usefulness of the documentary sources used in those studies—the federal census manuscripts—it provides unique information about the nonpersisters overlooked in previous work on economic mobility. The knowledge of the actual experiences of both persisters and nonpersisters offers a different perspective on economic mobility from works that have provided only conjectures as to the experiences of nonpersisters.

With the data introduced in this study, it is possible to trace patterns of occupational and financial mobility among both persisters and nonpersisters, since the individuals in the sample were located in 1860 whether or not they remained in the same community over the 1850s. By employing standard measures of mobility—movement among a handful of broad occupational classifications and the accumulation of property—and standard sources—the census manuscripts—this study will provide a sense of the bias produced by the exclusive concentration on persisters in previous studies of nineteenth-century U.S. economic mobility.

2. The average persistence rate in 63 community studies surveyed by Donald Parkerson was 38.3 percent. Parkerson, "Nineteenth-Century Americans," pp. 99–109.

3. Goodrich and Davidson, "Westward Movement I," pp. 161–185; and "Westward Movement II," pp. 61–116.

4. Goodrich and Davidson, "Westward Movement II," p. 114.

5. Ibid., p. 62.

6. Thernstrom, *Poverty and Progress*, p. 86.

The Problematic Nonpersisters

Although historians have been employing samples of individuals linked across successive documentary sources for nearly sixty years, the early focus of this work was on population turnover in rural communities.[7] With the publication of *Poverty and Progress*, attention shifted to urban places, and new questions were raised. Rather than simply calculating persistence rates and examining the characteristics of persisters and nonpersisters, these studies attempted to measure the occupational and financial mobility of nineteenth- century Americans by examining the experiences of persisters.[8] The experiences of individuals who changed locations was inferred from their appearance in and disappearance from these sources.

Even though making such inferences is like trying to learn the fate of characters in a play through their fleeting roles in the first act and their failure to appear in subsequent acts, the importance of the experiences of nonpersisters in the story of total economic mobility has required that guesses be made as to their fate. On the basis of the characteristics of those who left Newburyport, Thernstrom suggested that these individuals must have done no better in their next location.[9] In his later work on Boston, he asked whether these nonpersisters might not comprise a *"floating proletariat . . . of men ever on the move spatially but rarely winning economic gains as a result of spatial mobility."*[10]

These conjectures are unsatisfactory, however, because of both the overall mobility of nineteenth- century Americans and the vast differences in mobility exhibited in different places and by different groups. Previous studies of geographic mobility have found a wide range of persistence rates. In many of the places studied, persistence rates were less than 50 percent, including several places where less than a third of the population persisted over a decade.[11] Places with such low persistence rates included cities in the East (Philadelphia) and in the West (Chicago), and communities on the farming frontier (Trempeleau County, Wisconsin, and Sugar Creek, Illinois).[12] Conversely, persistence rates of more than 50 percent were not unusual either in the nineteenth century: they have been found in places as diverse as Hamilton, Iowa; East Central Kansas; Holland, Michigan; Poughkeepsie, New York; and Indianapolis.[13] Other studies have

7. Malin, "Turnover of Farm Population," pp. 339–372; Curti, *Making of An American Community*; Bogue, *Prairie to Cornbelt*.

8. Thernstrom, *Poverty and Progress*; Katz, *People of Hamilton West*; Griffen and Griffen, *Natives and Newcomers*; and Winkle, *Politics of Community*.

9. Thernstrom, *Poverty and Progress*, pp. 88–89, *passim*.

10. Thernstrom, *Other Bostonians*, p. 42 (italics added).

11. Blumin, "Mobility"; Curti, *Making of An American Community*; Galenson, "Economic Opportunity"; Faragher, *Sugar Creek*

12. Curti, *Making of An American Community*; Blumin, "Mobility"; Faragher, *Sugar Creek*; and Galenson, "Economic Opportunity."

13. Bogue, *Prairie to Cornbelt*; Malin, "Turnover of Farm Population"; Kirk and Kirk, "Transformation of the Occupational Structure"; Griffen and Griffen, *Natives and Newcomers*; Barrows, "Demographic Analysis."

shown vast differences in persistence rates across socioeconomic groups. For example, Thernstrom found that those in blue collar occupations were less likely to persist in Boston between 1880 and 1890 than white collar workers. Several studies have also observed a positive association between wealth and persistence.[14]

Since nonpersisters were a large fraction of the total nineteenth-century population, even a small error in guessing their fate would have a large influence on the accuracy of estimates of total economic mobility extrapolated from the experiences of persisters alone. At the same time, the low persistence rates of young, unskilled, unmarried workers suggests that nonpersisters may have merely been at an earlier stage in the life cycle than those who remained in the same city for a decade or more. This was suggested in an early discussion of Thernstrom's work on Boston by Engerman.[15] To account for this possibility, Kousser, Cox, and Galenson reexamined the cross-tabulations originally presented by Thernstrom in *The Other Bostonians*. Although Thernstrom noted that nonpersisters were young, unskilled, and unmarried, he was unable to control for the simultaneous influence of these effects. Once Kousser, Cox, and Galenson took account of the age of nonpersisters, the impact of occupational class differentials and marital status on persistence was greatly reduced. They suggested that a good deal of geographic mobility was simply the rational result of those who had the most to gain and the least to lose in forsaking a community relocating to seek opportunity elsewhere.[16] More recent studies that have examined geographic mobility have also simultaneously controlled for a variety of characteristics and found that only one or two (generally age and marital status) have a large influence on persistence.[17]

The best evidence with which to assess the experiences of nonpersisters would be actual information on how they fared after they left places like Newburyport. The last decade has seen a number of studies in which individuals who left a community were sought and located in other communities at a later census date.[18] These studies were made possible by technological improvements that have produced the "magical electronic device" that Thernstrom imagined would be necessary to follow nonpersisters—computers that can be brought directly to the evidence in libraries and archives—and the appearance of indexes to the census manuscripts.[19] The samples used in these studies, though, have been inappropriate for examining the economic mobility of nineteenth-century Americans.

The studies by Davenport and Knights were done with samples originally drawn from two specific communities—Schoharie County, New York, and Boston.[20] Unfortunately, the usefulness of these studies for determining the fate of nonpersisters generally is limited by the narrow scope of the locations from

14. Thernstrom, *Poverty and Progress*; Katz, *People of Hamilton West*; Barron, *Those Who Stayed Behind*; and Galenson, "Economic Opportunity."

15. Engerman, "Up or Out," pp. 483–484.

16. Kousser, Cox, and Galenson, "Log-Linear Analysis."

17. Galenson, "Economic Opportunity."

18. Davenport, "Out-Migrants"; Knights, *Yankee Destinies*; Steckel, "Census Matching"; Schaefer, "Statistical Profile"; Guest, "Notes."

19. Thernstrom, *Poverty and Progress*, p. 86.

20. Davenport, "Out-Migrants"; Knights, *Yankee Destinies*.

which the original samples of individuals to follow were drawn. Both Steckel and Schaefer have created national or regional samples by linking individuals drawn from the 1860 federal census manuscripts back into the 1850 manuscripts.[21] Unfortunately, these studies probably underrepresent young, unmarried, and childless individuals in 1850, which are just the groups that exhibited the geographic mobility that concerns us here. Both studies were forced to rely on state-by-state indexes for 1850 and thus used the birthplaces of children 10 and older to find the likely 1850 state of residence. The National Panel Study (NPS) linked individuals from the 1880 census manuscripts to the 1900 manuscripts, again using state-by-state census indexes.[22] The use of state indexes and the inability to search all state indexes for those who changed states, however, probably leave interstate migrants underrepresented in this sample. Guest reports that "only 160 out of 4,041 cases were found out-of- state."[23]

The sample employed here overcomes the shortcomings of these samples: it is national in scope, follows both young, single individuals and older individuals with families, uses a national index to the 1860 census to locate individuals regardless of where they moved, and follows both interstate and intrastate migrants. The information it provides on nonpersisters—particularly the unique information on long-distance movers—adds to our understanding of nineteenth-century economic mobility.

Measuring Persistence

Recent research has found extremely high rates of mobility, and low persistence rates, among a variety of immigrant groups. Esslinger found that only 16 percent of first- and second-generation immigrants persisted in South Bend, Indiana, between 1850 and 1860. The corresponding figures for 1860–70 and 1870–80 are 16 percent and 25 percent. Immigrants from different countries, however, were not equally likely to persist. Between 1870 and 1880, 30 percent of British immigrants, but only 18 percent of German immigrants, persisted in South Bend.[24] Galenson finds that British immigrants were 6.6 percentage points more likely to persist in Chicago between 1850 and 1860 than the native born, whereas German immigrants were 3.7 percentage points less likely to persist than the native born.[25] These same patterns have been found in rural places as well: Bogue finds that 46.5 percent of immigrants from the United Kingdom and Canada persisted in Bureau County, Illinois (a higher rate than that for the native born), as opposed to only 28 percent of immigrants from continental Europe.[26] These high rates result in

21. Steckel, "Census Matching"; Schaefer, "Statistical Profile."
22. Guest, "Notes."
23. Ibid., p. 65. These data are reexamined in Simkovich, "Inter-Generational Occupational Mobility."
24. Esslinger, *Immigrants*, p. 43.
25. Galenson, "Economic Opportunity," p. 585.
26. Bogue, *Prairie to Cornbelt*, p. 26.

part because many immigrants were either propertyless or unskilled, but the finding of greater mobility for some immigrant groups holds, even after controlling for wealth or occupation.[27]

Each of these studies uses a measure of persistence in which persisters are those located in the same county in both years and nonpersisters are those not located. This measure might be termed the "unconditional persistence rate," since it does not require that individuals meet the conditions of survival and enumeration to be included in the population at risk.[28] Nonpersisters could thus be individuals who actually left their original county of residence, but they could also have died in the intervening years or simply been missed by the census at the second date. To assess how persistence in the sample used here compares to these previous measures of persistence, we then need a measure that is constructed in a similar manner.

The individuals linked from the 1850 PUMS to the 1860 census are not useful for this purpose, since they only entered the sample if they were successfully located in 1860. The immigrants linked from the passenger ship lists can be used for this purpose, however. Immigrants who were located in the 1850 census but not in the 1860 census were included along with those linked to 1860 only and those linked to both censuses. A measure of persistence more comparable to that used previously, then, can be constructed for these immigrants. The denominator is all the immigrants linked from the ship lists to the 1850 census; the numerator is all those linked to the censuses of both 1850 and 1860.

The antebellum European immigrants examined here were quite mobile after their arrival in the United States. The top panel of Table 7-1 shows "unconditional" persistence rates calculated for the full sample and for regions, sizes of locations, and occupations. Since we will be interested in how unskilled workers like those who left Thernstrom's Newburyport sample fared after migration, occupations have been divided into three large groups: (1) unskilled workers (those in unskilled manual occupations and farm tenants); (2) those in skilled manual and white collar occupations; (3) and farm owners. The occupations included in each of these categories are shown in Appendix E. Farm tenants were distinguished from farm owners on the basis of the reported real estate holdings of those who described their occupation as "farmer." Farmers with no recorded real estate in the population schedules were classified as farm tenants, while farmers with positive real estate were classified as farm owners.[29] Since the individuals used here were not sought in the agricultural schedules, some of those classified as tenants here might have been farmers who just arrived in a community and had not had time to purchase a farm and put a crop in the ground before the census enumeration or were merely passing through it. The number of tenants described here is therefore probably an upper bound on the true number of tenants in the sample.

By this measure, no more than one out of seven immigrants was found in the

27. Galenson, "Economic Opportunity," p. 585; Engerman, "Up or Out," p. 478.
28. See Galenson and Levy, "Note on Biases," for a discussion of these issues.
29. This methodology is discussed in Bogue, *Prairie to Cornbelt*, pp. 63–64.

Table 7-1. Unconditional and conditional rates of persistence in 1850–60 of immigrant arrivals at New York, 1840–50.

Location	All N	All %	White Collar N	White Collar %	Skilled N	Skilled %	Farmer N	Farmer %	Unskilled N	Unskilled %
Unconditional										
Region										
Northeast	896	15.0	29	10.3	342	13.2	62	27.4	428	15.0
Northwest	440	13.9	—	—	132	9.9	144	17.4	129	12.4
Size of location										
Urban	900	14.4	40	15.0	390	13.3	27	18.5	394	15.0
Rural	556	13.0	—	—	132	6.1	183	20.2	210	11.4
Total	1,456	13.9	53	11.3	522	11.5	210	20.0	604	13.7
Conditional										
Region										
Northeast	332	40.4	—	—	104	43.3	24	70.8	184	34.8
Northwest	140	43.6	—	—	28	46.4	43	58.1	58	27.6
Size of location										
Urban	320	40.6	—	—	115	45.2	—	—	171	34.5
Rural	189	38.1	—	—	30	26.7	61	60.7	91	26.4
Total	509	40.0	—	—	145	41.4	67	62.7	262	31.7

Source: Male household heads and unaccompanied males in passenger ship arrival records at port of New York, 1840–1850, linked to 1850 and/or 1860 manuscript census schedules.

Notes: Cells with fewer than 20 observations are not reported. "Northeast" is New England and Middle Atlantic. "Northwest" is Midwest and Far West. "Urban" is a census subdivision with an 1850 population of 2,500 or more. The unconditional persistence rate is the ratio of the number of individuals located in the same county in 1850 and 1860 to the number of individuals observed in 1850; the conditional rate is the ratio of the number of individuals located in the same county in 1850 and 1860 to the number of individuals observed in both 1850 and 1860 (see text).

same county in both 1850 and 1860. Although these rates obscure much of the local variation in circumstances that produced the rates described in earlier studies, they are noteworthy because they are as low as the lowest rates observed elsewhere.[30] As in earlier studies of geographic mobility, unskilled workers were less likely to persist than farmers, but both white collar and skilled workers also had persistence rates below those of farmers. Both Chicago and San Francisco had persistence rates below 30 percent, whereas both of these places received large numbers of European immigrants and internal migrants. Persistence rates in the Northwest were below those in the Northeast, and nonfarmers in urban places were slightly more likely to remain in the same county than nonfarmers in rural places.

To account for the effects of mortality and underenumeration in the census and the census index, a second persistence rate is included in the bottom panel of

30. See Galenson, "Economic Opportunity," p. 584.

Table 7-1—the "conditional persistence rate." This is the fraction of all persons who were located in both 1850 and 1860 who remained in a particular county between 1850 and 1860. To see how the conditional, unconditional, and true persistence rates are related, suppose the entire 1850 population of a county is being sought in 1860. The numerator of the unconditional persistence rate is the number of people in the county in 1850 who meet four criteria: (1) they did not migrate out of the county between 1850 and 1860; (2) they survived to 1860; (3) they were enumerated within the county in the 1860 census; and (4) they appeared in the 1860 census index for the county. The denominator is the number of people in the county in 1850.

$$P_{unconditional} = \frac{(N_C)(P_{true})(S_C)(C_C)(I_C)}{N_C} = (P_{true})(S_C)(E_C) \qquad (1)$$

where $P_{unconditional}$ is the unconditional persistence rate, N_C is the county population in 1850, P_{true} is the true persistence rate (the ratio of N_C minus the number of out-migrants to N_C), S_C is the proportion of the population in the 1850 county that survived to 1860, C_C is the proportion of survivors enumerated within the county in the 1860 census, I_C is the proportion of those in the 1860 census for the county appearing in the 1860 census index for the county, and E_C is the total (census and index) enumeration rate in 1860 for the county. The conditional persistence rate has the same numerator, but its denominator is more restrictive: it is the number of people in the county in 1850 who meet three criteria: (1) they survived to 1860 anywhere in the United States; (2) they were enumerated in the 1860 census anywhere in the United States; and (3) they appeared in the 1860 census index anywhere in the United States:

$$P_{conditional} = \frac{(N_C)(P_{true})(S_C)(C_C)(I_C)}{(N_C)(S_{US})(C_{US})(I_{US})} = (P_{true})\left(\frac{S_C}{S_{US}}\right)\left(\frac{E_C}{E_{US}}\right) \qquad (2)$$

where $P_{conditional}$ is the conditional persistence rate, S_{US} is the proportion of the county population that survived to 1860 anywhere in the United States, C_{US} is the proportion of survivors enumerated in the 1860 census anywhere in the United States, I_{US} is the proportion of those in the 1860 census for the United States appearing in the 1860 census index for the United States, and E_{US} is the total (census and index) enumeration rate in 1860 for the total United States. Since the persistence rates presented in Table 7-1 were calculated for a variety of locations, S_C should be close to S_{US} and E_C should be close to E_{US} (by the Law of Large Numbers). Thus, the conditional persistence rate should be close to the true persistence rate, even if the survival rates and the enumeration rates are less than one. The relationship between the unconditional and conditional persistence rates can be seen by combining these two equations:

$$P_{unconditional} = (S_{US})(E_{US})(P_{conditional}) \qquad (3)$$

Both S_{US} and E_{US} will be less than one (since not everyone survived to 1860, and not everyone was enumerated in 1860), so $P_{unconditional}$ must be less than $P_{conditional}$, as in Table 7-1. We can use this equation to check the reasonableness of the implied rates of survival and census enumeration. We know that $P_{unconditional} = 0.139$ and $P_{conditional} = 0.400$ from Table 7-1. The 1860 census index was 95 percent accurate, so $I_{US} = 0.950$.[31] Thus,

$$0.139 = (S_{US}) (C_{US}) (0.950) (0.400) \tag{4}$$

which in turn implies that

$$0.366 = (S_{US}) (C_{US}) \tag{5}$$

This would be true, for example, with a Model West, Level 10 life table ($e_{20} = 38$) according to which 88 percent of the immigrants present in 1850 would have survived to 1860 and a census enumeration for immigrants that was 42 percent complete.[32]

The unconditional persistence rates in Table 7-1 are not directly comparable to those from other studies of nineteenth-century places for two reasons. The first is that these figures aggregate across a large number of individual communities, while other studies have focused instead on individual places. Much of the variation in the circumstances of individual communities that prompt differences in persistence rates is lost in such aggregation. Second, there is an additional reason here for the failure to locate an individual in 1860: inaccuracies in the 1860 census index. Although there is no reason to suspect that the shortcomings of the index should vary with region or size of place, this nonetheless imparts a downward bias of unknown magnitude to measured persistence, placing it below what it would be if linkage to 1860 had been done, as in these other studies, by directly comparing the enumerations in 1850 and 1860.

Since we will compare the postmigration experiences of persisters with nonpersisters, the conditional measure of persistence will be of greater interest here. It shows that nearly two-thirds of immigrants who survived and were enumerated changed counties between 1850 and 1860. The same patterns of persistence by occupation and urban/rural residence can be seen in the conditional rates in Table 7-1 as in the unconditional rates, but it is now less clear that those in nonfarm jobs were more likely to persist in the Northeast than in the Northwest. Unskilled workers were more likely to persist in the Northeast, skilled workers in the Northwest.

Having established the relationship between the unconditional and conditional persistence rates, and compared the unconditional rates here to those in other studies, we can abandon the unconditional rate and focus only on individuals located in both 1850 and 1860. The sample will now be expanded to include three components: (1) immigrants who were linked from ship lists to the 1850

---

31. See chapter 2, in this volume.
32. Coale and Demeny, *Model Life Tables.*

Table 7-2. Conditional rates of persistence in 1850–60 of natives and immigrant arrivals at New York, 1840–50, by occupation, region, and size of location.

1850 Location	All N	All %	White Collar N	White Collar %	Skilled N	Skilled %	Farmer N	Farmer %	Unskilled N	Unskilled %
Natives										
Region										
NE	881	64.7	56	64.3	231	65.4	252	78.6	320	55.0
MA	1,546	55.7	81	65.4	278	60.1	448	68.3	725	45.4
MW	873	49.4	34	52.9	89	44.9	384	61.2	356	37.9
SE	587	65.4	32	56.3	57	66.7	220	70.0	271	63.5
SC	363	52.1	—	—	25	56.0	178	60.1	152	42.1
Size of location										
Urban	664	57.1	84	66.7	238	58.0	65	78.5	248	49.2
Rural	3,607	57.2	126	57.1	449	61.0	1,419	67.0	1,587	47.7
Total	4,271	57.2	210	61.0	687	60.0	1,484	67.5	1,835	47.9
Immigrants										
Region										
NE	182	28.6	—	—	32	31.3	—	—	142	26.1
MA	509	33.0	—	—	139	43.2	39	69.2	314	22.9
MW	338	33.4	—	—	70	45.7	92	54.4	163	16.0
SE	52	25.0	—	—	—	—	—	—	28	14.3
SC	49	14.3	—	—	—	—	—	—	30	10.0
Size of location										
Urban	630	32.1	30	46.7	200	39.0	—	—	365	25.5
Rural	546	30.4	—	—	75	40.0	133	57.9	319	15.7
Total	1,176	31.3	43	46.5	275	39.3	141	58.9	684	20.9

Source: Males fifteen years and older in 1850 Public Use Microdata Series linked to the 1860 manuscript census schedules; male household heads and unaccompanied males in passenger ship arrival records at port of New York, 1840–1850, linked to 1850 and 1860 manuscript census schedules.

Notes. Cells with fewer than 20 observations are not reported. "NE" is New England; "MA" is Middle Atlantic; "SE" is Southeast; "SC" is South Central. "Urban" is a census sub-division with an 1850 population of 2,500 or more. The conditional rate is the ratio of the number of individuals located in the same county in 1850 and 1860 to the number of individuals observed in both 1850 and 1860 (see text).

and 1860 censuses; (2) immigrants linked from the 1850 PUMS to the 1860 census; and (3) natives linked from the 1850 PUMS to the 1860 census. Table 7-2 shows conditional persistence rates broken down by 1850 region, size of location, and occupation. The persistence rate is the number of those located in a county in the region or size of place who were found in that county again in 1860, divided by the number of people located in both 1850 and 1860.

The most striking finding in Table 7-2 is the generally low rate of persistence across all regions, sizes of places, and occupations for immigrants compared to natives. In many cases (for example, unskilled workers or those located in New England in 1850), the rate of persistence for immigrants was less than half of that for natives. There are some noteworthy exceptions to this generalization, however. In the Middle Atlantic states, immigrant farmers actually had a higher persistence rate than natives, while the same was true for skilled immigrants in the Midwest. Across all locations, though, white collar workers, skilled workers, and unskilled workers all had quite low rates, with fewer than 50 percent remaining in the same county over the 1850s. In contrast to the findings of previous studies of nineteenth-century communities where those lower in the occupational hierarchy were the most likely to relocate over the course of a decade, even white collar and skilled immigrants were more likely than not to relocate over a ten-year period.

The only groups with consistently high persistence rates are farmers. Farming entailed the largest capital investment after arrival of any of the occupations, so farmers had a large stake in initially choosing somewhere they could remain. Given the size of that investment and the costs associated with liquidating it, farmers might also have been more willing to remain in place, despite changes in the relative prices that made it a favorable place at the outset.

The generally low persistence rates for those apart from farmers are consistent with immigrants having a low overall persistence rate in the absence of compelling reasons (such as substantial location-specific investments or a lack of resources) not to relocate. The low persistence rates for most immigrants might seem paradoxical in light of the finding earlier that immigrants reached their observed 1850 locations quickly. They appear to have moved with great certainty to locations that most of them subsequently abandoned. Three points must be kept in mind, though.

First, some of the immigrants observed in 1850 were no doubt on their way to their 1860 location when they were observed by census marshals; they appear to have moved by 1860, but they were observed in transit in 1850. Second, as we will see, most immigrants remained in the same state and region between 1850 and 1860, and it was their 1850 state and region that they reached rapidly rather than a specific location within a state or region. Such movement as occurred is consistent with immigrants knowing generally where they wanted to settle, but making minor adjustments once they had time to evaluate conditions at their chosen destination or after they were able to amass the financial resources that would allow them to move from city to farm. Third, we should perhaps expect a great deal of mobility within states or regions among immigrants. At their arrival, they must have possessed some information about alternative locations in the United States. If conditions were unsatisfactory at the initial location, these immigrants would have possessed some knowledge of where else they could try.

The Correlates of Persistence

In order to assess the separate impact of factors such as age, marital status, occupation, and origin on persistence, Table 7-3 presents the results of a linear regres-

Table 7-3. Multivariate analysis of persistence in 1850–60 of natives and immigrant arrivals at New York, 1840–50.

Variable	Natives		Immigrants	
	(1)	(2)	(3)	(4)
Intercept	33.460***	31.344***	14.545	14.583
Age	0.567**	0.673**	−0.042	−0.042
Age^2 × 10^{-3}	−1.142	−2.137	8.259	8.322
Married	6.425***	8.952***	18.356***	20.357***
Family size	0.115	0.131	2.160***	2.232***
Occupation				
White collar	−0.941	−2.224	6.389	5.667
Skilled	1.886	2.595	5.774*	6.194**
Farmer	5.049***	6.029***	16.337***	19.169***
Real Wealth × 10^{-4}	—	25.530***	—	13.471
Real Wealth^2 × 10^{-8}	—	−5.877**	—	−2.166
Owned property	11.563***	—	10.411***	—
Origin				
Ireland	—	—	−10.444***	−11.008***
Germany	—	—	−5.783*	−6.005*
Other	—	—	2.270	2.229
Literate	−0.703	−0.585	−5.350	−4.758
Region				
New England	7.193***	8.223***	2.273	2.509
Midwest	−7.400***	−6.326***	−3.054	−2.068
Southeast	8.733***	9.323***	3.738	3.641
South Central	−3.945	−2.948	−12.980**	−12.992**
Far West	−23.013**	−21.217**	−15.417	−14.720
Urban	−3.791*	−4.636**	7.029***	6.160**
Adjusted R^2	0.105	0.103	0.224	0.219
N	4,270	4,270	1,175	1,175

Source: Males fifteen years and older in 1850 Public Use Microdata Series linked to the 1860 manuscript census schedules; male household heads and unaccompanied males in passenger ship arrival records at port of New York, 1840–1850, linked to 1850 and 1860 manuscript census schedules.

Note: The dependent variable takes a value of 100 if the individual remained in the same county between 1850 and 1860, and a zero otherwise. The coefficients measure the number of percentage points by which the probability of persisting increases or decreases in response to a unit change in the independent variable. All estimates were obtained by ordinary least squares regressions. Unmarried, illiterate, unskilled workers residing in the rural Middle Atlantic region in 1850 are the reference group in each regression. For immigrants, the British are the reference group. Probability that the true β is equal to zero: *<10%; **<5%; ***<1%.

sion in which the dependent variable is whether an individual persisted in the same county between 1850 and 1860. The definition of persistence used is the conditional one described previously. Separate regressions were run for immigrants and natives. All characteristics are measured in 1850. Columns 1 and 3 use a simple dummy variable for whether an individual owned any real estate in 1850; columns 2 and 4 use the actual value of real estate and its square instead.

For both natives and immigrants, several of the correlates of persistence discussed in other studies come through clearly. Marriage, a farm occupation, and the
possession of real estate all made individuals more likely to remain in the same
county. For example, married immigrants were 50 percent more likely to persist
than unmarried immigrants. An individual who owned property, whether an immigrant or a native, was 10 to 11 percentage points more likely to persist than one
who owned no property. Both immigrants and natives in the Southwest were also
more likely to migrate than others. The effects of marriage and a farm occupation
were considerably larger for immigrants than for natives, though.

There were other differences between natives and immigrants in the factors associated with persistence. Immigrants were more likely to persist if they had a family—each child increased the probability of persisting by more than 2 percentage
points. There was no corresponding family size effect on persistence for natives.
Immigrants' age had no apparent influence on the likelihood that they would persist, whereas age had a positive though diminishing effect on persistence among
natives. Though the quadratic term on age is negative, its size is so small that age's
impact is positive at all plausible ages. Immigrants were also far more likely to migrate than natives in the South Central. The impact of residence in the country's
other regions was similar for immigrants and natives. Among immigrants, the Irish
had the lowest persistence rates after controlling for other characteristics.
Germans were the most mobile of immigrants as previously reported by Esslinger
and others.[33] In this sample, however, the Irish were considerably more mobile
than any other group.

The dummy variable for property ownership suggests that individuals who
owned any property were more likely to persist. The regressions using the amount
of property owned, however, suggest that the effect of property ownership was
nonlinear, at least for natives. The impact of real wealth in column 2 achieves a
maximum at $21,000. It is positive before that point and negative after it. The ef-
fect for immigrants is also concave (peaking at $31,000), though not statistically
significant. The increase in persistence with greater wealth suggests that few individuals were constrained by wealth in deciding whether to relocate over the
1850s. As we saw in chapter 4, the cost of transportation was not likely to have
been an important constraint for either immigrants or natives. The cost of ob-
taining and establishing a farm was a far greater expense. But this was not a course
that internal migrants in this period had as their only option. The growth of cities
in this period allowed many poor Americans to change their county of residence
without having to incur the one significant cost that new farmers faced.

Patterns of Mobility

This raises the question of just where the natives and immigrants who relocated
were going. This is shown in Tables 7-4 and 7-5, where the 1850 and 1860 loca-

33. Esslinger, *Immigrants*, p. 43; Galenson, "Economic Opportunity," p. 585.

Table 7-4. Geographic mobility in 1850–60
of natives and immigrant arrivals at New York,
1840–50, by size of location.

| 1850 Location | N | 1860 Location | |
		Urban (%)	Rural (%)
Natives			
Urban	664	72.4	27.6
Rural	3,607	22.8	77.2
Immigrants			
Urban	630	74.3	25.7
Rural	546	41.9	58.1

Source: Males fifteen years and older in 1850 Public Use Microdata Series linked to the 1860 manuscript census schedules; male household heads and unaccompanied males in passenger ship arrival records at port of New York, 1840–1850, linked to 1850 and 1860 manuscript census schedules.

Note: "Urban" is a census subdivision with an 1850 population of 2,500 or more.

Table 7-5. Geographic mobility in 1850–60 of natives and immigrant arrivals at New York, 1840–50, by region.

| 1850 Location | N | 1860 Location | | | | | |
		NE (%)	MA (%)	MW (%)	SE (%)	SC (%)	FW (%)
Natives							
NE	881	91.5	2.6	4.5	0.1	0.0	1.2
MA	1,546	1.0	83.2	14.4	1.0	0.3	1.0
MW	873	1.0	4.7	88.9	0.5	2.1	3.0
SE	587	0.2	1.0	2.9	91.3	4.4	0.2
SW	363	0.0	0.3	12.1	2.5	84.3	0.8
FW	21	9.5	9.5	19.0	0.0	0.0	61.9
Immigrants							
NE	184	56.5	19.0	20.1	0.0	0.5	3.8
MA	525	11.2	60.2	22.5	1.9	2.1	2.1
MW	349	5.2	13.8	74.5	1.7	2.0	2.9
SE	55	12.7	18.2	25.5	32.7	7.3	3.6
SW	50	8.0	22.0	42.0	0.0	26.0	2.0
FW	13	7.7	0.0	23.1	0.0	30.8	38.5

Source: Males fifteen years and older in 1850 Public Use Microdata Series linked to the 1860 manuscript census schedules; male household heads and unaccompanied males in passenger ship arrival records at port of New York, 1840–1850, linked to 1850 and 1860 manuscript census schedules.

Note: "NE" is New England; "MA" is Middle Atlantic; "MW" is Midwest; "SC" is South Central; "SW" is Southwest; "FW" is Far West.

tions are shown for those immigrants and natives who were located in both census years. In terms of size of location, both immigrants and natives who began the 1850s in urban places were likely to end the decade in urban places. Only about a quarter of natives and immigrants moved from urban to rural places. There were sharp differences by nativity in where those who started the decade in rural places ended up, however. A quarter of natives made rural-to-urban moves over the 1850s, but more then 40 percent of immigrants left rural places for small towns and cities. Despite this disparity, net rural-to-urban migration as a fraction of the total native or immigrant population, was similar for both groups: just over 13 percent. The greater likelihood that immigrants would leave rural places for urban ones may reflect the seasonal agricultural employment mentioned in chapter 4. Immigrants may have served as marginal workers who could be drawn into farm work when conditions in farming relative to those in cities improved; when prosperity returned to cities, so too did the immigrants. The native born, however, were more closely tied to their rural locations. These were the places where they had spent their lives. Even a substantial shift in the terms of employment in cities versus those in farming may have drawn few into urban places. The cost, in terms of forsaking friends, family, and a familiar place, and perhaps giving up a farm that had been in the family for generations, was simply too high.

Many more immigrants than natives crossed regional boundaries over the decade: nearly half of immigrants located in New England in 1850 were elsewhere by 1860, with equal numbers having gone to the Middle Atlantic and Midwest states. Only 60 percent of immigrants who started the decade in the Middle Atlantic states, in turn, were found there in 1860, with most migrants moving west. Although most movement by immigrants was from east to west, nearly a fifth of those who were in the West in 1850 had moved to the East by 1860. The native born were less likely to leave their 1850 region, and were considerably less likely to move from west to east. This difference suggests that moves made by natives tended to be permanent, whereas a substantial fraction of immigrant moves was accounted for by short-term relocation to places where work could be found.

Who were those immigrants who made it to the West and then moved back to the East? Many of those who went west and to rural places were unmarried and unskilled. Along with the wealthier farmers with large families, they made up the bulk of those outside the East and outside cities. Many of those unmarried, unskilled immigrants were taking advantage of the high farm wages in the rural West to amass the capital either to buy their own farm or return to urban employment. This group of unattached laborers seems to constitute most of the group moving east and back into cities. Those who moved from rural places to urban places or from west to east were more often unmarried, were more often laborers, were more often Irish, and were considerably younger than those who remained in rural places and in the West.

Finally, since we know each individual's county of residence in 1850 and 1860, it is possible to calculate the distance that nonpersisters moved over the 1850s. Among natives, the majority of moves were short distance—under 149 miles. The balance of moves was divided equally between medium distance moves—150 to

400 miles—and long-distance moves—over 400 miles. The average move (among those who made a move) was 215 miles. Among immigrants, half of all moves were more than 400 miles, with the rest divided equally between short-distance and medium-distance moves. The average distance moved among immigrants who changed county was 472 miles. For individuals originating in New York City, a journey of 400 miles would have brought them as far west as Cleveland and Akron in Ohio. Those who were in urban places in 1850 traveled shorter distances on average when they moved than those in rural places, and unskilled workers moved farther than others. Among immigrants, the Irish moved the greatest distances over the 1850s.

The Occupational Mobility of Unskilled Workers

For unskilled workers, the easiest way to see how the occupational mobility of persisters and nonpersisters compared is to calculate the fraction of persisters and nonpersisters who were found in another occupation in 1860. Since an important determinant of the extent of upward occupational mobility is the state of the labor market, we should note the macroeconomic conditions of 1850 and 1860 before accepting the findings that follow as representative of the experiences of unskilled workers in the antebellum period. Ideally, we would like to be able to assess the mobility of the decade, controlling for cyclical, short-term, and structural effects. The best we can do here, however, is suggest how typical 1850 and 1860 were of the two decades before the Civil War. For example, if growth was particularly slow in 1850 and 1860, we might be more impressed by a given rate of economic improvement than if growth was robust. As chapter 3 noted, the emerging picture of the 1850s is a particularly difficult time for native-born skilled workers in eastern cities. Many faced intense competition from unskilled immigrants who could be employed using new, low-skill production techniques. In the following chapter, we will explore further the impact of immigrants on this sector of the U.S. labor market. For the present purpose it is perhaps sufficient to suggest that the relative economic performance of immigrants and natives over the 1850s may reflect changes in production technology that favored immigrants at the expense of natives.

Tabulations of occupational mobility for immigrants and natives are shown in Table 7-6, disaggregated by whether the individual had made a geographic move between 1850 and 1860. If an individual who was an unskilled worker in 1850 had become a skilled manual or white collar worker or had entered farming by 1860, this was counted as an upward move. Immigrants and natives may have been better off in 1860 than they had been in 1850 even if they did not make such a move up in occupational status. As Engerman notes, occupational mobility and economic betterment are not necessarily synonymous, especially if wages are rising in a variety of occupations.[34] The reader should bear in mind that we are exam-

34. See Engerman, "Up or Out," p. 482.

Table 7-6. Occupational and geographic mobility in 1850–60 of natives and immigrant arrivals at New York, 1840–50, by distance moved and 1850 occupation.

	Same County	Different County	Distance Between 1850 & 1860 Counties (miles)		
			1–149	150–400	Over 400
Upward mobility of unskilled workers[a]					
Natives					
N	697	799	430	181	188
% up	62.1	67.1**	62.8	72.4***	71.8***
Immigrants					
N	122	419	113	127	179
% up	48.4	52.7	46.0	54.3	55.9
Downward mobility of others[b]					
Natives					
N	1,744	1,031	563	207	261
% down	10.4	15.2	14.2**	19.3***	14.2*
Immigrants					
N	246	389	111	98	180
% down	8.5	31.4***	27.9***	36.7***	30.6***

Source: Males fifteen years and older in 1850 Public Use Microdata Series linked to the 1860 manuscript census schedules; male household heads and unaccompanied males in passenger ship arrival records at port of New York, 1840–1850, linked to 1850 and 1860 manuscript census schedules.

Note: Probability that the true percentage is identical to that for "Same County": *<10%; **<5%; ***<1%. [a]The percentage of 1850 unskilled workers (including farm tenants) who were found in white collar or skilled occupations or as farm owners in 1860. [b]The percentage of 1850 farm owners, white collar workers, or skilled workers who were found as unskilled workers (including farm tenants) in 1860.

ining but one dimension of an individual's experience: how he described his occupation when queried by a census marshal in 1850 and 1860. Although later we will also consider how the wealth of individuals changed when they moved, there is no presumption that we are able to measure improvements in peoples' lives over time in a comprehensive way.

The first surprise is that immigrant unskilled workers who changed county between 1850 and 1860 did better than those who remained in the same county: 53 percent of nonpersisters were white collar workers, skilled workers, or farmers by 1860, as opposed to only 48 percent of persisters. Although these differences in upward mobility rates are not statistically significant, they suggest that nonpersisters were doing no worse than persisters. The specific occupation entered by most immigrant unskilled workers when they moved up in occupational status was skilled worker: of the unskilled workers who moved up between 1850 and 1860, 53 percent became skilled workers. Another 28 percent became farm owners, but

of these, none had been farm tenants in 1850, so the movement into farm ownership was by those who had been outside the farm sector in 1850. There were no
striking differences by persister/nonpersister in the specific occupations immigrants entered when they moved up, which suggests that geographic mobility was
not associated with movement into particular occupations.

Perhaps even more surprising is the pattern of occupational mobility by distance moved for immigrants: those who moved the farthest were the most likely
to move up in occupation. More than half of all immigrant unskilled workers who
moved more than 400 miles between 1850 and 1860 moved up in occupational
status. Immigrants who remained in the same county were less likely to move up
than those who made medium-distance or long-distance moves.

These same patterns can be seen among native-born unskilled workers in even
more striking terms. Native-born unskilled workers who moved more than 150
miles over the 1850s saw their chances of moving up from unskilled worker to another occupation improve by 10 percentage points. Short-distance movers did
slightly worse than persisters (as was true among immigrants), but other movers
had brighter prospects than those who stayed behind. For natives, these differences in upward mobility are statistically significant.

The selectivity of long-distance migration provides one explanation for this
pattern: if the only migrants who were willing to travel a great distance to a new
community were those who possessed superior knowledge of opportunities there
or possessed characteristics that made it easier for them to adjust to conditions at
the new location, we might observe the pattern seen in Table 7-6. The trade-off
between return and variance is a central component of the model of migration developed by Paul David.[35] Alternatively, perhaps movement to more distant locations *was* in fact inherently more risky than remaining in the same place or moving to closer communities. The measure of occupational mobility used here—a
simple dichotomous variable for whether the individual moved up from the lowest occupational status to a higher status—may simply be unable to detect that
riskiness. An individual who moves to a distant location might face a wider variance in the returns he earns there—in terms of wealth, occupational prestige, income, or some other continuous underlying variable—but only the positive variance shows up in the movement from unskilled worker to white collar worker,
skilled worker, or farmer. If a long-distance mover could find work only in a less
desirable job within the class of unskilled workers than he held before migration,
this negative variance is not detected. To assess the validity of this explanation,
we will later examine how the wealth of persisters and nonpersisters compared.

The Occupational Mobility of White Collar Workers,
Skilled Workers, and Farmers

Unskilled workers were not the only non-persisters in nineteenth-century
America. Even though the unskilled were more likely to change county of resi-

35. See David, "Microeconomics of Migration."

dence than skilled workers, white collar workers, or farmers, individuals in these groups, too, changed locations. Although their overall conditional persistence rate in Table 7-2 was higher than the rate for unskilled workers, it is worth considering the impact of migration on the occupational mobility of white collar workers, skilled workers, and farmers as well. We have shown that the failure to observe the occupational mobility of unskilled workers may have led to a downward bias in measuring upward occupational mobility; if white collar workers, skilled workers, and farmers who were nonpersisters were more likely to move down in occupational status, previous studies will have produced a downward-biased measure of downward occupational mobility. The combination of these two biases would be a downward bias in total (upward and downward) occupational mobility, and a characterization of the antebellum labor market as less fluid than it actually was.

Table 7-6 shows the downward occupational mobility of white collar workers, skilled workers, and farmers by migration status and distance moved for nonpersisters. For all individuals, those who changed county of residence over the 1850s were more likely to make a downward occupational move than those who remained in the same county. These differences were all statistically significant. Although both natives and immigrants moved down in greater numbers when they moved out, the fraction falling to unskilled worker was greater among immigrants at every distance moved.

Most of the downward mobility experienced by white collar workers, skilled workers, and farmers was into the class of workers who described themselves simply as "laborers." Of the immigrant white collar workers, skilled workers, and farmers who moved downward between 1850 and 1860, 66 percent became laborers. Another 19 percent entered other unskilled occupations, 6 percent entered mining, and 9 percent became farm tenants. None of those who became farm tenants were farm owners in 1850, so this might represent the first step in a transition from a nonfarm occupation to eventual farm ownership. Two clear patterns emerge when the fractions entering specific occupation by persister/nonpersister are examined among immigrants: those who changed county were more likely to find themselves employed as unskilled workers than persisters, and nonpersisters were more likely to become miners (in fact, of the immigrants who entered mining, all changed county of residence between 1850 and 1860, and most moved more than 400 miles).

As was the case with unskilled workers, there are two possible explanations for the differences in occupational mobility between persisters and nonpersisters. The first is the riskiness of changing counties. If skilled workers, white collar workers, and farmers employed location-specific knowledge (of customers, markets, or weather and soil conditions, for example), a change in county of residence reduced the value of that knowledge. This forces us to ask why any white collar worker, skilled worker, or farmer would ever move, given this cost of migration. The alternative explanation that provides an answer is that the measure of occupational mobility used here is not sufficiently sensitive to detect the positive variance in circumstances that nonpersisters experienced. Those who moved into better positions within the class of white collar workers, skilled workers, and farmers after a move to a new community show up as merely retaining their premigration occupational status. The next section considers this possibility.

The Financial Mobility of Nonpersisters

Although the crude occupational mobility measure used above may be too imprecise to detect the subtle changes in the circumstances of nonpersisters that would explain why any unskilled workers stayed at their 1850 location and why any white collar workers, skilled workers, or farmers relocated, the sample used here provides another measure of economic performance: the census manuscripts in both 1850 and 1860 record the value of each individual's real estate wealth. Table 7-7 shows the increase or decrease in wealth experienced during the 1850s,

Table 7-7. Geographic mobility and change in real estate wealth in 1850–60 of natives and immigrant arrivals at New York, 1840–50, by distance moved and 1850 occupation.

	Same County	Different County	Distance Between 1850 & 1860 Counties (miles)		
			1–149	150–400	Over 400
Unskilled workers					
Natives					
N	697	799	430	181	188
ΔReal Estate	736.30	537.03	409.47**	791.46	576.46
Std. Dev.	3,713	1,864	1,396	2,172	2,390
Immigrants					
N	122	419	113	127	179
ΔReal Estate	258.89	537.03*	511.50	574.88*	526.30*
Std. Dev.	915	2,061	2,550	1,959	1,779
Others					
Natives					
N	1744	1031	563	207	261
ΔReal Estate	2,103.59	1,489.27*	1,878.23	897.63**	1,119.48
Std. Dev.	10,411	8,782	9,830	2,545	9,527
Immigrant					
N	246	389	111	98	180
ΔReal Estate	1,093.23	458.13***	440.81*	810.11	277.17***
Std. Dev.	3,888	2,708	1,375	3,758	2,643

Source: Males fifteen years and older in 1850 Public Use Microdata Series linked to the 1860 manuscript census schedules; male household heads and unaccompanied males in passenger ship arrival records at port of New York, 1840–1850, linked to 1850 and 1860 manuscript census schedules.

Note: Probability that the true average is identical to that for "Same County": *<10%; **<5%; ***<1%. "ΔReal Estate" is (Real Estate in 1860) − (Real Estate in 1850).

by migration status, distance moved, and 1850 location, as well as the standard deviation of the change in wealth.

Among immigrant unskilled workers, movers did better than persisters: their wealth grew more than twice as much as that of persisters, and this difference was statistically significant. The biggest gain came among medium-distance movers, but the gain for long-distance movers was only slightly smaller and also statistically significant. Among native unskilled workers, there are fewer differences by distance moved. The only group that saw its wealth grow more or less than persisters was short-distance movers, who saw slower wealth growth than other native unskilled workers. For white collar workers, skilled workers, and farmers, wealth grew by considerably less among nonpersisters than it did among persisters, but these differences are not large except among immigrants. Immigrant white collar workers, skilled workers, and farmers who moved more than 400 miles saw a real estate growth over the 1850s only a quarter as great as persisters. This difference, like most of those among white collar workers, skilled workers, and farmers, was statistically significant.

The standard deviation of the gain in wealth experienced by those who moved greater distances was greater than the standard deviation of the gain experienced by those who moved shorter distances for only one group: native-born unskilled workers. For them, the standard deviation rose continuously with distance from the 1850 location. This suggests that the simple measure of occupational mobility used above was indeed missing an important aspect of the experience of these migrants: the greater uncertainty they faced at greater distances from their original location. Although nonpersisters were more likely to move up from unskilled worker to white collar worker, skilled worker, or farmer, and added more to their wealth the farther they moved from their 1850 location, they were also more likely to see a drop in their wealth. For other groups, the trade-off of risk for return is less apparent. In fact, for immigrant unskilled workers, the standard deviation actually falls continuously with distance even though the wealth change was higher for movers than stayers, suggesting the possibility that, for this group, migration may have been highly selective. The lower standard deviation at greater distances would then reflect the superior ability or knowledge of those who chose to travel great distances between 1850 and 1860.

Multivariate Analysis of Occupational Mobility and Wealth Accumulation

Unskilled workers who moved between 1850 and 1860 moved up in occupational status more often than unskilled workers who stayed in the same county. Among white collar workers, skilled workers, and farmers, movers moved down to unskilled worker more often than stayers. These findings, however, do not allow us to say whether geographic mobility had an independent impact on occupational mobility. Other studies have shown that nonpersisters were disproportionately young and unattached, so the observed impact of geographic mobility on occupational mobility may reflect this characteristic of movers rather than the influence of movement by itself. For example, unskilled workers who moved more than 150 miles over the 1850s may have done better than stayers or short-distance movers because they were younger than stayers and short-distance movers and therefore at a stage in the life cycle when they were more willing to change occupation in order to take advantage of opportunities in more distant locations. Similarly, the poor performance of white collar workers, skilled workers, and farmers who crossed county boundaries during the 1850s may be the result of their relative youth: they were more likely to end up as unskilled workers because they were not yet firmly established in an occupation in 1850, rather than because of any inherent risk associated with geographic mobility.

Table 7-8 presents the results of several multivariate regressions that attempt

Table 7-8. Multivariate analysis of occupational mobility in 1850–60 by natives and immigrant arrivals at New York, 1840–50.

	Natives		Immigrants	
Variable	Unskilled	Others	Unskilled	Others
Intercept	19.141**	45.655***	43.581***	74.361***
Age	2.099***	−1.483***	1.318*	−2.993***
Age^2	−32.143***	19.326***	−28.825**	37.693***
Origin				
Ireland			−30.935***	17.641***
Germany			−1.290	−5.501
Other			−6.195	−6.010
Literate	14.775**	−8.758***	14.746**	−11.356
Region				
New England	4.774	−2.820*	2.252	9.305*
Midwest	7.838**	−4.272**	−2.058	−1.963
Southeast	1.809	−1.292	−3.134	−4.857
South Central	9.645**	−5.842**	−13.761	−3.209
Far West	−24.849	7.710	3.800	6.100
Urban	3.279	0.852	−4.419	−1.950
Changed County	4.995**	4.376***	6.297	18.098***
Adjusted R^2	0.023	0.021	0.083	0.143
N	1,495	2,774	540	634

Source: Males fifteen years and older in 1850 Public Use Microdata Series linked to the 1860 manuscript census schedules; male household heads and unaccompanied males in passenger ship arrival records at port of New York, 1840–1850, linked to 1850 and 1860 manuscript census schedules.

Note: For Unskilled Workers, the dependent variable takes a value of 100 if the individual moved into a job as something other than an unskilled worker between 1850 and 1860, and a zero otherwise. For Others, the dependent variable takes a value of 100 if the individual moved into a job as an unskilled worker between 1850 and 1860, and a zero otherwise. The coefficients measure the number of percentage points by which the probability of changing occupation increases or decreases in response to a unit change in the independent variable. All estimates were obtained by ordinary least squares regressions. Illiterate, unskilled workers residing in the rural Middle Atlantic region in 1850 and not changing county are the reference group in each regression. For immigrants, the British are the reference origin group. Probability that the true β is zero: *<10%; **<5%; ***<1%.

to separate the impact of geographic mobility from the influence of other personal characteristics on occupational mobility. The regressions control for age and its square (to allow the impact of age to increase or decrease with age), marital status, family size, literacy, country of origin, and 1850 location (region and urban or rural). Geographic mobility is measured by a dichotomous variable for whether the individual was found in a different county in 1860 than in 1850 (which allows the intercept to differ between movers and stayers). Separate regressions were estimated for unskilled workers and others. A simple linear probability ordinary least squares regression was used.[36] The dependent variable is 100 if an unskilled worker became a white collar worker, skilled worker, or farmer, or a white collar worker, skilled worker, or farmer became an unskilled worker and zero otherwise. The coefficients measure the percentage point change in the probability of changing occupations associated with a unit change in the independent variables.

For natives who were unskilled workers in 1850, the probability of becoming a white collar worker, skilled worker, or farmer by 1860 was greater for those who moved during the decade, even after controlling for other personal characteristics. The probability that a native unskilled worker would move up increased with age through age 33, and then decreased, reflecting the frequency with which individuals changed occupation early in their careers. Thus, a rural, native-born unskilled worker who was 30 years old in 1850 had a 53 percent probability of becoming a white collar worker, skilled worker, or farmer by 1860 if he remained in the same county between 1850 and 1860. The same immigrant had a 58 percent probability of becoming a white collar worker, skilled worker, or farmer if he moved to another county during the 1850s. Among immigrants, the coefficient on geographic mobility was positive, but statistically insignificant. Age was associated with only a slight increase in the probability of moving up. The Irish fared worse and the Germans better than the British.

Among both natives and immigrants, white collar workers, skilled workers, and farmers experienced downward occupational mobility when they moved, even after controlling for other personal characteristics. The effect of age was again nonlinear: the probability of moving down to unskilled worker fell through age 38 for natives and age 24 for immigrants, and then rose, reflecting the lower degree of occupational attachment among younger workers. For a rural, native-born white collar worker, skilled worker, or farmer who was 30 years old in 1850, the probability of moving down to unskilled worker by 1860 was 19.6 percent for nonmovers and 24 percent for those who moved over the decade. Among immigrants, the impact of a change in county was also negative, but even larger in size. The Irish were nearly twice as likely to move down to unskilled worker as the British or the Germans.

For native and immigrant white collar workers, skilled workers, and farmers, the pattern of wealth accumulation for movers and nonmovers shown in Table 7-9 is similar to the pattern of occupational mobility. Even after controlling for an

36. Logistic regressions produced qualitatively similar results. The linear probability results are presented here because of the straightforward interpretation of the coefficients, which facilitates comparison with the results on changes in wealth in Table 7-9.

Table 7-9. Multivariate analysis of change in real estate wealth 1850–60, by natives and immigrant arrivals at New York, 1840–50.

Variable	Natives		Immigrants	
	Unskilled	Others	Unskilled	Others
Intercept	−933.48	−2495.79	−1690.65***	−3232.62**
Age	133.08***	107.30	88.49***	238.37***
Age^2	−1739.53***	−897.32	−990.73**	−3569.70***
Origin				
Ireland			−187.22	−344.34
Germany			−3.63	−266.00
Other			334.72	−10.84
Literate	−115.12	1877.11**	382.53	756.32
Region				
New England	−111.10	−1050.09**	88.53	−422.51
Midwest	85.22	449.89	16.97	105.86
Southeast	−349.66	1043.23*	−279.29	−191.52
South Central	499.84**	703.72	−283.76	−29.77
Far West	−279.27	−566.92	48.49	−548.69
Urban	251.11	1299.80**	125.18	231.33
Changed County	−155.78	−408.95	456.10**	−591.28**
Adjusted R^2	0.021	0.004	0.019	0.019
N	1,495	2,774	540	634

Source: Males fifteen years and older in 1850 Public Use Microdata Series linked to the 1860 manuscript census schedules; male household heads and unaccompanied males in passenger ship arrival records at port of New York, 1840–1850, linked to 1850 and 1860 manuscript census schedules.

Note: The coefficients measure the dollar change in real estate wealth between 1850 and 1860 in response to a unit change in the independent variable. All estimates were obtained by ordinary least squares regressions. Illiterate, unskilled workers residing in the rural Middle Atlantic region in 1850 and not changing county are the reference group in each regression. For immigrants, the British are the reference origin group. Probability that the true β is zero: *<10%; **<5%; ***<1%.

immigrant's age, movers did worse than nonmovers, though this effect was statistically significant only for immigrants. For unskilled workers, however, shifting to a focus on wealth accumulation produces an important difference: immigrant unskilled workers saw their wealth rise more if they moved, unlike natives who, if they saw a wealth change as they moved, saw a fall. This contrasts with the lack of a statistically significant positive effect on upward occupational mobility for immigrant movers. Immigrant unskilled workers benefited from mobility, but in a different way from native-born unskilled workers.

These multivariate results demonstrate that there were important differences in the economic performance of movers and stayers, even after controlling for such observed personal characteristics as age, country of origin, literacy, and location. Unskilled workers clearly did better at moving into better occupations if they moved, and immigrant unskilled workers who moved also did better at accumulating real estate wealth than nonmovers. White collar workers, skilled workers, and farmers who moved did worse than nonmovers in terms of occupational mobility, regardless of how far they moved, and did worse than nonmovers in wealth accumulation. These findings do not rule out the possibility that unskilled workers who moved long distances were more ambitious, better informed, or more able than nonmovers and short-distance movers, or that white collar workers, skilled workers, and farmers who moved were less ambitious, worse informed, or less able than nonmovers. Rather, they point to the danger in making broad generalizations about the experiences of movers and stayers in the antebellum period. Clearly, not all unskilled workers who migrated were less successful at their new locations than the unskilled workers they left behind, while not all white collar workers, skilled workers, and farmers enjoyed greater economic success at their destinations than the white collar workers, skilled workers, and farmers who did not migrate.

Conclusions

Although we have learned a great deal from the community-based social mobility studies undertaken over the last three decades, there has been a nagging suspicion among many that an important part of the story was being missed because of the inability to observe the postmigration economic performance of those who left the communities on which those studies focused. This study has found some justification for those suspicions. When it is possible to observe the occupational mobility of nonpersisters, unskilled workers who left their 1850 county of residence were no less likely to move up in occupational status and, at least among immigrants, increased their wealth more rapidly than unskilled workers who did not move. Controlling for individual characteristics merely enhances these effects. White collar workers, skilled workers, and farmers who changed county of residence were more likely to move down in occupational status and accumulated less wealth than persisters. This was true for both immigrants and natives.

The magnitudes of these differences for unskilled workers are not large: native-born unskilled workers who changed county of residence between 1850 and 1860 were 5 percentage points more likely to move up in occupational status than persisters. These differences are also statistically insignificant in some cases. In Thernstrom's original work on Newburyport, only 20 percent of immigrants who were unskilled workers in 1850 were in skilled or nonmanual jobs by 1860, so the ability to observe the occupational mobility of nonpersisters would lead to only a modest upward revision in the rate of total (persister and nonpersister) occupational mobility if the persisters and nonpersisters in Newburyport had the same experience as those described here.[37]

But the importance of these findings lies not so much in what they show as in what they do not show: nonpersisters who began the 1850s as unskilled workers were *not* found to have done systematically worse than persisters, contrary to the

37. Thernstrom, *Poverty and Progress*, p. 100.

conjectures of many. The suggestion of previous studies, based on persisters, that observed upward occupational mobility among those who remained in a community represented an upward bound on the total upward mobility of persisters and nonpersisters does not appear true. Since white collar workers, skilled workers, and farmers who changed county of residence were more likely than persisters to move down in occupational status, the extent of total (upward and downward) mobility has probably been underestimated by the focus on persisters in previous work.

Even as we have seen the modifications that we might make to our views of nineteenth-century occupational mobility as a result of the inclusion of nonpersisters in the analysis, we have also seen the inadequacy of a simple measure such as occupational change. For example, the high proportion of upward occupational moves experienced by those who moved the greatest distances among unskilled workers obscures the significant risk in wealth terms that those long- distance migrants faced. Ignoring that risk would lead us to a very different interpretation of the experience of migrants. This suggests that in addition to moving away from an exclusive concentration on nonpersisters, research on economic mobility in nineteenth-century America must also examine a wider range of measures of economic performance.

8

The Impact of Immigration
on Natives, 1850–1860

The arrival of immigrants in the years before the Civil War did more than simply transform the immigrants themselves. As we have already seen, the immigration process resulted in substantial geographic, occupational, and financial changes among arrivals, but that process also had profound effects—both positive and negative—on the population of native-born Americans. The net benefits of immigration remain a contentious topic of debate today; they were no less an issue in the antebellum period. In the political realignment that occurred in the 1850s, immigration's role was seen by many as central.

This chapter shifts the focus from the immigrants themselves to the native-born Americans they joined at their arrival. It asks how immigration affected the economic fortunes of natives. Although this is an interesting question in its own right—especially because the data for the 1850s used here can circumvent many of the problems encountered in assessing immigration's impact today—it is an important part of the story of how immigrants entered the U.S. labor market. Many, particularly the Irish, faced intense discrimination, and the attitudes that produced that discrimination were shaped by native workers' perception that immigrants were a potent source of competition in the labor market. Understanding the objective reality behind that perception will help us understand the forces shaping natives' responses to immigrants' arrival, which in turn will make it easier to understand immigrants' relative economic performance.

The Issues: Present and Past

The negative effect of immigration on the wages and incomes of native-born workers feared by many has been difficult to find in recent data. Only two studies for the contemporary period, one examining 120 urban labor markets and one examining the aggregate U.S. labor market using national-level time series data, have found a negative association between an increase in the fraction foreign born and the change in the wages of natives.[1] The negative impact of immigration early in the twentieth century has been better documented. Using historical data on urban labor markets at the turn of the century, Goldin has found a clear negative impact from immigration, while Hatton and Williamson have used national-level time series data to demonstrate a similar negative effect.[2] These differences between the findings of contemporary and historical studies motivate the approach adopted here: examining another historical period when both the immigration rate was high—the highest in U.S. history—and the data are available to accommodate many of the criticisms of previous studies of immigration's impact.

Differences between the contemporary and historical results may be due to the much greater volume of immigration in the years around 1900. The immigration rate was more than twice as great in the early years of the twentieth century as it has been in recent years of peak immigration. Some of the difference may also reflect changes in the "absorptive capacity" of the U.S. economy—its ability to accommodate the arrival of large numbers of immigrants without suffering a large fall in wages among the native born—a capacity which Williamson suggests was particularly low at the beginning of this century.[3] Finally, some of the difference may result from differences in the factors omitted from these studies, such as the endogeneity of the location choices made by immigrants and natives in cross-sectional studies of local labor market data and differences between the wages of immigrants and natives in time series studies of national-level data.

Both Altonji and Card and Goldin attempt to account for immigrants' location choices, though Goldin accounts only for fixed city-specific effects that may attract or repel immigrants.[4] If immigrants tend to move to places where labor market conditions are good when they arrive, they may cause a positive relationship between the wages of the native born and the fraction foreign born in a sample of cities. This can happen if immigrants have no genuine effect, or even if they have a genuinely negative effect, on the wages of the native born in any particular labor market. If immigrants are drawn to places where labor market conditions are not good, the data can suggest a positive relationship between the fraction foreign born and the wages of natives, even if their actual effect on natives' wages in any particular labor market is positive. Such an effect might also amplify a negative effect of immigrants on natives' wages.

Neither Altonji and Card nor Goldin examine the internal migration of the native born in response to the arrival of immigrants. Internal migration would dissipate the impact of immigration if natives leave places where immigration has

---

1. Altonji and Card, "Effects of Immigration"; Borjas, Freeman, and Katz, "Labor Market Effects."
2. Goldin, "Immigration Restriction"; Hatton and Williamson, "Impact of Immigration."
3. Williamson, "Trade-Offs."
4. Borjas doubts the validity of the instrumental variables used by Altonji and Card to account for the endogeneity of the location choices made by immigrants. Borjas, "Economics of Immigration," pp. 1697–1698.

depressed wages. The effect could go in the opposite direction as well: internal migration could cause a negative association between the change in native wages and the change in the fraction foreign born if the native born migrate in greater numbers than immigrants to places where local labor market conditions are good. For the contemporary period, evidence on whether the association observed by Altonji and Card could be the result of natives' internal migration is mixed. Using 1980 census data, both Filer and White and Hunter found more out-migration and less in-migration of native-born workers in cities with large immigrant concentrations.[5] Frey reaches a similar conclusion using 1990 census data.[6] Studies by Butcher and Card and White and Liang, however, reach a different conclusion based on Current Population Survey data from the 1980s: they find that the in-migration of natives was greater in cities that received large numbers of immigrants in the 1980s.[7]

For the late nineteenth century, Goldin suggests that the internal migration of the native born is unlikely to have reduced the impact of immigration on wages, though she does not address the possibility that their migration may generate a negative association between the change in the immigrant share and the change in the native wage.[8] Friedberg and Hunt suggest that the estimates of immigration's impact in Altonji and Card are small compared to estimates of the effect of "generational crowding," a point that applies with equal force to Goldin's study which finds the impact roughly similar in magnitude to that in Altonji and Card.[9] Friedberg and Hunt suggest that Goldin's results "may be affected by the 'composition' problem": the city-level wages she uses combine the wages of both immigrants and natives, so wages could fall in a location with the entry of immigrants simply because they earn lower wages themselves rather than because of their impact on the wages of natives.[10] Goldin notes that her focus on occupations that few immigrants entered reduces this problem.[11] Both of the national-level time series studies also suffer from this "composition" problem.

This chapter examines the impact of immigration on natives in a setting where it should be possible to detect an impact if ever there was one: the antebellum period, when the immigration rate was more than twice as great as in the modern period. The scale of immigration in this period can be seen in Figure 3-1, which shows the absolute number of immigrants entering the United States each year from 1820 to 1992 (the immigration level) and the number of entering immigrants per thousand U.S. population in each year (the immigration rate). Although the level of immigration was higher in the 1980s than in the previous half century, the level was not high by historical standards until the early 1990s. Even then, the rate of immigration was no more than half the rate experienced in

5. Filer, "Immigrant Arrivals"; White and Hunter, "Migratory Response."
6. Frey, "New White Flight."
7. Butcher and Card, "Immigration and Wages"; White and Liang, "Internal Migration."
8. Goldin, "Immigration Restriction," p. 249.
9. Friedberg and Hunt, "Impact of Immigrants," p. 34.
10. Ibid., p. 31.
11. Goldin, "Immigration Restriction," p. 252–253.

the previous three great waves of immigration (in the 1850s, the 1880s, and the years just before 1910). The level and rate should be adjusted upward in the post-war years for undocumented immigrants. In recent years, the INS estimates that this would add 300,000 to the annual immigration total. The sharp increase in immigration after 1990 in Figure 3-1 does not represent an increase in the numbers arriving at the border. Rather, it reflects the transition to documented status under the immigration law reform of previously undocumented immigrants who had entered prior to 1991 and sought citizenship under the law's lottery provision.

The data available for the antebellum period introduced in chapter 2 make it possible to control for immigrants' location decisions and to examine both out-migrants and nonmigrants among the native born. Instrumental variable techniques are used to account for the possibility that immigrant inflows into a location are related to labor market conditions there. The inability to capture the impact of the geographic mobility of native-born workers has been a problem in virtually every study of immigration's impact at the level of local labor markets. As Borjas notes of studies of the impact of contemporary immigrants that treat local labor markets as essentially closed economies, "As long as native workers and firms respond to the entry of immigrants by moving to areas offering better opportunities, there is no reason to expect a correlation between the wage of natives and the presence of immigrants."[12]

This will be particularly important for the antebellum period, when internal migration rates were high by contemporary standards. Native-born workers were extremely mobile: as the preceding chapter showed, only 57 percent remained in the same county between 1850 and 1860. By contrast, the Census Bureau reports that 6 percent of Americans changed their county of residence between 1991 and 1992. Cumulating the implied persistence rate over 10 years as $(1-0.06)^{10}$ means that 53 percent would remain in the same county over a decade. A ten-year migration rate calculated on the basis of a single year rate overstates the true ten-year rate because most moves are accounted for by a small fraction of the population who move repeatedly, so decadal intercounty migration rates in the 1850s were probably considerably higher than those in the 1990s.[13] To see this, suppose that 6 percent of the population move every year, while the other 94 percent remain in the same location. The implied ten-year migration rate of 47 percent will be nearly eight times greater than the true fraction of people residing in different locations at the beginning and end of the decade. Cumulating the one-year rate to obtain a ten-year rate will overstate the true ten-year rate as long as some people move more than once. Internal migration was also probably *effectively* greater in the past because of the size of the relevant labor market. Since modern local labor markets often include several adjacent counties, while local labor markets in the antebellum period were probably no larger than a county, the rate of migration between local labor markets was also no doubt larger in the antebellum period than these figures indicate it is today: some contemporary intercounty

12. Borjas, "Economics of Immigration," p. 1699.
13. Tucker and Urton, "Geographic Mobility."

moves represent migration within a single local labor market. But the nature of the data—multiple observations on every individual in the sample, regardless of location—makes it possible to account for this effect, and also to assess how much of immigration's impact is missed by ignoring it.[14]

A potential objection to the comparison undertaken here between the impact of immigration in the antebellum period and its impact at the turn of the century and later is that changes in the economy's structure and in its "absorptive capacity" would make a comparison of immigration's impact across these eras misleading. The frontier was moving rapidly west before the Civil War, and urban growth was rapid in new, Midwestern cities. By 1900, the frontier had vanished, forcing immigrants and natives into closer competition without the outlet provided by free land and growing cities in the West.

Two responses can be offered to this objection. The first is that, according to Williamson's estimates, the economy's "absorptive capacity" was not much greater before the Civil War than at the turn of the century. He has calculated that the elasticity of demand for unskilled labor (a measure of "absorptive capacity") fell from -3.90 in 1850 to -3.25 by 1900, and fell again over the next three decades to -1.60 by 1929.[15] The decline between 1850 (the period examined here) and 1900 (a time at which both Goldin and Hatton and Williamson are able to detect a negative impact from immigration) is slight (only a sixth) compared to the changes that occurred by 1929 (a fall of nearly 50 percent).[16] Further, the absorptive capacity recovered significantly after the 1920s, making comparisons between the 1850s and the recent period less unreasonable than they might seem initially. The second response is that if this is a problem, it can to some extent be accounted for in the analysis. If the economy's capacity to accommodate immigrants without depressing the wages of natives reflects the availability of a farming frontier and rapidly growing cities just behind it, to which natives displaced by immigrants could move, the data used here will be able to capture these effects.

Apart from offering a new comparative perspective, the impact of immigration in this period is also interesting in its own right. As the next section shows, there were loud complaints in the popular press and in the political arena about the negative consequences of immigration for natives. Even though those complaints never produced the closing of the "Golden Door" that Goldin documents at the start of the twentieth century with the imposition of the quota system, they did produce an important political movement that led to the election of Lincoln and a Republican Party committed to ending slavery in the 1860 election.[17] In this sense, the long-run impact of immigration in the 1840s and 1850s is arguably greater than the impact of immigration at the turn of the century that resulted in the restriction of immigration.

The balance of this chapter provides an overview of the impact of immigration

14. Also, since the data are individual-level observations on the native born, the analysis does not suffer from the "composition" problem of other studies.

15. Williamson, "Trade-Offs," p. 273.

16. Goldin, "Immigration Restriction"; Hatton and Williamson, "Impact of Immigration."

17. Goldin, "Immigration Restriction."

in this period, a simple economic model in which income changes and migration probabilities are jointly determined, and both are affected by immigration, estimates of the impact of immigration on the incomes of the native born, allowing for the out-migration of those whose incomes change because of a change in the immigrant concentration in their local labor market, and some tentative conclusions and implications of the findings for (1) our understanding of how the impact of immigration has evolved over 150 years; and (2) how immigration affects the demand for immigration restriction.

Responses to Antebellum Immigration

As noted in chapter 3, the 1850s witnessed the highest immigration rates in U.S. history. The arrival of so many immigrants in so short a time, and their concentration in a few locations and occupations, no doubt placed enormous stress on local labor markets. Until now, we have not had quantitative evidence of that stress for more than a few locations or industries. Nonetheless, several pieces of circumstantial evidence—on the change in the ethnic composition of the work force, on the degradation of skilled work, on the attitude toward immigration in the popular press, on the rise of nativist political organizations, and on the response of organized labor—suggest that immigration's impact was substantial in some circumstances.

The first evidence of immigration's impact is the rapid change in the ethnic make-up of the labor force where it has been possible to measure workers' nativity. In the textile mills of Lowell, where 90 percent of workers were native born in 1849, only 35 percent were native born in 1855.[18] The same rapid transformation of the labor force can be seen in a variety of other craft industries: carpentry, iron casting, shoemaking, tailoring, and cabinetmaking.[19]

The labor history literature on "de-skilling" provides further evidence that immigration's impact was substantial. Fogel suggests that this was a period characterized by "the general degradation of skill premiums by the downgrading of once highly skilled operations."[20] He goes on to describe the "Berkshire system" under which skilled iron workers were gradually replaced by unskilled workers:

> Prior to the introduction of the system, iron casting was performed by highly skilled journeymen. Afterward, journeymen were required to hire unskilled helpers (called bucks), each journeyman working in teams with from one to five bucks. Although the bucks were supposed to be purely helpers, the high-priced journeymen were often replaced by low-priced bucks who, if given the opportunity, soon learned enough of the trade to be given a rammer (the tool used to pack sand around a mold pattern).[21]

18. Lazonick and Brush, "Early U.S. Manufacturing."
19. Hoagland, "Iron Molders' International Union"; Ernst, *Immigrant Life*; Ross, *Workers on the Edge*.
20. Fogel, *Without Consent or Contract*, p. 358.
21. Ibid.

This process was accelerated where changes in the manufacturing process made it easier for employers to replace skilled workers with unskilled workers:

> A very direct form of this competition seems to have occurred between native-born and immigrant skilled workers over jobs in the manufacturing sector. But this seemed less threatening than the conflict arising from technological innovation, which led to the displacement of skilled workers by semiskilled machine operators, many of them of foreign origin.[22]

This development will figure prominently in the attempt to measure immigration's impact below, as the income measure developed here will be able to detect the demotion of skilled workers to unskilled positions.

The pressures immigration placed on labor markets, particularly in the urban Northeast, produced a remarkable backlash in the 1850s. The first response of native workers was increased labor militancy: dozens of new labor organizations sprang to life between 1850 and 1854, and a wave of more than 400 strikes swept the country in 1853 and 1854.[23] The second response was political: increasing support for those who preached the nativist creed. Although nativism had been present on the fringes of American politics since the nation's inception, it now moved to center stage. Capitalizing on anti-immigrant, protemperance, and anti-slavery sentiment ignored by the two major political parties, the Order of the Star-Spangled Banner (popularly known as the "Know-Nothings") grew from a secret band of 43 adherents in 1852 to a national political organization boasting one million followers in 1854. The party "elected eight governors, more than one hundred congressmen, the mayors of Boston, Philadelphia, and Chicago, and thousands of other local officials."[24] The party asserted that immigration was driving native-born unskilled workers into pauperism:

> The effect of this immense influx of the laboring . . . immigrants, will inevitably depreciate the value of American labor. The price of labor depends upon the demand and supply, and it is indisputably true that for the last few years the supply has increased in a greater ratio than the demand, and consequently the value has been diminished, and . . . many, even among the native, who earn their livelihood by "the sweat of their brow," have been compelled to toil for barely sufficient to supply the actual necessaries of life.[25]

Surprisingly, the Know-Nothings did not advocate the restriction of immigration. They merely suggested extending the period before which immigrants could become naturalized (and therefore eligible to vote). Although this suggests a greater fear of immigrant's political power than of their economic impact, the party's rhetoric clearly appealed to northern workers, particularly in northern cities, who felt they had been injured by competition with immigrants.

Nativist prescriptions were not just the musings of political extremists. The

22. Lane, *Solidarity or Survival*, p. 22.
23. Commons et al., *History of Labour*, pp. 601–614; Fogel, *Without Consent or Contract*, p. 363.
24. Abinder, *Nativism and Slavery*, p. ix.
25. Busey, *Immigration*, pp. 78–79.

popular press took up the anti-immigrant cry with equal fervor: an editorial in the Philadelphia *Sun* asserted that

> the enormous influx of foreigners will in the end prove ruinous to American workingmen, by *reducing the wages of labor* to a standard that will drive them from the farms and workshops altogether, or reduce them to a condition worse than that of Negro slavery. (Nov. 3, 1854; emphasis in original)[26]

The balance of this chapter seeks evidence of the quantitative impact of immigration on native-born workers. In the process, it assesses the reasonableness of the circumstantial evidence presented above. It asks: Were native-born workers suffering from the influx of immigrants? If so, was the suffering general or localized? What does the impact of immigration in this period tell us about the impact observed at the turn of the century and in the contemporary period? Finally, why was the solution proposed by the Know- Nothings less extreme than the outright restriction that occurred sixty years later?

The Data

The data are individual-level observations on 2,897 native-born American males between the ages of 15 and 60 in 1850 located in 726 counties drawn from the new sample of males linked from the Public Use Micro Sample (PUMS) of the 1850 federal census of population to the 1860 federal census manuscript schedules described in chapter 2. The sample contains each individual's location (state, county, city, ward) and self-reported occupation in both 1850 and 1860. For each location, the county's distance from the frontier and the fraction of the population foreign born were obtained from the 1850 and 1860 published census volumes.[27] Finally, the data set contains incomes imputed for 157 occupational titles listed in Appendix D.

As Fogel notes, there are several problems in using wages to measure the economic welfare of native-born workers in this period, many of which obtain in the use of imputed incomes.[28] These problems result from differences across locations and over time in prices, unemployment, seasonality, and the length of the workweek, and in the distribution of workers across occupations (what he terms "deskilling"). The measure of income change used here suffers from many of these shortcomings. The income measures used here have been adjusted for differences across regions and over time in prices, using the regional price index of Coelho and Shepherd.[29] The imputed nominal incomes are assumed to be constant within occupations between 1850 and 1860, which abstracts from changes in unemployment, seasonality, or the length of the workweek. The income measure

26. For other examples of the nativism that became increasingly apparent among native-born craft workers, see Commons et al., *Documentary History*, pp. 88–90.

27. U.S. Census Office, *Seventh Census*; U.S. Census Office, *Eighth Census*.

28. Fogel, "Problems," pp. 482–484.

29. Coelho and Shepherd, "Regional Prices."

used here introduces an additional problem by ignoring changes in incomes resulting from positive age-income or tenure-income relationships.

Since one of the issues we are interested in is whether immigration's impact is felt by natives across occupations, the regression for the change in income will include both dummies for occupation and interactions between occupation and the share foreign born at the 1850 location. Three occupational groups will be used: white collar (professional, technical, and kindred; managers, officials, and proprietors; clerical; and sales), skilled workers (craft and kindred workers; operatives in factory jobs), and farmers (farmers; farm managers; and farm foremen). The omitted category is unskilled workers (operatives and kindred workers not in factory jobs; service workers; and laborers). Since the census did not provide a breakdown of age by nativity, it is not possible to use the most appropriate measure of the competition that native-born males faced from immigrants: the fraction of the male labor force age 15 to 60 that was foreign born. The measure of immigration's impact used here will instead be simply the fraction of the county's population that was foreign born.

The data are summarized in Table 8-1, which shows the characteristics of individuals and the communities in which they lived in 1850 and 1860, disaggregated by the fraction foreign born at the 1850 location. Although average age does not vary much across the different foreign-born concentrations, many of the other variables do. In particular, the fraction of natives who had made a previous interstate move rises with the fraction immigrant, while the average family size falls. Places with the highest immigrant shares had fewer farmers and more white collar and skilled workers among natives than places with fewer immigrants. Finally, the places with the highest immigrant concentrations were cities in the New England and Middle Atlantic states.

The two outcome measures that will be the focus of the empirical analysis, the change in the log of imputed income for natives and their out-migration rate, vary with the foreign-born concentration, though not always in the expected direction. Although the native-born out-migration rate was clearly highest in places with large immigrant concentrations, incomes in places with high immigrant concentrations grew more than twice as fast as in places with low immigrant concentrations, and grew as fast as in places with medium concentrations. Part of this difference may reflect the occupational mix in these places. Locations with low immigrant concentrations were mainly rural and southern, places in which the predominant occupation was farmer. Although natives in these places may have seen their incomes rise over the 1850s, the measure of income change used here captures only income changes resulting from changes in occupation. Places that had high immigrant concentrations were urban centers in the Northeast and Midwest in which the occupational distribution was wider. In these places, there was scope for considerable movement between occupations. If immigrants chose locations where economic growth was rapid, and if rapid growth in the 1850s was positively correlated with rapid growth in the late 1840s when most immigrants arrived, we would expect to see the same positive association between immigrant concentration and income growth. The higher share of negative income changes

Table 8-1. Characteristics of natives observed in both 1850 and 1860, by foreign-born share in 1850 county.

Characteristic	All	Foreign-Born Share in 1850 County		
		Under 5%	5% to 10%	Over 10%
Personal				
Age (1850)	31.507	31.105	31.934	31.772
Previous migrant	0.263	0.248	0.262	0.288
Family size (1850)	3.429	3.671	3.292	3.175
Literate	0.956	0.924	0.984	0.983
Occupation (1850)				
White collar	0.072	0.039	0.065	0.127
Skilled	0.254	0.179	0.264	0.360
Farmer	0.524	0.630	0.515	0.372
Unskilled	0.153	0.153	0.163	0.147
y_{1850}	6.612	6.695	6.587	6.507
y_{1860}	6.687	6.743	6.685	6.605
Δy 1850–60	0.075	0.048	0.098	0.098
Mover 1850–60	0.397	0.384	0.401	0.412
Location				
Population (1850)	7,074.27	527.042	994.128	21,615.07
Population (1860)	18,084.43	5,762.16	10,627.90	42,308.65
Miles to frontier	602.037	510.591	654.385	697.017
% Foreign (1850)	0.088	0.019	0.071	0.204
% Foreign (1860)	0.118	0.053	0.123	0.211
Region (1850)				
New England	20.6	13.6	22.2	29.9
Middle Atlantic	36.9	23.6	50.4	46.2
Midwest	20.8	19.5	25.5	19.0
Southeast	13.3	26.5	1.1	3.2
South Central	8.0	16.8	0.7	0.7
Far West	0.3	0.0	0.0	1.1
No. of obs.	2,896	1,314	698	884

Source: Native-born males fifteen years and older in 1850 Public Use Microdata Series linked to the 1860 manuscript census schedules.

Note: "Previous migrant" is an individual living outside his state of birth in 1850. "y_{1850}" and "y_{1860}" are the natural log of the income imputed on the basis of the individual's occupational title in 1850 and 1860 as described in Appendix D. "Mover" is an individual who changed county of residence between 1850 and 1860. "Miles to frontier" is the straight-line distance from the individual's 1850 county to 90° longitude.

in places with high immigrant concentrations is consistent with the first interpretation but not the second.

Measuring the Impact of Immigration on Natives

Critics of contemporary studies of immigration's impact on natives contend that
to see how immigration affects native-born workers, we must examine not only
the initial impact of immigration (such as a fall in natives' wages) but also natives'
response (such as out-migration).[30] In order to make this connection explicit, this
study adopts a simple "mover/stayer" framework for the empirical analysis.[31] The
model is constructed to exploit the fact that individuals in the sample are observed
at two points in time.

Suppose first that the log of the income of individual i at the origin (o), location j, at time t, can be written as a function of observed and unobserved individual and location characteristics:

$$y^o_{ijt} = \beta'_o X_{ijt} + \epsilon_i + \eta_j + v^o_{it} \tag{1}$$

where X is a vector of observed individual and location characteristics (age, literacy, fraction foreign born in the county, and interactions between occupation in
1850 and the fraction foreign born), ϵ is an unobserved individual-specific fixed
effect, η is an unobserved location-specific fixed effect, and v is an error term or-
thogonal to X, $E(v^o_{it}) = 0$, and with and finite variance.

The log of the income of individual i at time t' depends on whether he has
moved since time t. For movers (m), who go to location k

$$y^m_{ikt'} = \beta'_m X_{ikt'} + \epsilon_i + \eta_k + v^m_{it'} \tag{2}$$

For stayers (s), who remain in location j

$$y^s_{ijt'} = \beta'_o X_{ijt'} + \epsilon_i + \omega_j + v^o_{it'} \tag{3}$$

where X, ϵ, η, and v are as defined above, though the interaction between occupation and fraction foreign born in the county in X now uses 1850 occupation and
1860 fraction foreign born. This specification assumes that the parameter vector
β_o does not change between time t and time t'.

Assume that the individual chooses whether or not to migrate in order to max-
imize Δy. this will eleminate the individual specific effect ϵ_i for both movers and

30. Borjas, "Economics of Immigration"; Friedberg and Hunt, "Impact of Immigrants."
31. This framework has been used by Lee, "Unionism and Wages," to study union/nonunion wage
differentials, by Willis and Rosen, "Education," to examine the returns to schooling, and by Nakosteen
and Zimmer, ""Migration and Income," and Robinson and Tomes, "Interprovincial Migration," to
analyze migration and income.

stayers, and will eliminate the location specific effect ω_j for stayers. For movers (m), the change in the log of income is

$$
\begin{aligned}
\Delta y_i^m &= y_{ikt'}^m - y_{ijt}^o \\
&= \beta_m' X_{ikt'} - \beta_o' X_{ijt} + (\epsilon_i - \epsilon_i) + (\eta_k - \eta_j) + (v_{it'}^m - v_{it}^o) \\
&= \beta_m' X_{ikt'} - \beta_o' X_{ijt} + v_i^m
\end{aligned}
\tag{4}
$$

where $v_i^m = \eta_k - \eta_j + v_{it'}^m - v_{it}^o$ is an error term with $E(v_i^m) = 0$, $Var(v_i^m) = \sigma_m$. For stayers (s), the change in the log of income is

$$
\begin{aligned}
\Delta y_i^s &= y_{ijt'}^s - y_{ijt}^o \\
&= \beta_o' (X_{ijt'} - X_{ijt}) + (\epsilon_i - \epsilon_i) + (\eta_j - \eta_j) + (v_{it'}^o - v_{it}^o) \\
&= \beta_o' X_{ijt'} - \beta_o' X_{ijt} + v_i^s
\end{aligned}
\tag{5}
$$

where $v_i^s = v_{it'}^o - v_{it}^o$ is an error term with $E(v_i^s) = 0$, $Var(v_i^s) = \sigma_s$.

The individual migrates if an index of the net benefit of migration, I^*, is positive:

$$
\begin{aligned}
I_i^* &= \delta_1 C_i + \delta_2 (\Delta y_i^m - \Delta y_i^s) - v_i \\
I_i^* &= \delta Z_{ijt} - v_i \\
I_i &= 1 \; iff \; I_i^* > 0 \Rightarrow \delta Z_{ijt} > v_i \\
I_i &= 0 \; otherwise
\end{aligned}
\tag{6}
$$

where C includes individual and location characteristics associated with the net benefits of migration, I_i is a dummy variable indicating whether the individual migrated, Z includes all the regressors in C and X, and v_i is an error term with $E(v_i) = 0$, $Var (v_i) = \sigma_v$. The vector C includes age, literacy, family size, whether a previous interstate move was made by the individual, distance from the 1850 location to the frontier, and the change between 1850 and 1860 in the fraction at the 1850 location who were foreign born. Family size should raise the cost of moving (both the direct cost of transportation and the set-up cost at the new location), though it should be uncorrelated with the change in income.[32] Similarly, whether a previous interstate move was made before 1850 (determined by comparing the reported state of birth and the 1850 state of residence) should capture the impact of any unobserved characteristics associated with a high propensity to migrate, but should be uncorrelated with the change in income between 1850 and 1860. The propensity to migrate will also be influenced by proximity to better locations. To capture this effect, the regressions include a measure of the distance from location j to the frontier for those located in rural places in 1850.[33] The change in the frac-

32. Robinson and Tomes, "Interprovincial Migration," p. 480, suggest that the presence of school-age children will increase the cost of migration if changing schools is costly. The presence of a spouse will inhibit migration "since a member of a family unit has to take into account the change in earnings of other family members."

33. Distance to the frontier was defined as the straight-line distance from location j to 90° longi-

tion foreign born is included to allow for the possibility that even if immigrants have no direct effect on the incomes earned by natives, natives are averse to living in places that receive a large influx of immigrants.

This is a "Type 5 Tobit model." Estimation proceeds in five steps.[34] First, assume that v_i^m, v_i^s, v_i follow a trivariate normal distribution. Equations (4) and (5) can now be rewritten as

$$\Delta y_i^m = \beta_m' X_{ikt'} - \beta_o' X_{ijt} + v_i^m \quad iff \ \delta Z_{ijt} > v_i \tag{7}$$

$$= \beta_m' X_{ikt'} - \beta_o' X_{ijt} + \rho_m \sigma_m \left[\frac{\phi(\delta Z_{ijt})}{\Phi(\delta Z_{ijt})} \right] + \mu_i^m$$

$$\Delta y_i^s = \beta_o'(X_{ijt'} - X_{ijt}) + v_i^s \quad iff \ \delta Z_{ijt} \le v_i \tag{8}$$

$$= \beta_o'(X_{ijt'} - X_{ijt}) + \rho_s \sigma_s \left[\frac{-\phi(\delta Z_{ijt})}{1 - \Phi(\delta Z_{ijt})} \right] + \mu_i^s$$

where $\rho_m = Corr\,(v_i, v_i^m)$, $\rho_s = Corr\,(v_i, v_i^s)$, $Var(v_i)$ has been normalized to 1, $E(\mu_i^m) = E(\mu_i^s) = 0$, ϕ is the standard normal density function, Φ is the cumulative normal distribution function, and the error terms μ_i^m, μ_i^s are heteroskedastic (since they depend on δZ_{ijt}).

Second, estimate equation (6) by Probit Maximum Likelihood to obtain the parameters $\hat{\delta}$. Use this vector, together with Z_{ijt} to calculate the inverse Mills ratio:

$$\frac{\phi(\hat{\delta} Z_{ijt})}{\Phi(\hat{\delta} Z_{ijt})} \tag{9}$$

Third, estimate equations (7) and (8) by weighted least squares (to account for the heteroskedasticity), including the inverse Mills ratio as a regressor, as in the Heckman two-step estimator for selection, to obtain $\hat{\beta}_o$, $\hat{\beta}_m$, $\hat{\rho}_m \hat{\sigma}_m$, $\hat{\rho}_s \hat{\sigma}_s$.

Fourth, use these parameters as starting values in the joint ML estimation of equations (6), (7), and (8), providing more efficient estimates than the separate estimates used by Lee (1978).[35]

Fifth, estimate $\Delta \hat{y}_i^m$ and $\Delta \hat{y}_i^s$ for each observation using $\hat{\beta}_o'(X_{ijt'} - X_{ijt})$, $\hat{\beta}_o' X_{ijt}$, $\hat{\beta}_m' X_{ikt'}$, insert these into equation (6), and reestimate equation (6) by Probit ML to obtain the structural parameters $\hat{\delta}_1$, $\hat{\delta}_2$, and correct the standard errors for the fact that some of the regressors are estimated values.[36]

---

tude. Locations west of this longitude (Minnesota, the Dakota Territory, western Wisconsin, western Illinois, Iowa, Kansas, Nebraska, Colorado, the western two-thirds of Missouri, Arkansas, Louisiana, Texas, Arizona, New Mexico, California, Oregon, and Washington) were assigned a value of zero.

34. Maddala, *Qualitative Variables*, pp. 234–240; Amemiya, *Advanced Econometrics*, pp. 395–400.

35. Amemiya, *Advanced Econometrics*, p. 400; Lee, "Unionism and Wages."

36. Maddala, *Qualitative Variables*, pp. 252–256.

This strategy suffers from a few difficulties when applied empirically. The first is the identification of the parameters in the migration decision equation, equation (6). In order to identify δ_1, there must be at least one variable contained in X that does not appear in C. Since X includes interactions between an individual's occupation at time t and the fraction foreign born in the county at time t and time t', but these interactions are excluded from C, this condition is satisfied. In order to identify δ_2, there must be at least one variable contained in C that does not appear in X. Since C includes an indicator for previous interstate migration and measures of family size, and distance to the frontier, but these are excluded from X, this condition is satisfied.

Another problem is that the "mover/stayer" framework imposes some strong restrictions when used to analyze migration.[37] The most important is the need to limit the number of origins and destinations, even though the logic of the model suggests at least the possibility of a different wage equation for each origin and each alternative location. The origins have been defined broadly to keep the sample sizes reasonably large. The two origins examined here will be "urban places (population $> 2,500$) in the Northeast (New England and Middle Atlantic)" and "rural places in the Northeast."[38] All alternative locations have been aggregated into a single alternative location for each origin. For those originating in the urban Northeast, the "other" location is rural places in the Northeast or any location outside the Northeast; for those originating in the rural Northeast, the "other" location is urban places in the Northeast and any location outside the Northeast. This framework also imposes some restrictive assumptions on the error structure of equations (7) and (8).[39]

The estimation procedure itself imposes further restrictions. Ideally, we would like a model that produces coefficients that directly measure $\partial\Delta y/\partial\Delta X_F$ (the difference in the change in income associated with a given change in the foreign-born concentration) for both movers and stayers. This would require that the vector X include a term $F_{1860} - F_{1850}$ for both movers and stayers. But in order to allow for the possibility that the parameter vector β differs between the origin and the destination, the *level* of all variables in 1860 and the negative of the *level* of all variables in 1850 must be included in the regression for movers (rather than the *differences* as is the case for stayers). Our measure of $\partial\Delta y/\partial\Delta X_F$ for movers, then, must be calculated using the coefficients on F_{1860} and $-F_{1850}$. The advantage of this procedure is that it allows us to test whether the impact of immigrants on natives' wages at the origin differs according to whether an individual later migrated out of that location. To derive $\partial\Delta y/\partial\Delta X$ for an element of the vector X, rewrite equation (7) as

37. Robinson and Tomes, "Interprovincial Migration," pp. 477–478.

38. Separate analyses (not presented here) were also performed for those originating in the rural Midwest and the rural Southeast. The findings were similar to those described below for the rural Northeast.

39. See Robinson and Tomes, "Interprovincial Migration," pp. 479–480, for a discussion of these issues.

$$\Delta y_i^m = \frac{1}{2}(\beta_m - \beta_o)'(X_{ikt'} + X_{ijt}) +$$
$$\frac{1}{2}(\beta_m + \beta_o)'(X_{ikt'} - X_{ijt}) + \rho_m \sigma_m \lambda_i^m + \mu_i^m \qquad (10)$$

where $\lambda_i^m = \phi(\delta Z_{ijt})/\Phi(\delta Z_{ijt})$. Since $\Delta X_i = X_{ikt'} - X_{ijt}$, the desired partial derivative is

$$\frac{\partial \Delta y^m}{\partial \Delta X} = \frac{1}{2}(\beta_m + \beta_o) \qquad (11)$$

For movers, if the regression includes the 1860 values of the vector X and the negative of the 1850 values of the vector X, the impact of ΔX_F is then the simple average of the coefficients on the 1860 value of X_F and the coefficient on the negative of the 1850 value of X_F. For stayers, the impact of ΔX_F can be read directly as the coefficient on ΔX_F.

A final problem is endogeneity. The vector X contains the fraction foreign born in the county in 1850 and 1860. This will be correlated with the error terms in equations (7) or (8) if immigrants choose where to settle on the basis of an unobserved location specific effect associated with the level of income earned by native-born males. To eliminate this correlation, the fraction foreign born at time t or time t' is replaced with an instrument created using the ratio of white females age 20 to 29 to white females age 30 to 39 in the county, as well as polynomials up to fifth order in this ratio. The resulting instrument should be correlated with the fraction foreign born (as immigrants are disproportionately prime-age), but not with the error term in income equations for *male natives*. Note that for stayers, first differencing has eliminated any permanent location specific effect. The instrument needs only to be correlated with the fraction foreign born and uncorrelated with transitory location specific effects. Separate instruments are created for the fraction foreign born in 1850 and 1860. This is different from the procedure used by Altonji and Card who created a single instrument for the *difference* in the immigrant share between two dates in each location using the immigrant share at the initial date.[40] Here, because some fraction of the sample moves between 1850 and 1860, the *levels* are each instrumented separately and the instrument for the difference is taken as the difference in the instruments. For movers, there is no reason to expect that the immigrant share in the initial year should be correlated with the change in the immigrant share movers face as a result of changing locations. The table in note 41 shows the regressions used to create the instruments for 1850 and 1860. The regressors are linear and higher order terms in the ratio of females in the county age 20 to 29 to females in the county age 30 to 39. The dependent variable in each case is the fraction of the county's population foreign born.[41]

40. Altonji and Card, "Effects of Immigration."
41. The regression coefficients and their standard errors (S.E.) are:

Regression Results

Taken together, the parameters of equations (6), (7), and (8) allow us to assess the total impact of immigrants, after accounting for the effect of outmigration. To see this, differentiate equation (8) with respect to the change in the foreign-born share ΔX_F, which yields:

$$\frac{\partial(\Delta y^s)}{\partial \Delta X_F} = \beta_{oF} - \delta_F \rho_s \sigma_s \frac{-\phi(\delta Z)}{1 - \Phi(\delta Z)}\left(\delta Z + \frac{-\phi(\delta Z)}{1 - \Phi(\delta Z)}\right) \qquad (12)$$

where β_{oF} is the coefficient on the change in the immigrant share between 1850 and 1860 for stayers and δ_F is the coefficient on the change in the immigrant share between 1850 and 1860 from the structural probit equation. This includes the direct effect of immigrants' arrival on the income change experienced by stayers and the effect induced by immigration on the probability that an individual will be a stayer (the second term). Since the change in the fraction foreign born *at the origin* enters the vector Z rather than the change between the 1850 share at the origin and the 1860 share at the destination, the full effect of a change in the 1850 share at the origin and the 1860 share at the destination for movers is simply the quantity in equation (11). The total effect of immigration is a weighted sum of equation (12) and β_{mF}. If the difference between equation (12) and β_{mF} is small, little of immigration's impact would be missed in this period by concentrating only on those who remained in the same location.

For stayers, the effect in equation (12) is similar to that estimated in most studies of the impact of contemporary migrants which ignore the impact of out-

	1850		1860	
	β	S.E.	β	S.E.
intercept	0.8209[†]	0.1125	0.4079[†]	0.0465
(20–29)	−1.0479[†]	0.1835	−0.2548[†]	0.0811
(20–29)²	0.4773[†]	0.1052	0.0106	0.0517
(20–29)³	−0.0876[†]	0.0255	0.0181	0.0135
(20–29)⁴	0.0069[†]	0.0026	−0.0027[*]	0.0014
(20–29)⁵	0.0002[‡]	0.0001	0.0001[‡]	0.0001
Adjusted R²	0.0584		0.0731	
N	1,593		2,015	

Probability the true β = 0: [†]<1%; [‡]<5%; [*]<10%.

For movers, the instrumented values for 1850 and 1860 are entered directly into the regressions. For stayers, the difference between the instruments for 1860 and 1850 are entered. The following analysis was also performed using an instrument created using the method of Altonji and Card, "Effects of Immigration," and the arbitrary assumption that the instrumented value for the change in the foreign-born concentration faced by movers was the simple average of the instrumented changes at the origin and destination. All of the substantive results that follow were replicated.

migration. In these studies, since individual migration decisions are not observed for the native born, immigration's impact on the change in income might indeed be negative ($\beta_{oF} < 0$), but the observed impact could be zero or positive if the second term is sufficiently large and negative. One important difference between equation (12) and the measure of immigration's impact in contemporary studies is that the latter measure allows for native-born in-migrants. The measure used here holds the composition of the native-born population fixed between 1850 and 1860, so it measures immigration's impact only on nonmigrants who remained in a particular location between 1850 and 1860. The difference between this measure and contemporary measures turns on the impact of immigration on native-born in-migration rates.

The results from estimating equations (7) and (8) for the observations located in the urban Northeast are presented in Table 8-2.[42] The first two columns use instrumental variables in place of the foreign-born share in 1850 and 1860 to eliminate the correlation between the foreign-born share and the transitory component of the error term in the income equations. The third and fourth columns use the actual levels of the foreign born instead. The excluded occupations are unskilled and farmer. Skilled workers saw their incomes grow significantly less rapidly than the omitted group, but much of this difference probably reflects regression to the mean due to the nature of the income measure: unskilled workers had nowhere to go but up, while both white collar and skilled workers could move down.

Of greater interest are the coefficients on the fraction foreign born in 1850 and 1860 for movers and the coefficient on the change in the fraction foreign born for stayers. For both movers and stayers in the omitted group, incomes grew more rapidly when the fraction foreign born grew. The implied value of $\partial \Delta y / \partial \Delta X_F$ calculated using equation (11) is 6.781 for movers; the value of $\partial \Delta y / \partial \Delta X_F$ for stayers is 5.564. It is not possible to reject the null hypothesis that these effects are identical ($t = 0.260$, $p = 0.795$). For skilled workers, though, increases in immigration were associated with slower income growth. This was true for both movers and stayers. The implied value of $\partial \Delta y / \partial \Delta X_F$ for skilled workers was -3.972 for movers; for stayers, the impact was -3.025. Again, the difference in these effects is not statistically significant ($t = -0.124$, $p = 0.902$). The similarity of the effects for movers and stayers suggests that immigration's impact could be accurately measured by examining only those who remained in the same location over the 1850s. The magnitudes of the coefficients for the omitted group suggest that an increase of 1 percentage point in the foreign born share was followed by a 6 to 7 percent increase in income; for skilled workers, the same increase in the fraction

---

42. Note that although age and literacy were hypothesized to effect the level of income, the values of these variables change by the same amount between 1850 and 1860 for every individual in the sample (10 years for age and zero for literacy, since no observations became literate between 1850 and 1860). The intercept term in the first difference regressions will capture all such effects. Age was included separately in the first difference regressions to allow for a nonlinear impact of age on the level of income.

Table 8-2. Estimates of the parameters of the structural earnings equations for movers and stayers in the urban Northeast.

Variable	Using Instruments for % Foreign Born		Using Actual Level of % Foreign Born	
	Δy^m	Δy^s	Δy^m	Δy^s
Intercept	−1.828**	0.348**	0.222	−0.276**
	(0.932)	(0.184)	(0.497)	(0.124)
Age	−0.001	0.002	−0.001	0.001
	(0.007)	(0.003)	(0.007)	(0.002)
White collar	−0.551	−0.514	0.092	0.064
	(4.204)	(0.333)	(1.163)	(0.146)
Skilled	−2.834**	−0.434	0.618***	0.411***
	(1.272)	(0.305)	(0.236)	(0.107)
$-F_{1850}$	14.174***		0.051	
	(4.973)		(2.299)	
$-F_{1850} \times$ White collar	−22.176		−1.247	
	(46.122)		(7.211)	
$-F_{1850} \times$ Skilled	−31.055***		−0.057	
	(11.398)		(2.976)	
F_{1860}	−0.613		3.299	
	(5.873)		(2.820)	
$F_{1860} \times$ White collar	−10.420		−5.096	
	(39.759)		(7.056)	
$F_{1860} \times$ Skilled	9.550		−3.895	
	(9.777)		(3.149)	
ΔF		5.564**		−1.491***
		(2.640)		(0.373)
$\Delta F \times$ White collar		−4.716		1.710***
		(5.639)		(0.668)
$\Delta F \times$ Skilled		−8.589*		2.173***
		(4.916)		(0.552)
σ	0.711***	0.467***	0.645***	0.456***
	(0.267)	(0.026)	(0.204)	(0.023)
ρ	−0.741**	−0.291	−0.574	0.253
	(0.356)	(0.410)	(0.539)	(0.341)
Log−likelihood	−449.902		−440.321	
No. of obs.	386		386	

Source: Native-born males fifteen years and older in 1850 Public Use Microdata Series linked to the 1860 manuscript census schedules.

Note: The entries are estimates obtained by maximum likelihood of the parameters of equations (7) and (8). Heteroskedasticity-corrected standard errors (White 1980) in parentheses. "White collar" and "Skilled" are 1850 occupations. F_t is the fraction foreign born in the county in year t; ΔF is the change in the fraction foreign born in the county between 1850 and 1860. Probability that the true parameter is zero: *<10%; **<5%; ***<1%.

foreign born led to a 3 to 4 percent drop in income. Although large in magnitude, the impact for white collar workers was not statistically significant.

When the actual level of the foreign born is used instead, the negative effects of immigration on skilled workers are reduced to statistical insignificance. In the case of stayers, the effect is actually reversed: in column 4, a rise in the immigrant concentration is associated with a higher rate of income growth for skilled workers who did not move. For the omitted occupational group, the sign also changes between columns 2 and 4 on the change in the foreign-born share: the change in the foreign-born share is now associated with slower income growth than it was when using instrumental variables for the foreign-born shares in 1850 and 1860. These sign changes in going from the instrumented to the actual levels are consistent with immigrants choosing locations that are good for native skilled workers and bad for native unskilled workers.[43]

Results for the rural Northeast are shown in Table 8-3. The results are strikingly different from those in Table 8-2: there is no strong negative impact from the change in the immigrant concentration. In fact, the implied $\partial \Delta y / \partial \Delta X_F$ is actually positive for movers in the omitted occupational group when the actual levels are used and for stayers when the instruments are used. Older movers saw slower income growth, while skilled natives saw faster growth when the actual foreign-born shares were used whether they were movers or stayers.[44] The absence of an impact from immigration in the rural Northeast (and in an identical analysis of the rural Midwest) suggests that there is no need to take into account the arrival in the rural Northeast and Midwest of natives from the urban Northeast displaced by immigrants in analyzing immigration's impact.

Using the coefficients from Tables 8-2 and 8-3, it is possible to estimate the coefficient vector δ in equation (6) to determine the impact of potential differences in income growth and other factors as determinants of migration patterns. The results of this exercise are shown in Table 8-4.[45] For the urban Northeast, the most important determinant of migration is having made a previous interstate move: previous interstate migrants were 9 percentage points more likely to move than others, and this difference was statistically significant. The change in the for-

43. The coefficients on σ and ρ in column 1 of Table 8-2 indicate that movers are negatively selected: their income change is smaller than the change that stayers would have earned had they migrated. Since the coefficients on ρ are essentially zero in columns 2, 3, and 4, it is not possible to say anything definitive about the nature of the selection among stayers when instruments for the foreign born are used and among movers and stayers when the actual foreign-born concentrations are used.

44. The coefficients on σ and ρ in Table 8-3 suggest the positive selection of movers using both predicted and actual foreign-born concentrations (they earn more than stayers would have earned if they had migrated), but once again leave the sign of the selection effect for stayers indeterminate.

45. This calculation requires predicted values of both Δy^m and Δy^s for all observations, while both depend on the foreign-born concentration in 1850 and 1860 at the origin and the destination. For both movers and stayers, the 1860 foreign-born concentration at the origin (necessary to obtain Δy^s) can be easily obtained, as can the 1860 foreign-born concentration at the destination for movers (necessary to obtain Δy^m for movers). For stayers, it is not clear what to use for the 1860 foreign-born concentration in calculating their income in the event of migration. For this exercise, it was arbitrarily assumed that they would move to a place with an 1860 foreign-born concentration equal to the average 1860 foreign-born concentration in the places to which movers relocated.

Table 8-3. Estimates of the parameters of the structural earnings equations for movers and stayers in the rural Northeast.

Variable	Using Instruments for % Foreign Born		Using Actual Level of % Foreign Born	
	Δy^m	Δy^s	Δy^m	Δy^s
Intercept	−0.052	0.201	−0.488***	−0.052
	(0.241)	(0.169)	(0.178)	(0.100)
Age	−0.004*	−0.002	−0.005**	−0.002
	(0.003)	(0.002)	(0.003)	(0.002)
Skilled	1.009	0.200	0.284*	0.362***
	(0.688)	(0.299)	(0.164)	(0.109)
$-F_{1850}$	0.583		−0.058	
	(2.324)		(0.485)	
$-F_{1850} \times$ Skilled	7.401		−0.438	
	(8.427)		(0.997)	
F_{1860}	−0.740		1.095***	
	(1.569)		(0.432)	
$F_{1860} \times$ Skilled	−2.452		−0.263	
	(4.017)		(0.621)	
ΔF		2.837**		−0.463
		(1.458)		(0.435)
$\Delta F \times$ Skilled		−1.626		0.707
		(4.609)		(0.994)
σ	0.592***	0.561***	0.654***	0.561***
	(0.037)	(0.013)	(0.055)	(0.012)
ρ	0.394**	−0.073	0.653***	−0.001
	(0.205)	(0.209)	(0.141)	(0.055)
Log-likelihood	−1,907.089		−1,864.595	
No. of obs.	1,281		1,281	

Source: Native-born males fifteen years and older in 1850 Public Use Microdata Series linked to the 1860 manuscript census schedules.
Note: The entries are estimates obtained by maximum likelihood of the parameters of equations (7) and (8). Heteroskedasticity-corrected standard errors (White 1980) in parentheses. "Skilled" is 1850 occupation. F_t is the fraction foreign born in the county in year t; ΔF is the change in the fraction foreign born in the county between 1850 and 1860. Probability that the true parameter is zero: *<10%; **<5%; ***<1%.

eign-born share at the origin was associated with a lower probability of migration, though this effect was statistically distinguishable from zero only at the 85 percent level when instruments were used and at the 89 percent level when actual levels were used. The point estimate suggests that a 1 percentage point increase in the fraction foreign born would decrease the out-migration propensity by between 1 and 2 percentage points. The partial derivative of the migration probability with respect to the difference in the income change for movers and stayers, though neg-

Table 8-4. Estimates of the parameters of the structural migration equation for movers and stayers in the Northeast(partial derivatives evaluated at sample means).

Variable	Using Instruments for % Foreign Born		Using Actual Level of % Foreign Born	
	Urban	Rural	Urban	Rural
Intercept	−1.087	−1.778***	−1.168	−1.253
	(9.681)	(0.583)	(9.672)	(1.048)
Age	0.001	−0.005***	0.001	−0.005***
	(0.002)	(0.002)	(0.002)	(0.002)
Literate	0.934	−0.198*	0.945	−0.194*
	(9.703)	(0.116)	(9.704)	(0.116)
Family size	−0.004	0.002	−0.003	0.003
	(0.011)	(0.007)	(0.011)	(0.007)
Previous migrant	0.093*	0.101**	0.088*	0.099**
	(0.054)	(0.050)	(0.054)	(0.050)
ln(miles to frontier)		0.281***		0.776
		(0.086)		(0.553)
ΔF	−2.007	7.482***	−1.251*	2.495***
	(1.410)	(0.922)	(0.777)	(0.488)
$\Delta \hat{y}^m - \Delta \hat{y}^s$	−0.029	0.295*	−0.015	0.012
	(0.045)	(0.184)	(0.085)	(0.158)
Log-likelihood	−198.884	−832.261	−198.897	−854.447
χ^2	6.664	93.003***	6.637	48.632***
No. of obs.	386	1,281	386	1,281

Source: Native-born males fifteen years and older in 1850 Public Use Microdata Series linked to the 1860 manuscript census schedules.

Note: The entries are estimates obtained by maximum likelihood of the partial effects of the parameters of equation (6), evaluated at the sample means for all variables. Uncorrected standard errors in parentheses. ΔF is the change in the fraction foreign born in the origin county between 1850 and 1860. "Previous migrant" is an individual living outside his state of birth in 1850. "Miles to frontier" is the straight-line distance from the individual's 1850 county to 90° longitude. Probability that the true parameter is zero: *<10%; **<5%; ***<1%.

ative, is statistically insignificant. For the rural Northeast, age and literacy were both associated with a lower propensity to migrate whether using instruments or actual levels for the foreign born. Previous interstate migration and an increase in the foreign-born share were also associated with more migration whether using instruments or levels, while proximity to the frontier increased migration using instruments for the foreign born. The sign on the difference in income growth between movers and stayers is of the anticipated (positive) sign in both columns 2 and 4, though it is statistically significant only when the predicted foreign born share is used.[46]

46. The standard errors in Table 8-4 have not been corrected for the fact that one of the regres-

The apparently negative relationship in the urban Northeast between the change in immigrant concentration and the change in skilled workers' incomes and the positive relationship for the unskilled deserve further exploration. We now seek the mechanism by which that impact came about. Were skilled workers displaced by competition from skilled immigrants, or was it competition from unskilled workers eager to take their jobs (if not their occupational titles) as in the "de-skilling" story emphasized by labor historians? We can exploit the substantial differences across ethnic groups in the proportion possessing craft skills to provide a tentative answer. Chapter 2 shows that only 6 percent of Irish immigrants arriving between 1840 and 1850 reported a skilled occupation at arrival, whereas 20 percent of British immigrants and 24 percent of German immigrants did so over the same period. If we see a greater impact on native-born skilled workers from British and German immigration than from Irish immigration, this suggests that the impact of immigration came through competition within the skilled class of workers, with immigrants replacing natives in skilled jobs, and natives having to assume lower-income jobs as a result. If the impact is greatest from the Irish, the de-skilling explanation is more likely.

Table 8-5 shows the coefficients on interactions between an individual's occupation and the share of the population that was (1) Irish and (2) British and German at the 1850 and 1860 locations for movers and the changes in (1) and (2) for stayers.[47] This specification is identical to that in Table 8-2, but for the in-

---

sors (the estimated Δy^m-Δy^s) is an estimated value; Maddala, *Qualitative Variables*, pp. 252–256. In general, this correction has a substantial impact only on the standard error for Δy^m-Δy^s; Maddala, *Qualitative Variables*, p. 238.

47. The census did not report the distribution of countries of origin for the foreign born at the county level in 1850 or 1860. It provided such a breakdown only for about 30 cities in both years. It was thus necessary to estimate the Irish share of the population for each county, based on the Irish share in each state and the accommodations reported by Roman Catholic churches in each state and county. For 1850 and 1860, separate weighted linear least squares regressions of the state's Roman Catholic church space on the state's Irish population were estimated using $1/\sqrt{P}$ as the weight, where P is the state's total population in 1850 or 1860 (standard errors in parentheses):

1850: Irish = −4320.82 + 1.76 (*church space*)
        (4391.73) (0.20)
        Adj. R^2 = 0.71 N = 32
1860: Irish = −9125.61 + 1.43 (*church space*)
        (7337.68) (0.16)
        Adj. R^2 = 0.72 N = 36

The reported Roman Catholic church accommodations for each county were then used together with these regression coefficients to estimate the Irish population of each county. The resulting number was divided by the county's foreign-born population to estimate the ratio of Irish-born residents to total foreign-born residents in the county. The logistic transformation $e^X/(1 + e^X)$ was then used so this ratio would lie between zero and one. The transformed ratio was then multiplied by the instrumented foreign-born population and the actual foreign-born population to divide those figures into (1) Irish and (2) all other (British and German) components. In using this instrument, it is assumed that the foreign-born population of a county is endogenously determined by factors affecting the error term in the wage equations for natives, but that the division of the foreign-born population into Irish and all other immigrants is not.

Table 8-5. Estimates of the parameters of the structural earnings equations for movers and stayers in the urban Northeast (using instruments for % foreign born).

Variable	Δy^m	Δy^s
$-\text{Irish}_{1850}$	11.448*	
	(6.285)	
$-\text{Irish}_{1850} \times$ White collar	−11.346	
	(141.420)	
$-\text{Irish}_{1850} \times$ Skilled	−31.863***	
	(12.688)	
Irish_{1860}	0.201	
	(6.063)	
$\text{Irish}_{1860} \times$ White collar	−19.605	
	(72.812)	
$\text{Irish}_{1860} \times$ Skilled	2.010	
	(13.724)	
ΔIrish		−2.755
		(1.811)
ΔIrish x White collar		5.722
		(4.027)
ΔIrish x Skilled		4.882*
		(2.605)
$-\text{Other}_{1850}$	13.311**	
	(6.500)	
$-\text{Other}_{1850} \times$ White collar	2.712	
	(119.130)	
$-\text{Other}_{1850} \times$ Skilled	−22.643	
	(15.743)	
Other_{1860}	−2.770	
	(6.361)	
$\text{Other}_{1860} \times$ White collar	−5.631	
	(62.396)	
$\text{Other}_{1860} \times$ Skilled	9.601	
	(12.251)	
ΔOther		3.819
		(2.553)
ΔOther $\times$ White collar		−5.082
		(6.496)
ΔOther $\times$ Skilled		−7.823
		(4.989)
Log-likelihood	−434.208	
No. of obs.	386	

Source: Native-born males fifteen years and older in 1850 Public Use Microdata Series linked to the 1860 manuscript census schedules.

Note: The entries are estimates obtained by maximum likelihood of the parameters of equations (7) and (8). Heteroskedasticity-corrected standard errors (White 1980) in parentheses. "White collar" and "Skilled" are 1850 occupations. Irish_t is the fraction Irish born in the county in year t; "ΔIrish" is the change in the fraction Irish born in the county between 1850 and 1860. "Other_t" is the fraction British or German born in the county in year t; "ΔOther" is the change in the fraction British or German born in the county between 1850 and 1860. The intercept term and coefficients on age, occupation, σ, and ρ are not shown. Probability that the true parameter is zero: *<10%; **<5%; ***<1%.

clusion of two categories of immigrants (Irish and all others) and the inclusion of the corresponding interactions with occupation. Among those in the omitted occupational group, the arrival of non-Irish immigrants raised incomes for both movers and stayers, while the arrival of the Irish raised movers' incomes but reduced stayers' incomes. The results reveal that the largest negative impact of immigration was among skilled movers, and that this impact came mostly through the Irish. The implied $\partial\Delta y/\partial\Delta X_F$ for the increase in the Irish share is -9.102 for skilled movers. For skilled stayers, the effect of an increase in the Irish fraction is a faster rate of income growth. This group shows a negative impact of -4.003 from the non-Irish instead.

The threat to native-born skilled workers who left the cities of the Northeast, then, came not from similarly skilled British or German immigrants, but from largely unskilled Irish immigrants. Among those who remained in northeastern cities, by contrast, the British and Germans were a greater problem. Although the results for movers are consistent with the de-skilling story, the results for stayers are not. In fact, the arrival of Irish immigrants was associated with faster income growth for stayers. Further attention must be devoted to the characteristics of the places left by movers to learn why the Irish had an impact on some skilled workers but not on others.[48] The individual-level data in the present sample are inadequate to answer this question.

Industry and the Irish

The labor history literature on de-skilling suggests where we might turn for an answer. Where unskilled workers were used to squeeze out skilled workers, the Irish were generally recognized as the unskilled workers most likely to be used in this manner. They were the most likely group to be used in employers' attempts to transform industries dominated by small-scale hand production by artisans to large-scale machine production by operatives:

> The urban artisans, as serious casualties of change and economic depression, were able to identify a particular group, the Irish, as being largely responsible for their decline in occupational, political, and social status. . . . [T]he Irish were identified as agents in the process of economic modernization. The adoption of task differentiation and mechanization was facilitated by this increasing supply of cheap, unskilled labor, notably in industries like sewing, shoemaking, cabinetmaking, and carpentry. . . . [T]he Irish were perceived less as fellow laborers than as the minions of capital.[49]

48. Goldin, "Immigration Restriction," p. 251, finds that the arrival of mostly unskilled immigrants reduced the wages of nonunion artisans between 1890 and 1903, and reduced the wages of union artisans between 1907 and 1923. This is not comparable to the negative effect of unskilled immigrants on artisans described here. Goldin's results pertain to wage changes within the artisan class, whereas the results presented here are for individuals who were artisans in the base year (1850) whether or not they remained in this group over the 1850s.

49. Lane, *Solidarity or Survival*, pp. 26–28.

This suggests that the growth of large-scale, low-skill manufacturing, made possible by the appearance of cheap, unskilled Irish workers, was the mechanism through which immigration depressed the incomes of skilled native-born workers in the urban Northeast. If this is true, then we should observe an association at the county level between the scale of manufacturing and the share of the population born in Ireland. Although the published census volumes of 1850 and 1860 do not make such an analysis possible (since the number of manufacturing establishments was not tabulated at the county level in 1850), they do allow an examination of the relationship between the share of the population employed in manufacturing and the share of the population born in Ireland, born in other countries, and born in the United States.

To formalize this notion, suppose that Mfg_{it}, the share of the population in county i employed in manufacturing at time t, is a function of the share of the population from Ireland at time t, the share from Other countries at time t, and a location specific effect α_i that reflects endowments of resources, proximity to markets, and other factors that are fixed in the short run:

$$Mfg_{it} = \alpha_i + \beta_I Irish_{it} + \beta_O Others_{it} + \epsilon_{it} \qquad (13)$$

where ϵ_{it} is a transitory error term with the usual properties. There are two difficulties with estimating the parameters β_I and β_O: the presence of the unobserved fixed effect α_i and the possibility that immigrants choose where to live on the basis of the presence of manufacturing jobs. The unobserved location specific effect can be eliminated by first differencing:

$$\Delta Mfg_i = \beta_I \Delta Irish_i + \beta_O \Delta Others_i + (\epsilon_{it'} - \epsilon_{it}) \qquad (14)$$

The correlation between the regressors and the transitory location specific effects can be eliminated by using instrumental variables in place of the actual changes in the Irish and Other populations.

In this context, the instrumenting procedure used by Altonji and Card is appropriate.[50] They created a single instrument for the difference in the immigrant share between two dates in each location using the level of the immigrant share at the initial date. Bartel found that the best predictor of where an immigrant would settle in the 1970s was the fraction foreign born in a location.[51] Goldin also observed a statistically significant relationship between immigrant flows into cities between two dates and the share at the initial date around the turn of the century, but the direction of the relationship changed between 1890 and 1920: from 1890 to 1900 it was negative, from 1900 to 1910 it was positive, and from 1910 to 1920 it was again negative.[52] For the Irish, the regressors used to create the instruments are linear and higher order terms in the share of the county's 1850 population born in Ireland (see note 47) and the dependent variable is the change

---

50. Altonji and Card, "Effects of Immigration."
51. Bartel, "New U.S. Immigrants."
52. Goldin, "Immigration Restriction," p. 243.

from 1850 to 1860 in the fraction of the county's population born in Ireland. The regression for Other foreign born is defined similarly.[53]

Estimation of equation (14) for 192 urban counties (1850 population > 10,000) in the Northeast using instruments for *Irish* and *Other* produced an estimated β_I of 0.206 ($t = 1.671$, $p = 0.096$) and an estimated β_O of 0.109 ($t = 0.752$, $p = 0.453$). This suggests that an increase of 1 percentage point in the fraction of a county's population born in Ireland resulted in a 0.2 percentage point increase in the fraction of the county's population employed in manufacturing. The increase caused by the same size increase in the non-Irish immigrant population was only half as great.

These findings are consistent with the arrival of unskilled Irish immigrants making it easier for employers to transform their methods of production in some industries in order to eliminate skilled workers, and skilled workers seeing a fall in their incomes as their jobs were eliminated and choosing to migrate out of those places as a result. Places that received more non-Irish immigrants saw less growth in manufacturing. In these places, the competition between natives and immigrants was within the class of skilled workers. Native-born skilled workers chose to remain in such places, perhaps because employment in small-scale production remained an option, even though they now faced competition from British and German skilled workers. More detailed data on the changing distribution of workers across industries are necessary to provide a more definitive explanation for the different impacts on native skilled workers from Irish and non-Irish immigration.

Finally, since the regressions in Table 8-2 control for the selectivity of out-migration, it is possible to assess the importance of geographic mobility among native-born workers in diminishing the negative impact of immigration. A large historical literature has debated the value of the farming frontier as a "safety valve" for dissatisfied urban unskilled workers in the nineteenth century.[54] More recent research has uncovered extraordinary economic opportunity in urban places in the Midwest.[55] Did the presence of the farming frontier or rapidly growing cities

53. The regression coefficients and their standard errors (S.E.) are:

	Irish		Other	
	β	S.E.	β	S.E.
intercept	0.001*	0.001	0.002	0.001
[1850 share]	0.404[†]	0.138	1.175[†]	0.116
[1850 share]^2	−20.109[†]	3.801	−9.589[†]	1.745
[1850 share]^3	193.809[†]	35.362	29.918[†]	9.100
[1850 share]^4	−721.207[†]	128.801	−44.531[†]	18.959
[1850 share]^5	882.970[†]	158.441	24.295*	13.180
Adjusted R^2	0.271		0.197	
N	1,593		1,593	

Probability the true $\beta = 0$: [†]<1%; *<10%.

54. Turner, *Frontier in American History*.
55. Galenson, "Economic Opportunity."

like Chicago, Milwaukee, and Cincinnati provide relief to native-born skilled workers squeezed by the arrival of unskilled Irish workers in northeastern cities?

The importance of mobility can be seen by comparing the direct effect of immigration on income growth for movers and stayers.[56] When instruments are used for the foreign-born share, a comparison of the coefficients in columns 1 and 2 in Table 8-2 suggests that movers were considerably more sensitive to the arrival of immigrants at their 1850 location: for skilled workers, the coefficient on the immigrant share in 1850 (the sum of the coefficient for the omitted group and the coefficient on the interaction between skilled occupation and the immigrant share in 1850) is more than five times greater for movers than for stayers.[57] If moving had not been an option so movers would have had to remain at their 1850 location, their income growth would have been even more negative than it actually was.[58] This suggests that internal migration may indeed have been an important mechanism dissipating the impact of immigration, though in this case it is the internal migration of skilled workers rather than the unskilled workers whose movement Turner emphasized. Even though movers and stayers saw the same impact on their incomes from immigration, it was the outlet provided by migration out of the urban Northeast that made that equalization possible.

Implications

The tremendous volume of immigration in the late 1840s produced an immigration rate that was more than twice as great as it has been in the 1990s. As a result, we might expect that if immigration ever had an impact, it would have been manifested in the years between 1850 and 1860. The results do show great distress among skilled native-born workers in northeastern cities, but little apparent negative impact elsewhere. In fact, immigration was actually associated with faster income growth among unskilled workers. Since the income measure used here captures only the large changes in income associated with changes in occupation and not the within-occupation income changes that immigration might also cause, the effect of immigration is probably an underestimate of its true effect in this period. Although the negative effect for skilled workers could be increased

56. Note that this is different from the econometric question posed at the start of this section: How much of immigration's impact would be missed if we were unable to observe the behavior of outmigrants? Here, a counterfactual is posed: How different would things look if migration had not been possible?

57. For skilled workers, the difference between the 1850 effect of immigrant arrivals for movers and the 1850 effect for stayers is 13.856; this difference is statistically significant at the 78 percent level ($t = 1.239, p = 0.216$).

58. The difference between the impact of immigration for stayers and the 1850 impact for movers is probably an overstatement of how much worse movers would have fared if migration had not been an option, though. It is likely that skilled workers facing a deterioration in their positions as a result of the arrival of immigrants and unable to move to a more favorable environment would take steps to ameliorate that impact.

somewhat by taking account of changes in income within occupations, it is difficult to imagine how such an adjustment could reverse the large, positive, and statistically significant effect for unskilled workers.

These findings are in contrast to the conclusions of Goldin and Hatton and Williamson who both found a clear, generalized negative impact from immigration on wages in the U.S. labor market at the turn of the century.[59] That such a widespread impact cannot be detected in the antebellum period when the immigration rate was slightly higher than at the turn of the century indicates that some structural change occurred between 1850 and 1900. One possibility is the reduction in the economy's "absorptive capacity" suggested by Williamson.[60] As noted earlier, though, the elasticity of demand for unskilled labor fell only modestly over these fifty years. An alternative explanation is that the process of industrial transformation that the arrival of immigrants facilitated and that produced a negative effect for skilled workers in the 1850s was largely complete by the turn of the century. By that time, immigrants and natives were more likely to be in competition for jobs within a particular occupational class. The lack of an unambiguously negative effect from immigration today may reflect the increase in the economy's "absorptive capacity" since then calculated by Williamson.[61]

The results also reveal that little of the impact of immigration is missed by examining stayers and treating local labor markets as essentially closed economies. Hatton and Williamson suggest that the inability to detect immigration's impact in studies of local labor markets today results from the failure to account for the impact of geographic mobility (of both capital and labor).[62] The results presented here indicate that, at least for skilled workers, mobility attenuates the negative effects of immigration—movers would have had worse outcomes if migration had not been an option—but the overall impact of immigration is the same for movers and stayers. Taking account of the endogeneity of immigrants' location decisions, however, does make a considerable difference: the sign of the relationship between the arrival of immigrants and the income change experienced by natives is generally reversed when instruments are used for the arrival of immigrants.

Finally, the findings presented here also illuminate two aspects of antebellum political economy: the reluctance to restrict immigration, and the coming of the Civil War. As was noted above, the staunchest of nativists in the years between 1850 and 1860, the Know-Nothings, never advocated a solution to the "immigration problem" more radical than lengthening the time until immigrants could become naturalized. Nothing like the outright restriction of immigration imposed after 1921 was even considered. The isolated impact of immigration found here may explain why: with immigration's negative effects limited to one occupation group (skilled workers) in urban places in one region, it was difficult to make the case for restriction to a nation that otherwise derived significant benefits from immigration.

59. Goldin, "Immigration Restriction"; Hatton and Williamson, "Impact of Immigration."
60. Williamson, "Trade-Offs."
61. Ibid.
62. Hatton and Williamson, "Impact of Immigration."

The rise of the Know-Nothings did have a lasting impact, however, even though they shunned anti-immigrant legislation after their electoral victories in 1854, and passed from the political scene by 1856. Their effect was to drive voters into the Republican Party in the election of 1860, a party by then dedicated to anti-slavery positions initially advanced by the Know-Nothings. Fogel attributes much of the rise of the Know-Nothings to the competition faced by native-born skilled workers in northern cities in the 1850s.[63] The distress they responded to was an important force shaping the Know-Nothing agenda and the Republican Party's attempt to win over disaffected native workers. The Republicans' success in that conversion paved the way for the Civil War.

63. Fogel, *Without Consent or Contract.*

9

Conclusions

The early years of antebellum immigrants' experience in the United States were years of change. From their arrival at the docks of New York until up to twenty years later, they changed their locations, their occupations, and their wealth holdings, and changed them in ways consistent with an effort to find their niche in the economy of their adopted homeland. Some groups had a more difficult time than others in making these transitions: by virtually every measure, the Irish fared considerably worse than the British or Germans who arrived over the 1840s. But even the Irish experienced the extensive mobility characteristic of antebellum immigrants in the years immediately after their arrival in the United States.

It was possible to observe these transformations experienced by immigrants with a new body of data on antebellum Europeans who arrived at the port of New York between 1840 and 1850. Using passenger ship records and the manuscript schedules of the 1850 and 1860 federal population censuses, a longitudinal picture of immigrants' economic progress was created. These data allowed an examination of the patterns of geographic, occupational, and financial mobility in light of immigrants' characteristics at arrival and their time in the United States. This perspective is better suited to reveal the transformations that are an inherent part of the immigration process than conventional sources that allow us to observe immigrants only at a single point in time.

A companion sample of native-born Americans linked from the 1850 census to the 1860 census was developed and used as well, as a contrast to the performance seen among immigrants. But this new native-born sample produced some unique results in its own right. The ability to follow specific individuals over the 1850s without regard for where they settled made it possible to assess the link between geographic and occupational and financial mobility, for example. The focus on specific individuals also allowed an investigation of the impact of immigrants' arrival on the labor market outcomes of native-born workers.

The immigrants in the sample employed in this study all arrived at the port of New York, but most—probably 65 percent among those arriving at the end of the 1840s—left the city immediately. Those who remained in New York were either too poor to move on or had a specific reason for remaining. The Irish dominated the former group, while the latter consisted mainly of merchants and clerks who sought employment in the city's commercial houses. The majority of arrivals, however, took advantage of frequent and inexpensive transportation out of New York, traveling either to other locations along the Atlantic Coast or to points in the interior.

More than half of all immigrants in the sample went to just three states—New York, Ohio, and Pennsylvania. A greater percentage of immigrants than of the total U.S. population went to cities and small towns. Immigrants reached these locations quite rapidly. There are no marked differences in the regional distribution of the immigrants in the sample by how long they had been in the United States. The immigrants who were most likely to go west were those who arrived with the most resources and those who arrived with the least. Immigrants who were neither rich nor poor were more likely to remain in the East.

The attraction of the West for the immigrants who arrived with significant resources was the availability of large tracts of farmland. Only the immigrants who arrived with the means to buy, clear, and stock the land, and provision a family for a year or two until the first crop could be brought in, however, were able to avail themselves of this opportunity. The attraction of the West for the poorest immigrants—particularly unskilled, unmarried, Irish workers—was the opportunity to earn the region's high wages, either on its farms or in its cities. Many of these immigrants later returned to the East or to the cities with their earnings, to set themselves up as they had been too poor to do at arrival.

The vast majority of the immigrants in the sample—nearly 70 percent—changed counties between 1850 and 1860. This figure represents genuine mobility rather than the effects of mortality and census underenumeration that often bias the measurement of geographic persistence. Immigrants were considerably more geographically mobile than natives over the 1850s: only 43 percent of natives made an intercounty move over the decade. These conclusions on mobility were made possible by the use of samples of specific individuals located in both 1850 and 1860. The groups most likely to remain in the same county over the decade were farmers—because they had made a considerable investment in real estate at their 1850 location—and those who had sunk roots into the community in other ways, by marrying or acquiring property. These effects were similar for both immigrants and natives.

Most of the movement that occurred for immigrants was within regions, as if they had a general idea at their arrival where they wanted to go, or where their resources would allow them to go, but made minor adjustments after their initial choice. More than three quarters of immigrants remained in the same region between 1850 and 1860. Those who changed regions were far more likely to change occupational status than those who remained in the same county, state, or region. At the same time, those who changed regions were the ones who made the largest gains in wealth. Among natives, interregional migration was far less frequent. Roughly 90 percent of natives remained in the same region over the 1850s.

In terms of the sizes of the places to which immigrants and natives went, immigrants were far more likely to make rural-to-urban moves than natives, even though this was a decade that saw significant growth in urban places. This suggests the tenuous connection between immigrants and the locations in which they were found. Far more often than natives, they were willing to pull up stakes and make a significant change in their circumstances, perhaps in response to changes in relative wages in the city and on the farm. A significant number of immigrants also appear to have moved to rural places in anticipation of a subsequent move back into an urban area. Unskilled, unmarried, Irish workers were particularly likely to make such moves, returning to the city to settle down after a few years earning a living in agriculture.

In considering occupational mobility, a quarter of those who described themselves as white collar or skilled workers at their departure from Europe were found in a lower-status occupation in 1850. And though nearly half of those who described themselves as unskilled workers in Europe were in higher-status jobs by 1850, most of this upward mobility might be accounted for by misreporting of European occupations. The dominant tendency among new arrivals was downward occupational mobility.

Yet there were clear differences by country of origin in how successfully immigrants were able to rise or avoid a fall in status between their European and American occupations. Far fewer British and Germans moved down in status and far more moved up than was true for the Irish. This is consistent with the Irish having the most difficulty fitting into the American economy, perhaps because of the vast differences in terms of development between the U.S. and Irish economies.

Most of the occupational mobility experienced by the Irish and Germans seems to have come at arrival—their first job in the United States was either higher or lower than their reported occupation at departure from Europe. There is no obvious temporal pattern of occupational change between arrival and 1850 for these groups. The British, though, were increasingly likely to achieve a higher-status occupation with greater duration in the U.S. economy. Because immigrants were observed at several dates (arrival, 1850, and 1860), it was possible to isolate the impact of duration in the United States from the effect of changes over the 1840s in the propensity of successive immigrant cohorts to move up in occupational status irrespective of their time since arrival. This analysis suggested that Germans who arrived in the late 1840s, in the wake of the failed revolutions of 1848, were far more likely to improve their occupational status immediately after arrival than Germans who had arrived earlier in the 1840s. This is consistent with the revolutions producing a change in the average quality of German immigrants, as previously well-positioned skilled and white collar workers, who under normal circumstances would not have set sail for America, chose to do just that in fear of what a postrevolution Germany would look like.

Perhaps surprisingly, the Irish famine beginning in 1846 did not produce a negative impact on the ability of Irish immigrants to improve their occupational status. Perhaps the degree of discrimination against the Irish had been so severe during the 1840s that a drop in average quality led to no decrease in the fraction able to escape unskilled work. Or perhaps the famine's effects had yet to be felt in the quality of immigrants coming to America. For the most destitute Irishmen, a trip across the Irish Sea to England was often a more economically feasible alternative than direct migration to America. Only after earning some money in England's cities or waiting for a relative who had previously gone to America to forward passage fare could those lower in the Irish economic hierarchy make their way to the United States.

The immigrants in the sample continued to experience extensive occupational mobility into their second decade in the U.S. economy. Between 1850 and 1860, a quarter of white collar and skilled workers again fell in status, while just over a third of those who began as unskilled workers rose from that rank. As was the case between arrival and 1850, though, the British and Germans experienced most of the upward mobility while the Irish experienced most of the downward mobility.

Previous studies of occupational mobility in the nineteenth century have focused on individuals who remained in the same community over the course of a decade or more. In this study, immigrants and natives who left their 1850 county were located again in 1860, so it is possible to say how the concentration on persisters may have influenced the results of other studies on occupational mobility. The natives and immigrants in this sample who were most likely to move either up or down in occupational status were those who changed their county of residence over the 1850s. This movement suggests that the exclusive focus on persisters in other studies may have imparted a significant bias to the magnitudes of both upward and downward occupational mobility.

Immigrants were able to accumulate significant amounts of wealth with greater duration in the United States. Their wealth increased an average of nearly 15 percent with every year since their arrival among the most recent arrivals. The impact of duration remained positive for an immigrant's first twenty years in the United States. This duration effect is not the result of an unobserved cohort effect—that is, it is not simply the result of later arrivals possessing less wealth at arrival than had earlier arrivals irrespective of accumulation in the years after arrival. Because of the immigrants located in both 1850 and 1860, it was possible to isolate the effect of duration in the United States from this cohort effect. Nor is it simply the result of Germans' learning English, as the British were also able to increase their wealth with greater duration in the United States, and actually saw greater increases for each year in the United States than the Germans. And it is not the result of unobserved heterogeneity among the immigrants, as both fixed and random effects models on immigrants located in both 1850 and 1860 produced similar results.

There was a clear duration effect across all regions and occupations in wealth accumulation. Part of the return to duration apparently represented a return to duration in specific, fast-growing, local economies in the western states. Immigrants who settled in cities such as St. Louis and Milwaukee and remained there over the 1850s were several times wealthier in 1860 than immigrants who settled in the East, who changed location over the decade, and who settled and remained in places that grew more modestly.

By 1860, any differences in wealth between the Irish and the British and Germans that could not be accounted for by occupation had been erased. Thus, although the Irish had on average 35 percent of the wealth of the British and Germans in 1850, by 1860 that deficit had shrunk to statistical and substantive insignificance after accounting for occupation. The remaining deficit could be explained by the large number of Irish immigrants who were unskilled workers, rather than by the overall poverty of the Irish.

Farmers, white collar workers, and skilled workers all possessed more wealth in both 1850 and 1860 than unskilled workers, but the gap between these groups and unskilled workers widened considerably by 1860. Those who settled in the West were also wealthier than those in the East, and by a greater margin in 1860 than in 1850. Though this may simply have resulted from the faster rates of wealth accumulation with duration in particular occupations and locations, it may point to something more. When coupled with the increase between 1850 and 1860 in the age when wealth attained a maximum, these other differences between the 1850 and 1860 results may have been the product of better matches between immigrants and both the occupations in which they worked and the places in which they lived. By 1860, more such matches had been made, as immigrants continued the process of adjustment which they had begun at their arrival.

The immigrants themselves were not the only ones transformed by the process of immigration. The results in chapter 8 showed a substantial impact on native-born skilled workers from the arrival of immigrants over the 1850s. This is consistent with other research on the difficulties experienced by these workers in the antebellum period. It is also among the few times it has been possible to detect such a negative impact from immigration. The injury suffered by native-born skilled workers should not surprise us: the 1850s saw the highest rates of immigration in U.S. history (more than 15 immigrants per thousand U.S. population), and were also a time when employers were adopting new production techniques that could easily employ unskilled labor. Irish immigrants were apparently crucial in this process of industrial transformation. Although their arrival apparently led to some down-grading of skilled native workers, they may also have paved the way for less-skilled natives to enter factory work, by being available just as employers were preparing to change their production processes.

Overall, immigrants experienced a significant transformation in the years after they disembarked at New York. They sought out opportunities in distant locations, adjusted the skills they had brought with them when the need arose, and moved and adjusted again when they were unsuccessful. One measure of their success in making these changes is the rise in their wealth as the number of years since arrival increased. The frequent changes of location and occupation might be taken for mere rootlessness, but for the advances in wealth and occupation those changes occasioned. In this light, they appear more as calculated calibrations to improve immigrants' circumstances than the desperate flight of the unsuccessful. The improvements in immigrants' circumstances as their time in the United States increased also allow us to make more sense of the reasonableness of the immigrants' decision to come to the United States. The picture of immigrants huddled and disoriented and unable to escape the crushing poverty of immigrant ghettos in cities like New York, painted by some early historians of the immigrant experience, have made us wonder how desperate these people must have been in Europe to have traded it all for this fate. The successes enjoyed by immigrants and their quite rapid escape from New York and entry into rapidly growing cities in the West, however, suggest that desperation was not the only reason for migration for many.

The arrival of several million new Americans in the years before the Civil War led to a very vocal debate on the merits of immigration: Will these people become more like us and add to the American experience or will they merely take our jobs and fill our jails and poorhouses? The next great wave of immigration just after the turn of the century produced a similar discussion, as has the resurgence of immigration in the late 1980s and 1990s. Even though the origins of those entering the United States have changed over the 150 years from 1840 to 1990, the questions have not.

Clearly, at least for those arriving in the years before the Civil War, many of the fears were unjustified. Over time, immigrants did increasingly come to resemble the native born in their economic appearance. Though some of them aided in a process of industrial transformation that produced economic catastrophe for native-born skilled workers, the ultimate benefits of that transformation may more than outweigh the costs. And the paths that they marked into America's factories, into its growing western cities, and eventually into the respectability of its emerging middle class, were to be followed by generations more in the years to come.

Appendix A

Separating the Effects of Duration in the United States and Arrival Cohort

This is an example of a more general problem in economics: separating the influence of time in an environment from the influence of changes in the characteristics of individuals at their arrival in that environment. This difficulty appears in the analysis of immigrants' geographic mobility (where the preferences of successive cohorts for initial locations may change over time as new locations become available), immigrants' occupational mobility (where the average skill level of arrivals may change from one year's arrivals to the next's), and in the analysis of immigrant's wealth accumulation (where wealth at arrival may vary across cohorts). We will illustrate the problem and some solutions for the case of wealth accumulation. It is assumed that we observe the date of arrival for immigrants. We then observe some at one later date, some at another later date, and some at both dates. We observe their wealth at these dates, but not at arrival.

Suppose that the wealth at time t of an immigrant i who has been in the United States for Y years can be written as

$$W_{it} = W_{i0}\, e^{\delta Y_{it}} \tag{A1}$$

where δ is the annual percentage rate of growth in wealth and W_{i0} captures all other influences on wealth. Suppose also that

$$W_{i0} = e^{\beta X'_{it} + \mu_{it}} \tag{A2}$$

where X_{it} is a vector of individual characteristics such as age, location, and occupation, β is a vector of unknown parameters to be estimated, and μ_{it} is an error

term with the usual properties that captures the impact of unobserved characteristics such as wealth at arrival.[1]

This specification is particularly convenient, as it is linear in its logarithms:

$$\ln(W_{it}) = \beta X'_{it} + \delta Y_{it} + \mu_{it} \tag{A3}$$

The percentage impact on wealth of a one-unit change in one of the independent
variables can be determined directly from the regression. This specification has
been employed in numerous studies of wealth in the nineteenth century.[2]

The regression specification in equation (A3) has an important shortcoming,
however: it combines two effects in the term δY_{it}. The first is the actual effect of
wealth accumulation since arrival. The second is the effect of changes in the quality or wealth at arrival of successive cohorts of immigrants. This difficulty arises if
the term μ_{it} is changing systematically over time. This would be the case if some
structural change occurred, such that the average value of wealth at arrival is no
longer fully described by the term $\beta X'_{it}$ when evaluated at the values for the individual at the time of arrival, or if the state of the labor market that immigrants
enter at their arrival has a large impact on their level of wealth even after several
years in the United States.[3]

Suppose wealth at arrival is falling over time so that those for whom year of arrival takes on a larger value have a lower μ_{it}. Specifically, suppose

$$\mu_{it} = \gamma(Year\ of\ Arrival)_i + \eta_{it}, \quad \gamma < 0 \tag{A4}$$

where η_{it} captures the influence of unobserved characteristics other than wealth
at arrival. In a a sample of observations drawn in a single year t, duration in the
United States and year of arrival are linearly related: $(Year\ of\ Arrival) = t - Y_{it}$.
Substituting this relationship back into equation (A3) and regrouping terms
yields

$$\ln(W_{it}) = \gamma t + \beta X'_{it} = (\delta - \gamma)Y_{it} + \eta_{it} \tag{A5}$$

1. It is conventional to add a third term to W_{i0} in addition to the vector of individual characteristics and the individual-specific error term: a term ϵ_t that captures any peculiarity of the year in which
the cross section was drawn. Since we are concerned with wealth, which exhibits greater stability over
time than income and is thus less likely to be subject to the periodic fluctuations embodied in the term
ϵ_t, we will assume in what follows that ϵ_t equals zero.

2. See Atack and Bateman, "Egalitarianism"; Galenson, "Economic Opportunity"; Galenson and
Pope, "Economic and Geographic Mobility"; Pope, "Households" and "Coming to Zion"; and Steckel,
"Poverty and Prosperity" (1988).

3. There is some evidence suggesting that immigrants who arrived in the early 1840s entered a better labor market than those who arrived later. See the discussion in chapter 5. The procedures discussed here to isolate the duration and cohort effects will account for both changes in the average
wealth or quality at arrival of successive cohorts of immigrants and changes in the state of the labor
market immigrants entered over the 1840s. These issues are discussed in Heckman and Robb, "Using
Longitudinal Data." A simple change in the value of initial wealth caused by a change in the share of
immigrants arriving with a particular characteristic X_{it} (a composition effect) presents no such problem, since the influence of all observed personal characteristics is controlled for in the regressions.

Thus although the coefficent for individual characteristics β is identified in a single cross section, it is not possible to separate the duraction and cohort effects, δ and γ. In fact, in the case where $\gamma < 0$, it is possible for the estimated coefficent on duration in the United States ($\delta - \gamma$) to be positive even if the the true duration effect δ is zero.[4]

Since several hundred of the immigrants in the sample used here were located in both 1850 and 1860, it is possible to overcome this difficulty using two econometric approaches. The first approach is to estimate a model that takes account of any factor common to the immigrants who arrived in a particular year. This approach decomposes the disturbance term μ_{it} into two parts: a term α_j common to all arrivals in year j and a random disturbance η_{it}:

$$\ln(W_{it}) = \beta X'_{it} + \delta Y_{it} + \sum_{j=1840}^{1850} \alpha_j D_{ij} + \eta_{it} \qquad (A6)$$

where D_{ij} takes on a value of one if immigrant i arrived in year j and a zero otherwise, and t = 1850,1860. The parameter α_j measures the amount by which the average unexplained wealth for immigrants who arrived in year j differs from the average unexplained wealth for those who arrived in the excluded year. This allows us to identify separately the effect of years since arrival and any unobserved effect common to all arrivals in a particular year, such as average wealth at arrival, average ability by year of arrival, or the state of the U.S. labor market that immigrants entered at their arrival.

A more extreme version of the same procedure is also employed: again focusing on the 500 immigrants linked to both 1850 and 1860, but now allowing an individual-specific, time-invariant effect α_i for each immigrant:

$$\ln(W_{it}) = \beta X'_{it} + \delta Y_{it} + \alpha_i + \eta_{it} \qquad (A7)$$

This will allow us to account for unobserved individual heterogeneity, such as differences in ability, ambition, and luck, rather than simply heterogeneity related to arrival in a particular year. Two models will be estimated: a fixed-effects model and a random-effects model.

The fixed-effects model allows a different intercept term α_i for every individual in the sample by including a dummy variable in the regression for each cross-sectional unit. Unfortunately, the impact of any characteristic that does not change over time (such as country of origin) is captured in such an individual-

4. This is the basis of George Borjas's criticism of Barry Chiswick's finding that the earnings of twentieth-century immigrants increased with greater duration in the United States; see Borjas, "Self-Selection"; and Chiswick, "Americanization." Borjas offered evidence showing that the quality of immigrant arrivals was falling over the decades examined by Chiswick. In the terminology used here, Borjas contended that the most recent arrivals were of lower quality than earlier arrivals, so the coefficient on duration estimated for a single cross section could have been positive, even if δ was actually zero or negative.

specific intercept, so estimation of a fixed-effects model will not allow us to identify the impact of these characteristics.

In the random-effects model, the individual-specific term α_i and the term ω_{it}
are both random disturbances, distributed normally and independently in the
population with variances σ_α^2 and σ_η^2. This specification creates a correlation
across time between the residuals for a single cross-sectional unit:

$$\mu_{it} = \rho\mu_{it-1} + \eta_{it} \tag{A8}$$

where ρ is a correlation coefficient. The random-effects model allows us to identify the impact of time-invariant personal characteristics, but it is inappropriate
if the unobserved individual-specific effect is correlated with any of the other
regressors.

The specification chosen—fixed- or random-effects—should reflect the nature of the process generating the data and the corresponding nature of the residual μ_{it}.[5] If the residual simply reflects random variation because of the omission
of information not known to the observer on individuals in a sample drawn from
a large universe, information that is uncorrelated with the other independent
variables and reflects simple sampling error, then the appropriate specification is
the random-effects model. This would be the case, for example, if μ_{it} largely reflects luck which is distributed randomly in the population regardless of observable personal characteristics. The random-effects model makes it possible to capture the impact of this omitted variable.

If the residual instead reflects the presence of an unobserved individual-specific characteristic that is correlated with the other independent variables, then
the appropriate specification is the fixed-effects model. Since the process generating the observations on immigrant wealth used in this study is probably the result of both stochastic forces such as luck and time-invariant personal characteristics such as wealth at arrival and ambition that may be correlated with the other
independent variables such as occupation, both specifications will be used.

A number of specification tests have been developed to help choose among a
simple model with a single intercept, a fixed-effects model, and a random-effects
model. Whether the fixed-effects model is superior to a model with only one intercept can be determined by calculating the F-ratio:

$$F = \frac{(R_f^2 - R_c^2)/(n-1)}{(1-R_f^2)/(nT-n-K)} \tag{A9}$$

where R_f^2 is the R^2 from the fixed-effects regression, R_c^2 is the R^2 from a regression
in which a common intercept is used, n is the number of observations, T is the
number of time periods, and K is the number of regressors apart from the constant.
Under the null hypothesis (that a single-intercept model is appropriate), this sta-

5. See Hsiao, *Analysis*, p. 41–47.

tistic follows an F-distribution with $(n-1)$ and $(nT-n-K)$ degrees of freedom.[6]

Whether a random-effects model is superior to a model with only one intercept can be determined by calculating Breusch and Pagan's Lagrange multiplier test for homoskedasticity:

$$LM = \left(\frac{nT}{2(T-1)}\right)\left[\frac{\sum\limits_{i=1}^{n}\left(\sum\limits_{t=1}^{T}e_{it}\right)^2}{\sum\limits_{i=1}^{n}\sum\limits_{t=1}^{T}e_{it}^2}-1\right]^2 \qquad (A10)$$

where the e_{it} are the residuals from the single-intercept model. Under the null hypothesis (that the errors are homoskedastistic and therefore the single-intercept model is appropriate), this statistic follows a χ^2 distribution with one degree of freedom.[7]

Finally, whether a fixed-effects or random-effects model is preferred can be determined by calculating the Hausman statistic:

$$H = [\beta_f - \beta_r]'\left[\text{Var}[\beta_f] - \text{Var}[\beta_r]\right]^{-1}[\beta_f - \beta_r] \qquad (A11)$$

where β_f is the K-vector of estimated coefficients from the fixed-effects regression (except the constant), β_r is the corresponding K-vector from the random-effects regression, and K is the number of regressors in the fixed-effects regression apart from the individual-specific intercepts. Under the null hypothesis (that there is no correlation between the error term and the regressors, so the random-effects specification is appropriate), this statistic has a χ^2 distribution with K degrees of freedom.[8]

6. Greene, *Econometric Analysis*, p. 468.
7. Breusch and Pagan, "Simple Test."
8. Hausman, "Specification Tests."

Appendix B

A Continuous Time Duration Model with Discrete Observations

There are some circumstances when it is necessary to infer the time at which an event occurred on the basis of three pieces of information: an initial state, a terminal state, and the amount of time that has passed between the observation of the initial and terminal states. This situation occurs in the analysis of immigrants' departure from New York. We observe them on the day of their arrival in the United States, and know they were located in New York on that day. We then observe them again in the 1850 census, which tells us whether they were still located in New York. By comparing the date of the census to the date of arrival, we can estimate the amount of time between the initial and terminal states, but we do not know when in that interval a transition occurred; for individuals who have not yet left New York, we do not know when such a transition will take place. The same difficulties arise in analyzing immigrants' entry into the western states, and the occupational mobility they experienced in the years after their arrival. We will describe this problem and its solutions in the context of occupational mobility.

In order to analyze the timing and correlates of occupational mobility among immigrants after their arrival, we need to calculate the probability that an immigrant with a particular set of characteristics would be observed in a particular occupation at each date since arrival. If we know the date at which changes in occupation occur, this is a straightforward exercise: it involves estimating a duration model which yields a hazard function, the probability that a change will occur at each date. Since we do not know the date at which immigrants changed occupation (we know only whether they had changed occupation between departure from Europe and 1850 or 1860 and how long they had been in the United States by those dates), the standard duration model must be modified slightly to account for the fact that immigrants are not observed continuously but are instead observed only at two or three discrete dates.

To form the hazard function for the transition from occupation 1 to occupation 2 with discrete observations, consider a sample of individuals who are identical in all respects, except the length of time they spend after arrival in the United States in occupation 1 before moving into occupation 2.[1] This time t is distributed in the population according to a density function $f(t)$ which has a corresponding distribution function $F(t)$. For every t, $f(t)$ gives the probability that an immigrant will experience a completed spell in an occupation of length t. The distribution function $F(t)$ is defined as

$$F(t) = \int_0^t f(u) \ du \qquad (B1)$$

where $F(t)$ gives the probability that an immigrant will experience a completed spell in an occupation of length no greater than t. Thus, the probability that an immigrant is still in occupation 1 after time t (i.e., the probability that an immigrant experiences a completed spell in occupation 1 of length greater than t) is given by $[1-F(t)]$. The "instantaneous hazard rate"

$$\lambda_{12}(t) = \frac{f(t)}{1 - F(t)} \qquad (B2)$$

is the probability of an immigrant changing occupation at time t given that the immigrant had been in occupation 1 until time t. For a small increment dt,

$$\lambda_{12}dt = Prob[in\ occupation\ 2\ at\ time\ t + dt \mid in\ occupation\ 1\ at\ time\ t] \qquad (B3)$$

is the probability that an immigrant in occupation 1 at time t will move into occupation 2 by time $t + dt$. We can use this to write the probability of observing an immigrant in occupation 1 at time $t + dt$ as the product of two terms: the probability that the immigrant has remained in occupation 1 until time t, and the prob-

---

1. This procedure is described in Amemiya, *Advanced Econometrics*, pp. 440–442, and Sheps and Menken, *Mathematical Models*, pp. 110–114. The procedure has been applied in another context by Gönül, "Labor Force Participation Decisions." The approach is similar to that employed in recent historical work by Carter and Savoca, "Labor Mobility," and Jacoby and Sharma, "Employment Duration," but with an important difference: the approach used here does not require knowledge of the date at which the transition from one state to another occurred. This approach can be applied in other situations, where a transition between two states is possible but the researcher knows only whether the transition occurred and the amount of time an individual was at risk to make the transition, rather than the exact time when the transition occurred. For example, this approach will be used to determine the probability that immigrants returned to their premigration occupations at different times since their arrival given their date of arrival in New York and occupation at arrival and in 1850 or 1860. It could also be used to determine the probability of marriage at different ages for a sample of individuals given their ages and whether they were married at some known date.

ability that the immigrant will remain in occupation 1 in the interval dt (i.e., *not* move to occupation 2 in the interval dt). Thus,

$$P_{11}(t + dt) = P_{11}(t)(1 - \lambda_{12}(t) \, dt) \tag{B4}$$

Dividing both sides by dt, rearranging terms, and taking the limit as dt goes to zero yields

$$\frac{\partial P_{11}(t)}{\partial t} = -P_{11}(t)\lambda_{12}(t) \tag{B5}$$

The solution to this differential equation is

$$P_{11}(t) = \exp\left(\int_0^t -\lambda_{12}(u) \, du\right) \tag{B6}$$

Since the probabilities for the two events must sum to one, we can write the second probability as

$$P_{12}(t) = 1 - \exp\left(\int_0^t -\lambda_{12}(u) \, du\right) \tag{B7}$$

All that remains is to specify the hazard function $\lambda_{12}(u)$—how the probability of changing occupation at any date t depends on personal characteristics and on the amount of time since arrival t. Three approaches can be pursued at this point: a nonparametric approach, a semiparametric approach, and a fully parametric approach.[2] The advantage of the first two is that they are less sensitive to misspecification of the distribution of the hazard. The advantage of the latter is that it can be pursued with a relatively small number of observations, as in the present case. The fully parametric approach will be adopted here, but two different distribution functions will be examined to reduce the possibility of misspecification.

First, assume that the hazard follows a *Weibull* distribution, and that individual characteristics enter the hazard multiplicatively. For individual i with characteristics described by the vector X, the hazard can then be written as:

$$\lambda_{12}(t_i; X_i) = \alpha(\exp(X_i'\beta)t_i)^{\alpha-1} \tag{B8}$$

---

2. For examples of the nonparametric and semiparametric approaches with continuously observed samples, see Meyer, "Semiparametric Estimation."

where β and α are parameters to be estimated. This allows the hazard to change as the time at risk increases. In particular, if $\alpha < 1$, the hazard rate falls as t increases; if $\alpha > 1$, the hazard rate rises as t increases; and if $\alpha = 1$, the hazard rate does not change as the time at risk increases. Note, however, that the change in the hazard is monotonic: the Weibull hazard does not allow for the possibility that the hazard may increase for some time after arrival before it falls. Now, given a sample of N individuals, the log-likelihood function for the sample is

$$L(\beta, \alpha) = \sum_{i=1}^{N} (y_i) \ \ln(\exp(-\exp(X_i'\beta)t_i)^\alpha) + \tag{B9}$$

$$(1 - y_i) \ \ln(1 - \exp(-\exp(X_i'\beta)t_i)^\alpha)$$

where y_i is a binary variable equal to one if the individual was in occupation 1 after t years in the United States and equal to zero if the individual was in occupation 2 after t years.

A second approach uses the *log-logistic* hazard. Individual characteristics again enter the hazard multiplicatively. For individual i with characteristics described by the vector X, the hazard can now be written as

$$\lambda_{12}(t_i; X_i) = \frac{\alpha[\exp(X_i'\beta)t_i]^{\alpha-1}}{1 + [\exp(X_i'\beta)t_i]^\alpha} \tag{B10}$$

This specification permits a nonmonotonic hazard. If $\alpha < 1$, the hazard decreases monotonically from ∞ at time zero as t increases; if $\alpha = 1$, the hazard decreases from $\exp(X_i'\beta)$ at time zero to zero as t increases; and if $\alpha > 1$, the hazard increases from zero at time zero to a single maximum at time $[(\alpha-1)/\exp(X_i'\beta)]^{1/\alpha}$, and then decreases to zero as t increases.[3]

---

3. See Lancaster, *Econometric Analysis*, pp. 44–45, for a discussion of the Weibull and log-logistic hazard functions.

Appendix C
Estimates of White Male Life Expectation in the United States by Region, Urban/Rural, and Nativity

As part of the 1850 federal census of population, census marshals were instructed to ask at each household they visited whether any member of that household had died in the preceding twelve months. The published totals based on this question have been examined by Condran and Crimmins who concluded that these data need to be used with care.[1] The enumeration of deaths was probably better in areas that had been settled longer, better after infancy and before old age, and more accurate for deaths that occurred closer in time to the date of the census.

Since the published mortality totals did not provide breakdowns of life expectancy by region, size of location, and nativity, and these were necessary to estimate the fraction of the ship list sample and the 1850 PUMS that should have survived to 1860, I used a sample of the data from the manuscript mortality schedules to provide new estimates of life expectation along these dimensions. The sample was created by Accelerated Indexing Systems, and for 1850 consists of 30,713 decedents in 593 counties in 17 states. The sample contains 18 counties (7 urban) in the Northeast, 272 counties (none urban) in the Northwest, and 303 counties (2 urban) in the South. Urban counties had an 1850 population of 35,000 or more. The 17 states were: Connecticut, Delaware, and Vermont (Northeast); Illinois, Indiana, Michigan, Ohio, and Utah (Northwest); and Arkansas, Florida, Georgia, Kentucky, Louisiana, Mississippi, Tennessee, Texas, and Virginia (South).

In order to reduce the errors found by Condran and Crimmins, resulting from the retrospective process by which the data were collected, the life expectations were based only on those who died in the six months immediately before the census. Each death in these months was multiplied by two to return the mortality rate to a full-year basis. A second adjustment to the mortality-by-age totals in each

1. Condran and Crimmins, "Mortality Data."

Table C-1. Life expectancies by sex, location, and nativity, 1830–60.

Survivors	Life Expectancies		
	e_{20}	e_{30}	e_{40}
Native Born Males, 1850			
weighted	44.4	37.7	30.9
unweighted	45.4	38.8	32.1
Urban			
weighted	38.0	30.9	24.3
unweighted	38.2	31.3	25.2
Northeast	38.2	31.0	24.1
Northwest	44.0	37.0	31.4
South	29.8	23.7	19.5
Rural			
unweighted	47.2	40.7	33.9
weighted	47.6	41.1	34.2
Northeast	43.4	36.0	28.3
Northwest	47.6	41.2	34.4
South	49.5	43.4	36.9
Foreign Born Males, 1850			
weighted	35.7	31.2	27.3
unweighted	38.7	33.8	29.1
Urban	30.6	27.5	24.9
Rural	45.3	38.1	31.6
Total U.S. 1830-60[a]	40.9	34.5	—
Total U.S. 1830-60[b]	42.8	36.0	—
Total U.S. 1850[c]	40.1	33.6	27.1
Total U.S. 1850[d]	37.6	31.0	—
Total U.S. 1860[e]	44.0	37.4	—
Model West, Level 13[f]	41.5	34.0	26.6

Sources: Native Born, 1850, and Foreign Born, 1850: author's calculations from 1850 manuscript mortality schedules of the 1850 federal census of population; [a]Meech, *Tables of Life*; [b]Pope, "Adult Mortality"; [c]Jacobson, "Expectation of Life"; [d]Haines, "Model Life Tables"; [e]Vinovskis, "Mortality Rates"; [f]Coale and Demeny, *Model Life Tables*.

Note: e_x are life expectancies at age x.

county was made necessary by the absence of records for the deaths of some individuals from the sample. The shortfall of deaths (the difference between the published total deaths for the white population and the total in the sample) was apportioned to each age, sex, and nativity group in the county according to that group's share in the region's population. The population shares were derived from the 1850 PUMS. The missing records resulted from illegibility and missing pages in the manuscripts.

The life expectations estimated for prime-age males are shown in Table C-1.

Rates for infants and the elderly (not shown) are certainly too high. For the present purpose, the first of these is not a problem, since we are interested in the survival of males age 10 and older in 1850. The understatement of the mortality rate for the elderly will be overcome by assuming a 100 percent mortality rate by 1860 for those age 65 and over in 1850 when estimating the number of survivors from the ship lists and the 1850 PUMS. The life expectancies shown in the table are probably too high for the urban Northeast (since the sample's urban places in the Northeast do not include the largest cities, such as New York, Philadelphia, or Boston) and too low for the urban South (since one of the ten urban counties in the South is Orleans Parish, which contains the City of New Orleans, an unusually unhealthy place). The differences between the native-born and immigrants seem reasonable.

The differences between these new rates and those previously calculated for the antebellum period may reflect shortcomings of the sample of mortality records used here, but those differences might also reflect differences in coverage. For example, the figures for the Northeast presented here are identical to Jacobson's estimates from Massachusetts and Maryland when the urban and rural populations are combined using their population shares as weights.[2] The weighted life expectations for natives and immigrants are only a half year greater at age 20 than the expectation from Pope's sample.[3]

2. Jacobson, "Expectation of Life."
3. Pope, "Adult Mortality."

Appendix D
Imputing Income By Occupation

Neither the 1850 census nor the 1860 census collected information on income for individuals. Other documentary sources provide information on earnings, but only for individuals in particular occupations, places, or industries. In order to assess the impact of immigration in the 1850s, then, we need a measure of income by occupation that we can use to infer the income earned by an individual on the basis of a reported occupational title. Fortunately, the 1850 census reported real estate wealth that can be used to derive such a measure.

The 1850 census asked each respondent to report the value of his or her real estate holdings. The Public Use Micro Sample (PUMS) of the 1850 census provides individual-level observations on roughly 32,000 males between the ages of 20 and 65 who reported occupations.[1] A regression was estimated using these data with the natural log of real estate wealth as the dependent variable and age, age squared, and age cubed, controls for region of residence and size of location, along with dummy variables for 157 occupation titles, as regressors.

The coefficients on the occupational dummies, evaluated at age 30, were taken to represent differences in income within three broad occupational classes: white collar, skilled, and unskilled. These dummies were inflated to reflect the white collar/skilled and skilled/unskilled premia found by Goldin and Margo for clerks, artisans, and laborers.[2] To make their wage figures comparable to the coefficients from the wealth regression, the Goldin and Margo estimates for average nominal daily wages for clerks, artisans, and laborers were weighted by the population shares from the 1850 IPUMS in each of the regions they defined (Northeast, Midwest, South Atlantic, and South Central) to create a national average for

1. Ruggles et al., *IPUMS-95*.
2. Goldin and Margo, "Wages, Prices, and Labor Markets."

Table D-1. Imputed income scores by three-digit occupational code and title.

Code	Title	Income
Professional, Technical, and Kindred		
000	Accountants & auditors	$488.95
001	Actors & actresses	488.95
003	Architects	488.95
004	Artists & art teachers	502.60
005	Athletes	488.95
006	Authors	488.95
007	Chemists	488.95
009	Clergymen	775.22
010	College presidents & deans	488.95
018	Professors, mathematics	488.95
028	Professors, nonscientific subject	488.95
029	Professors, subject not specified	488.95
031	Dancers & dance teachers	488.95
032	Dentists	298.03
033	Designers	488.95
035	Draftsmen	488.95
036	Editors & reporters	484.85
043	Engineers, civil	488.95
046	Engineers, mechanical	488.95
051	Entertainers not elsewhere classified	488.95
054	Funeral directors & embalmers	488.95
055	Lawyers & judges	1281.49
057	Musicians & teachers	502.60
073	Pharmacists	759.35
074	Photographers	488.95
075	Physicians & surgeons	1191.52
092	Surveyors	931.15
093	Teachers not elsewhere classified	502.60
099	Professional, technical, and kindred workers not elsewhere classified	484.85
Farmers & Farm Managers		
100	Farmers	1175.86
123	Farm managers	576.18
Managers, Officials, & Proprietors		
201	Buyers & shippers	1073.70
203	Conductors, railroad	716.49
210	Inspectors	748.00
230	Managers, building	748.00
240	Officers, pilots, etc., ship	716.49
250	Public officials not elsewhere classified	748.00
270	Postmasters	1111.78
290	Managers, officials, and proprietors not elsewhere classified	1073.70

Table D-1. (*continued*)

Code	Title	Income
Clerical & Kindred		
300	Agents not elsewhere classified	749.71
304	Baggagemen, transportation	711.74
305	Bank tellers	711.74
310	Bookkeepers	352.20
320	Cashiers	711.74
321	Collectors, bill & account	711.74
335	Mail carriers	711.74
340	Messengers & office boys	711.74
342	Shipping & receiving clerks	711.74
360	Telegraph messengers	711.74
365	Telegraph operators	711.74
380	Ticket agents	749.71
390	Clerical & kindred not elsewhere classified	748.00
Sales & Kindred		
410	Auctioneers	$1027.11
430	Hucksters & peddlers	557.59
450	Insurance agents	1027.11
460	Newsboys	557.59
470	Real estate agents	1027.11
490	Salesmen & clerks not elsewhere classified	714.48
Craftsmen & Kindred		
500	Bakers	352.79
501	Blacksmiths	502.32
502	Bookbinders	396.67
503	Boilermakers	589.90
504	Brick masons & tile setters	492.75
505	Cabinetmakers	501.15
510	Carpenters	489.84
511	Cement finishers	299.16
512	Compositors & typesetters	478.77
521	Engravers	309.10
522	Excavating operators	492.15
523	Foremen not elsewhere classified	233.88
524	Forgemen & hammermen	299.16
525	Furriers	299.16
532	Inspectors, log & lumber	299.16
533	Inspectors not elsewhere classified	299.16
534	Jewelers, watchmakers, etc.	453.40
541	Locomotive engineers	299.16
544	Machinists	352.45
553	Mechanics, railroad car shop	299.16
554	Mechanics not elsewhere classified	469.37

Table D-1. (*continued*)

Code	Title	Income
555	Millers	546.99
560	Millwrights	491.71
561	Molders, metal	405.61
563	Opticians, lens grinders	299.16
564	Painters, construction	418.74
565	Paperhangers	299.16
570	Pattern makers, except paper	309.44
571	Photoengravers	299.16
573	Plasterers	497.12
574	Plumbers & pipe fitters	465.89
575	Pressmen & plate printers	299.16
580	Rollers & roll hands, metal	356.45
581	Roofers & slaters	299.16
582	Shoemakers, except factory	413.22
583	Stationary engineers	363.63
584	Stone cutters & carvers	279.16
590	Tailors & tailoresses	362.06
591	Tinsmiths & coppersmiths	417.13
592	Tool & die makers	299.16
593	Upholsterers	513.71
594	Craftsmen not elsewhere classified	410.45
595	Armed forces	270.01
Operatives & Kindred		
602	Apprentice carpenters	$ 389.36
611	Apprentices, building trades	389.36
614	Apprentices, other trades	389.36
615	Apprentices, trade not specified	470.85
623	Boatmen & lock keepers	360.91
624	Brakemen, railroad	389.36
625	Bus drivers	260.75
632	Deliverymen & routemen	517.11
633	Dressmakers, except factory	389.36
634	Dyers	317.14
635	Filers, grinders, polishers	389.36
641	Furnacemen & pourers	469.09
642	Heaters, metal	389.36
643	Laundry operatives	389.36
644	Meat cutters	430.00
645	Milliners	389.36
650	Mine operatives & laborers	253.70
661	Motormen	389.36
670	Painters	362.68
673	Sailors & deck hands	387.46
674	Sawyers	431.63

Table D-1. (*Continued*)

Code	Title	Income
675	Spinners, textile	145.52
680	Stationary firemen	300.55
681	Switchmen, railroad	389.36
682	Taxicab drivers	434.52
683	Truck & tractor drivers	329.21
684	Weavers, textile	220.02
685	Welders & flame-cutters	389.36
690	Operatives and kindred workers not elsewhere classified	431.17
Service Workers		
710	Laundresses	270.90
720	Private household workers	457.43
730	Attendants	270.90
732	Attendants, recreation	270.90
740	Barbers, beauticians, etc.	640.41
750	Bartenders	662.26
752	Boarding house keepers	287.09
763	Guards & watchmen	258.79
764	Housekeepers	424.91
770	Janitors & sextons	270.90
771	Marshals & constables	335.91
773	Policemen & detectives	335.91
780	Porters	485.81
781	Practical nurses	270.90
782	Sheriffs & bailiffs	335.91
784	Waiters & waitresses	485.81
785	Watchmen, bridge tenders	258.79
790	Service workers not elsewhere classified	457.43
Farm Laborers		
810	Farm foremen	404.61
820	Farm laborers	490.86
Laborers		
910	Fishermen & oystermen	598.43
930	Gardeners	468.96
940	Longshoremen	511.84
950	Lumbermen	598.43
970	Laborers, not elsewhere classified	327.60

Source: Calculated from regressions on real estate wealth in 1850 Public Use Microdata Series and data on earnings from Goldin and Margo, "Wages, Prices, and Labor Markets."

each occupation using their 1850 figure. For each occupation, daily wages were multiplied by 312 to obtain annual wages. Finally, the occupational dummy for common laborers was inflated to equal the resulting Goldin and Margo national average annual wage for laborers, and the dummies for all unskilled occupations were adjusted by the same factor. The same was done for skilled workers, with the income of carpenters pegged to the Goldin and Margo skilled wage, and for white collar workers, with the income of clerks pegged to the Goldin and Margo clerks wage. The results of these imputations for 157 occupational titles are shown in Table D-1. These incomes were then adjusted using the 1851 and 1861 price levels by region to reflect differences across locations and over time in prices.[3]

3. Coelho and Shepherd, "Regional Prices."

Appendix E
Coding of Occupations in the Ship Lists and the Census

White Collar

Professional

Artist	Professor	Clergyman	Lawyer
Publisher	Dentist	Priest	Physician
Attorney	Teacher	Minister	Doctor
Other			

Commercial

Agent	Wholesaler	Merchant	Broker
Other	Trader	Importer	Banker
Salesman	Clerk		

Proprietary

Baker	Victualer	Druggist	Contractor
Jeweller	Barber	Peddler	Florist
Keeper	Grocer	Builder	Tobacconist
Owner	Dealer	Furrier	Landlord
Huckster	Butcher	Confectioner	Manufacturer

Skilled

Beamer	Sawyer	Gainer	Blower
Smelter	Hatter	Brewer	Sorter
Layer	Engraver	Engineer	Refiner
Fisherman	Machinist	Saddler	Founder
Currier	Upholsterer	Painter	Cutler
Weaver	Plasterer	Dresser	Operator
Printer	Mason	Carver	Clothier
Miller	Cooper	Turner	Gilder
Binder	Shoemaker	Grinder	Boiler
Smith	Joiner	Carder	Spinner
Puddler	Finisher	Mechanic	Roller
Fitter	Lithograph	Molder	Cutter
Warper	Paver	Distiller	Wright
Plumber	Dyer	Carpenter	Tailor
Measurer	Candler	Tanner	Millwright
Cordwainer			

Farmer

Unskilled

Milkman	Boatman	Logger	Fireman
Carrier	Postman	Heaver	Coachman
Policeman	Drayman	Waiter	Watchman
Hostler	Mariner	Whitewasher	Laborer
Miner	Digger	Carman	Lightman
Gardener	Carter	Servant	Packer
Domestic	Quarryman	Driver	Porter
Waterman	Teamster	Seaman	

References

Abinder, T. *Nativism and Slavery: The Northern Know Nothings and the Politics of the 1850s.* New York: Oxford University Press, 1992.

Altonji, Joseph G., and David Card. "The Effects of Immigration on the Labor Market Outcomes of Less-Skilled Natives." In *Immigration, Trade, and the Labor Market,* edited by John M. Abowd and Richard B. Freeman. Chicago: University of Chicago Press, 1991.

Amemiya, Takeshi. *Advanced Econometrics.* Cambridge: Harvard University Press, 1985.

Atack, Jeremy, and Fred Bateman. *To Their Own Soil: Agriculture in the Antebellum North.* Ames: Iowa State University Press, 1987.

———. "Egalitarianism, Inequality, and Age: The Rural North in 1860." *Journal of Economic History* 41 (March 1981): 85–93.

Baines, Dudley. *Migration in a Mature Economy.* Cambridge: Cambridge University Press, 1985.

Barron, Hal S. *Those Who Stayed Behind: Rural Society in Nineteenth Century New England.* Cambridge: Cambridge University Press, 1984.

Barrows, R. G. "A Demographic Analysis of Indianapolis, 1870–1920." Ph.D. diss., Indiana University, 1977.

Bartel, Ann P. "Where Do the New U.S. Immigrants Live?" *Journal of Labor Economics* 7 (1989): 371–391.

Bateman, Fred, and Thomas Weiss. *A Deplorable Scarcity: The Failure of Industrialization in the Slave Economy.* Chapel Hill: University of North Carolina Press, 1981.

Berry, Thomas S. *Production and Population Since 1789: Revised GNP Series in Constant Dollars.* Richmond: Bostwick Press, 1988.

Birch, Brian P. "The Editor and the English: George Sheppard and English Immigration to Clinton County." *Annals of Iowa* 47 (1985): 620–642.

Blumin, Stuart M. "Mobility in a Nineteenth-Century American City: Philadelphia, 1820–1860." Ph.D. diss., University of Pennsylvania, 1968.

Board of Aldermen of the City of New York. *Documents, 1834-1865*. New York: City of New York, 1834–1865.

Bodnar, John. *The Transplanted: A History of Immigrants in Urban America*. Bloomington: Indiana University Press, 1985.

Bogue, Allan G. *From Prairie to Corn Belt: Farming in Illinois and Iowa in the Nineteenth Century*. Chicago: University of Chicago Press, 1963.

Borjas, George J. "Self-Selection and the Earnings of Immigrants." *American Economic Review* 77 (September 1987): 531–553.

———. "The Economics of Immigration." *Journal of Economic Literature* 32 (December 1994): 1667–1717.

———. "The Self-Employment Experience of Immigrants." *Journal of Human Resources* 21 (1986): 485–506.

Borjas, George J., Richard B. Freeman, and Lawrence F. Katz. "On the Labor Market Effects of Immigration and Trade." In *Immigration and the Work Force: Economic Consequences for the United States and Source Areas*, edited by George J. Borjas and Richard B. Freeman. Chicago: University of Chicago Press, 1992.

Breusch, T. S., and A. R. Pagan. "A Simple Test for Heteroskedasticity and Random Coefficient Variation." *Econometrica* 47 (November 1979): 1287–1294.

Busey, Samuel C. *Immigration: Its Evils and Consequences*. New York: DeWitt and Davenport, 1856.

Butcher, K. F., and David Card. "Immigration and Wages: Evidence from the 1980s." *American Economic Review* 81 (May 1991): 292–296.

Carter, Susan B., and Elizabeth Savoca. "Labor Mobility and Lengthy Jobs in Nineteenth-Century America." *Journal of Economic History* 50 (March 1991): 1–16.

Chiswick, Barry R. "A Longitudinal Analysis of the Occupational Mobility of Immigrants." In *Proceedings of the Thirtieth Annual Meeting of the Industrial Relations Research Association, December 28–30, 1977*. Madison, Wisc.: The Association, 1978.

———. "The Effect of Americanization on the Earnings of Foreign-Born Men." *Journal of Political Economy* 86 (October 1978): 897–921.

———. "The Performance of Immigrants in the United States Labor Market." In *Economic Aspects of International Migration*, edited by Herbert Giersch. Berlin: Springer-Verlag, 1994.

Coale, Ansley, and Paul Demeny. *Regional Model Life Tables and Stable Populations*. New York: Academic Press, 1966.

Coelho, Philip, and James Shepherd. "Differences in Regional Prices: The United States, 1851–1880." *Journal of Economic History* 34 (September 1974): 551–591.

Cohn, Ray L. "The Occupations of English Immigrants to the U.S., 1836–1853." *Journal of Economic History* 52 (1992): 377–387.

Commissioners of Emigration of the State of New York. *Annual Report*. New York: State of New York, 1854.

Commons, J. R., U. B. Phillips, E. A. Gilmore, H. L. Sumner, and J. B. Andrews, eds. *A Documentary History of American Industrial Society, Vol. VII*. Cleveland: Arthur H. Clark, 1910.

Commons, J. R., D. J. Saposs, H. L. Sumner, E. B. Mittelman, H. E. Hoagland, J. B. Andrews, and S. G. Perlman. *History of Labour in the United States*. New York: Macmillan, 1918.

Condran, Gretchen A., and Eileen Crimmins. "A Description and Evaluation of Mortality Data in the Federal Census: 1850–1900." *Historical Methods* 12 (1979): 1–23.

Conway, Alan. "New Orleans as a Port of Immigration." *Louisiana Studies* 1 (1975): 1–22.

Curti, Merle. *The Making of an American Community: A Case Study of Democracy in a Frontier County.* Stanford: Stanford University Press, 1959.

Davenport, David. "Tracing Rural New York's Out-Migrants, 1855–1860." *Historical Methods* 17 (1984): 59–67.

David, Paul A. "Fortune, Risk, and the Microeconomics of Migration." In *Nations and Households in Economic Growth,* edited by Paul A. David and Melvin W. Reder. New York: Academic Press, 1974.

Drake, Michael. "We Are Yankeys Now." *New York History* 45 (1964): 222–264.

Engerman, Stanley L. "Up or Out: Social and Geographic Mobility in the United States." *Journal of Interdisciplinary History* 5 (1975): 483–484.

Erickson, Charlotte. "The Uses of Passenger Lists for the Study of British and Irish Emigration." In *Migration Across Time and Nations,* edited by Ira Glazier and Luigi De Rosa. New York: Holmes and Meier, 1986.

———. "Emigration from the British Isles to the U.S.A. in 1841: Part I." *Population Studies* 43 (1989): 347–367.

———. "Emigration from the British Isles to the U.S.A. in 1831." *Population Studies* 35 (1981): 175–197.

———. *Invisible Immigrants.* Coral Gables: University of Miami Press, 1970.

Ernst, Robert. *Immigrant Life in New York City, 1825–1863.* New York: King's Crown Press, 1949.

Esslinger, Dean R. *Immigrants and the City: Ethnicity and Mobility in a Nineteenth-Century Midwestern Community.* Port Washington, N.Y.: Kennikat, 1975.

Faragher, John M. *Sugar Creek: Life on the Illinois Prairie.* New Haven: Yale University Press, 1986.

Ferrie, Joseph P. "A New Sample of Males Linked from the Public Use Microdata Sample of the 1850 U.S. Federal Census of Population to the 1860 U.S. Federal Population Census Manuscript Schedules." *Historical Methods* 16 (1996): 141–56.

Ficker, Christian Traugott. "Friendly Adviser for All Who Would Emigrate to America and Particularly to Wisconsin." *Wisconsin Magazine of History* 25 (1941): 215–236, 331–353, 455–475.

Filer, Randall K. "The Effect of Immigrant Arrivals on Migratory Patterns of Native Workers." In *Immigration and the Work Force: Economic Consequences for the United States and Source Areas,* edited by George J. Borjas and Richard B. Freeman. Chicago: University of Chicago Press, 1992.

Flick, R. "Reliability of Census Indexes." Brigham Young University, 1982.

Fogel, Robert W. *Without Consent or Contract: The Rise and Fall of American Slavery.* New York: Norton, 1989.

———. "Problems in Measuring the Real Wages of Native Non-Farm Workers in the North, 1846–1855." In *Without Consent or Contract: The Rise and Fall of American Slavery—Evidence and Methods,* edited by Robert W. Fogel, Ralph A. Galantine, and Richard L. Manning. New York: Norton, 1992.

Frey, William H. "The New White Flight." *American Demographics* 16 (1994): 40–48.

Friedberg, Rachel M., and Jennifer Hunt. "The Impact of Immigrants on Host Country Wages, Employment, and Growth." *Journal of Economic Perspectives* 9 (Spring 1995): 23–44.

Galenson, David W. "Economic Opportunity on the Urban Frontier: Nativity, Work, and

Wealth in Early Chicago." *Journal of Economic History* 51 (September 1991): 581–603.

Galenson, David W., and Daniel S. Levy. "A Note on Biases in the Measurement of Geographic Persistence Rates." *Historical Methods* 19 (1986): 171–179.

Galenson, David W., and Clayne L. Pope. "Economic and Geographic Mobility on the Farming Frontier: Evidence from Appanoose County, Iowa, 1850–1870." *Journal of Economic History* 49 (September 1989): 635–655.

Gates, Paul. *The Illinois Central and Its Colonization Work.* Cambridge: Harvard University Press, 1934.

Gjerde, Jon. *Peasants to Farmers.* Cambridge: Cambridge University Press, 1985.

Glazier, Ira A. *The Famine Immigrants: Lists of Irish Immigrants Arriving at the Port of New York, 1846–1851.* Baltimore: Genealogical Publishing, 1983.

Glazier, Ira A., and P. William Filby. *Germans to America: Lists of Passengers Arriving at U.S. Ports, 1850–1855*, Volume 1, January 1850—May 1854. Wilmington, Delaware: Scholarly Resources, 1986.

Goldin, Claudia. "The Political Economy of Immigration Restriction in the United States, 1890 to 1921." In *The Regulated Economy: A Historical Approach to Political Economy*, edited by Claudia Goldin and Gary D. Libecap. Chicago: University of Chicago Press, 1994.

Goldin, Claudia, and Robert A. Margo. "Wages, Prices, and Labor Markets Before the Civil War." In *Strategic Factors in Nineteenth Century American Economic History*, edited by Claudia Goldin and Hugh Rockoff. Chicago: University of Chicago Press, 1992.

Gönül, F. "Dynamic Labor Force Participation Decisions of Males in the Presence of Layoffs and Uncertain Job Offers." *Journal of Human Resources* 24 (1989): 195–220.

Goodrich, Carter, and Sol Davidson. "The Wage Earner in the Westward Movement I." *Political Science Quarterly* 50 (1935): 161–185

———. "The Wage Earner in the Westward Movement II." *Political Science Quarterly* 51 (1936): 61–116.

Greene, William. *Econometric Analysis.* New York: Macmillan, 1990.

Griffen, Clyde, and Sally Griffen. *Natives and Newcomers: The Ordering of Opportunity in Mid-Nineteenth Century Poughkeepsie.* Cambridge: Harvard University Press, 1978.

Guest, Avery. "Notes From the National Panel Study." *Historical Methods* 20 (1987): 63–77.

Haines, Michael R. "The Use of Model Life Tables to Estimate Mortality for the United States in the Late Nineteenth Century." *Demography* 16 (1979): 289–312.

Hatton, Timothy J., and Jeffrey G. Williamson. "The Impact of Immigration on American Labor Markets Prior to the Quotas." National Bureau of Economic Research Working Paper No. 5185, 1995.

Hausman, Jerry. "Specification Tests in Econometrics." *Econometrica* 46 (November 1978): 1251–1271.

Heckman, James J., and Richard Robb. "Using Longitudinal Data to Estimate Age, Period, and Cohort Effects in Earnings Equations." In *Analyzing Longitudinal Data for Age, Period, and Cohort Effects*, edited by H. Winsborough and O. Duncan. New York: Academic Press, 1983.

Hoagland, H. E. "The Rise of the Iron Molders' International Union." *American Economic Review* 3 (1913): 296–313.

Hsiao, Cheng. *Analysis of Panel Data.* Cambridge: Cambridge University Press, 1986.

Hutchinson, Edward P. "Notes on Immigration Statistics of the United States." *Journal of the American Statistical Association* 53 (July 1958): 963–1025.

Jackson, Ronald V. "Index to the Seventh Census of the United States." Salt Lake City: Accelerated Indexing Systems International, 1981.

———. "Index to the Eighth Census of the United States." Salt Lake City: Accelerated Indexing Systems International, 1991.

Jacobson, P. H. "An Estimate of the Expectation of Life in the United States in 1850." *Milbank Memorial Fund Quarterly* 35 (1957): 197–201.

Jacoby, Sanford, and Sunil Sharma. "Employment Duration and Industrial Labor Mobility in the United States, 1880–1980." *Journal of Economic History* 52 (1992): 161–180.

Jenks, William L. "Michigan Immigration." *Michigan History Magazine* 28 (1944): 67–100.

Kamphoefner, Walter D. *Westphalians: From Germany to Missouri.* Princeton: Princeton University Press, 1987.

———. "The Volume and Composition of German-American Return Migration." In *A Century of European Migrations: 1830-1930,* edited by Rudolph J. Vecoli and Suzanne Simke. Urbana: University of Illinois Press, 1991.

Kamphoefner, Walter D., Wolfgang Helbich, and Ulrike Sommer. *News From the Land of Freedom: German Immigrants Write Home.* Ithaca: Cornell University Press, 1991.

Kapp, Friedrich. *Immigration and the Commissioners of Emigration of the State of New York.* New York: The Nation Press, 1870.

Katz, Michael B. *The People of Hamilton West, Canada: Family and Class in a Mid-Nineteenth Century City.* Cambridge: Harvard University Press, 1975.

King, Miriam, and Steven Ruggles. "American Immigration, Fertility, and Race Suicide." *Journal of Interdisciplinary History* 20 (1990): 347–369.

Kirk, Gordon, and C. T. Kirk. "Migration, Mobility, and the Transformation of the Occupational Structure in an Immigrant Community: Holland, Michigan, 1850–80." *Journal of Social History* 7 (1974): 142–164.

Knights, Peter. *Yankee Destinies.* Chapel Hill: University of North Carolina Press, 1991.

———. "Accuracy of Age Reporting in the Manuscript Federal Censuses of 1850 and 1860." *Historical Methods* 4 (1971): 79–83.

Kousser, J. Morgan, Gary W. Cox, and David W. Galenson. "Log-Linear Analysis of Contingency Tables: An Introduction for Historians With An Application to Thernstrom On the 'Floating Proletariat.'" *Historical Methods* 15 (1982): 152–169.

Kremers, Gerhard. "Letters." *Wisconsin Magazine of History* 21 (1937): 68–84.

Kuznets, Simon, and Ernest Rubin. *Immigration and the Foreign Born.* New York: National Bureau of Economic Research, 1954.

Lancaster, Tony. *The Econometric Analysis of Transition Data.* Cambridge: Cambridge University Press, 1990.

Lane, A. T. *Solidarity or Survival? American Labor and European Immigrants, 1830–1924.* New York: Greenwood Press, 1987.

Lazonick, William, and T. Brush. "The 'Horndahl Effect' in Early U.S. Manufacturing." *Explorations in Economic History* 22 (1985): 53–96.

Lebergott, Stanley. "The Demand for Land." *Journal of Economic History* 45 (June 1985): 181–212.

Lee, L. F. "Unionism and Wages: A Simultaneous Equations Model with Qualitative and Limited Dependent Variables." *International Economic Review* 19 (1978): 415–433.

Levine, B. *The Spirit of 1848: German Immigrants, Labor Conflict, and the Coming of the Civil War.* Urbana: University of Illinois Press, 1992.

Lucas, Henry S. "The Journey of an Immigrant Family from The Netherlands to Milwaukee in 1854." *Wisconsin Magazine of History* 29 (1945): 201–223.

Lynch, B. T., and W. L. Arends. "Selection of a Surname Coding Scheme for the SRS

Record Linkage System." Sample Survey Research Branch, Research Division Statistical Reporting Service, U.S. Department of Agriculture. Washington, 1977.

Maddala, G. S. *Limited Dependent and Qualitative Variables in Econometrics.* Cambridge: Cambridge University Press, 1983.

Mageean, Deidre M. "Nineteenth-Century Irish Emigration: A Case Study Using Passenger Ship Lists." In *Irish Studies IV: The Irish in America: Emigration, Assimilation, and Impact,* edited by P. J. Drudy. Cambridge: Cambridge University Press, 1984.

Mahr, August C. "Down the Rhine to Ohio: The Travel Diary of Christoph Jacob Munk, April 21—August 17, 1832." *Ohio State Archaeological and Historical Quarterly* 57 (1948): 266–310.

Malin, James. "The Turnover of Farm Population in Kansas." *Kansas Historical Quarterly* 20 (1935): 339–372.

Margo, Robert A. "Wages and Prices During the Antebellum Period: A Survey and New Evidence." In *American Economic Growth and Standards of Living Before the Civil War,* edited by Robert E. Gallman and John J. Wallis. Chicago: University of Chicago Press, 1992.

Meech, L. *Systems and Tables of Life Insurance.* New York: Spectator, 1898.

Meyer, Bruce D. "Semiparametric Estimation of Hazard Models." Massachusetts Institute of Technology, 1986.

Miller, Kirby. *Emigrants and Exiles.* New York: Oxford University Press, 1985.

Mirer, Thad. "The Age-Wealth Relation Among the Aged." *American Economic Review* 69 (June 1979): 435–443.

Mokyr, Joel, and Cormac Ó Gráda. "Emigration and Poverty in Pre-Famine Ireland." *Explorations in Economic History* 19 (1982): 360–384.

Nadel, Stanley. *Little Germany: Ethnicity, Religion, and Class in New York City, 1845–80.* Urbana: University of Illinois Press, 1990.

Nakosteen, R. A., and M. Zimmer. "Migration and Income: The Question of Self-Selection." *Southern Economic Journal* 46 (1980): 840–851.

Neal, Larry, and Paul J. Uselding. "Immigration: A Neglected Source of American Economic Growth: 1790–1912." *Oxford Economic Papers* 24 (1972): 68–88.

Ostergren, Robert. *A Community Transplanted.* Madison: University of Wisconsin Press, 1988.

Page, Thomas Walker. "Distribution of Immigrants in the United States Before 1870." *Journal of Political Economy* 20 (1912): 676–694.

———. "Some Economic Aspects of Immigration Before 1870, Part I." *Journal of Political Economy* 20 (1912): 1011–1028.

Parkerson, Donald. "How Mobile Were Nineteenth-Century Americans?" *Historical Methods* 15 (1982): 99–109.

Pope, Clayne L. "Adult Mortality in America Before 1900: A View from Family Histories." In *Strategic Factors in Nineteenth Century American Economic History,* edited by Claudia Goldin and Hugh Rockoff. Chicago: University of Chicago Press, 1992.

———. "Coming to Zion: The Economic Fortunes of the Foreign-Born in Utah." Brigham Young University, 1991.

———. "Households on the American Frontier: The Distribution of Income and Wealth in Utah, 1850-1900." In *Markets in History: Economic Studies of the Past,* edited by David W. Galenson. Cambridge: Cambridge University Press, 1989.

Robinson, C., and N. Tomes. "Self-Selection and Interprovincial Migration in Canada." *Canadian Journal of Economics* 15 (1982): 474–502.

Ross, S. J. *Workers on the Edge: Work, Leisure, and Politics in Industrializing Cincinnati, 1788–1840*. New York: Columbia University Press, 1985.

Ruggles, Steven, M. Sobek, P. K. Hall, and C. Ronnander. *Integrated Public Use Microdata Series: IPUMS-95 Version 1.0*. Computer file and user's guide. Minneapolis: Social History Research Laboratory, Department of History, University of Minnesota, 1995.

Schaefer, Donald. "A Statistical Profile of Frontier and New South Migration, 1850–1860." *Agricultural History* 59 (1985): 563–578.

Schafer, Joseph. *Four Wisconsin Counties*. Madison: State Historical Society of Wisconsin, 1927.

Sheps, Mendel C., and Jane A. Menken. *Mathematical Models of Conception and Birth*. Chicago: University of Chicago Press, 1973.

Simkovich, Boris. "Long-Term Trends in American Inter-Generational Occupational Mobility." Harvard University, 1993.

Sokoloff, Kenneth L., and Georgia C. Villaflor. "The Market for Manufacturing Workers During Early Industrialization: The American Northeast, 1820 to 1860." In *Strategic Factors in Nineteenth Century American Economic History*, edited by Claudia Goldin and Hugh Rockoff. Chicago: University of Chicago Press, 1992.

Soltow, Lee. *Men and Wealth in the United States*. New Haven: Yale University Press, 1975.

Steckel, Richard. "Poverty and Prosperity: A Longitudinal Study of Wealth Accumulation, 1850–1860." *Review of Economics and Statistics* 72 (May 1990): 275–285.

———. "Census Matching and Migration: A Research Strategy." *Historical Methods* 21 (1985): 52–60.

———. "Poverty and Prosperity: A Longitudinal Study of Wealth Accumulation, 1850–1860." Ohio State University, 1988.

———. "The Quality of Census Data for Historical Inquiry: A Research Agenda." *Social Science History* 15 (1991): 580–599.

Swierenga, Robert P. "Dutch International Migration Statistics: An Analysis of Linked Multinational Nominal Files." *International Migration Review* 15 (1981): 445–470.

———. "Dutch International Migration and Occupational Change: A Structural Analysis of Multinational Linked Files." In *Migration Across Time and Nations*, edited by Ira Glazier and Luigi De Rosa. New York: Holmes and Meier, 1986.

———. "Reply to Gemery-Schofield: 'Under-Reporting of Dutch Immigration Statistics: A Recalculation.'" *International Migration Review* 21 (1987): 1596–1599.

Taylor, Philip. *The Distant Magnet: European Emigration to the U.S.A.* New York: Harper and Row, 1971.

Thernstrom, Stephan. *Poverty and Progress: Social Mobility in a Nineteenth Century City*. Cambridge: Harvard University Press, 1964.

———. *The Other Bostonians: Poverty and Progress in the American Metropolis, 1880–1970*. Cambridge: Harvard University Press, 1973.

Thistlethwaite, Frank. "Migration from Europe Overseas in the Nineteenth and Twentieth Centuries." In *Rapports du XIe Congrès International des Sciences Historiques, Vol. 5, Histoire Contemporaine*. Stockholm: Almqvist & Wiksell, 1960.

Thompson, D. R. *Hints to Emigrants; or to Those Who May Contemplate Emigrating to the United States of America, and California*. London: Francis Whelpton, 1849.

Tucker, C. J., and W. L. Urton. "Frequency of Geographic Mobility: Findings from the National Health Interview Survey." *Demography* 24 (1987): 265–270.

Turner, Frederick J. *The Frontier in American History*. New York: H. Holt, 1920.

U.S. Census Bureau. *Historical Statistics of the United States: Colonial Times to 1970.* Washington: Government Printing Office, 1975.

———. *Statistical Abstract of the United States: 1995.* Washington: Robert Armstrong, 1995.

U.S. Census Office. *Seventh Census of the United States: 1850.* Washington: Robert Armstrong, 1853.

———. *Compendium of the Seventh Census of the United States: 1850.* Washington: B. Tucker, 1854.

———. *Eighth Census of the United States, 1860.* Washington: Government Printing Office, 1864.

———. *Compendium of the Eighth Census of the United States: 1860.* Washington: Government Printing Office, 1864.

U.S. Department of the Treasury. *Immigration Into the United States, 1820 to 1903.* Washington: Government Printing Office, 1910.

U.S. Senate [Aldrich, N. W.]. *Wholesale Prices, Wages, and Transportation.* 52d Cong., 2d sess., Senate Report No. 1394. Washington: Government Printing Office, 1893.

Uselding, Paul J. "Studies in the Technological Development of the American Economy During the First Half of the Nineteenth Century." Ph.D. diss., Northwestern University, 1970.

Vinovskis, Maris A. "Mortality Rates and Trends in Massachusetts Before 1860." *Journal of Economic History* 32 (1972): 184–213.

Wells, David A. *Our Burden and Our Strength.* New York: Loyal Publication Society, 1864.

White, Halbert. "A Heteroskedasticity-Consistent Covariance Matrix Estimator and a Direct Test for Heteroskedasticity." *Econometrica* 48 (1980): 817–838.

White, M. J., and L. Hunter. "The Migratory Response of Native-Born Workers to the Presence of Immigrants in the Labor Market." Brown University, July 1993.

White, M. J., and Z. Liang. "The Effect of Immigration on the Internal Migration of the Native-Born Population, 1981–1990." Brown University, August 1993.

Willcox, Walter. *Studies in American Demography.* Ithaca: Cornell University Press, 1940.

Williamson, Jeffrey G. "Immigrant-Inequality Trade-Offs in the Promised Land: Income Distribution and Absorptive Capacity Prior to the Quotas." In *The Gateway: U.S. Immigration Issues and Policies,* edited by Barry R. Chiswick. Washington: American Enterprise Institute, 1982.

Willis, Robert J., and Sherwin Rosen. "Education and Self-Selection." *Journal of Political Economy* 87 (1979): S7–S36

Winkle, Kenneth. *The Politics of Community: Migration and Politics in Antebellum Ohio.* Cambridge: Cambridge University Press, 1988.

Wittke, Carl F. *Refugees of Revolution: The German Forty-Eighters in America.* Philadelphia: University of Pennsylvania Press, 1952.

Zimmerman, Gary J., and Marion Wolfert. *German Immigrants: Lists of Passengers Bound from Bremen to New York, 1847–1854.* Baltimore: Genealogical Publishing, 1985.

Index

Abinder, T., 162

absorptive capacity of the U.S. economy
  with respect to immigrants, 157, 160,
    183

age-wealth relationship
  controlling for changes in
    characteristics, 1850–60, 124
  controlling for years since arrival, 110
  differences between 1850 and 1860, 127
  differences between immigrants and
    natives, 105
  differences by country of origin, 120
  estimates from other studies, 112, 113

Altonji, Joseph G., 157, 158, 170, 180

Amemiya, Takeshi, 168

Arends, W. L., 29

arrival of immigrants
  and return migration, 22–23
  and time spent in New York City, 40,
    42–46, 53
  and transformation of host country, 4
  and wealth, 47, 69, 114–115
  ascertaining date of, 10, 11–12
  impact on natives, 36, 38, 156–184
  in interior of United States, 62–64
  occupational status at, 8, 36, 71, 81

arrival records
  linking to census manuscripts, 12–14,
    18–20

quality of, 15–18, 80
  sources, 5, 10, 13

Atack, Jeremy, 58, 63, 101, 106, 112

average quality of immigrants at arrival
  and effect of duration in United States,
    99
  and events in Europe, 84, 89, 90, 187,
    188

Baines, Dudley, 23

Barron, Hal S., 133

Barrows, R. G., 132

Bartel, Ann P., 180

Bateman, Fred, 37, 58, 63, 101, 106,
    112

benefits of immigration, 156

Berry, Thomas S., 37

Birch, Brian P., 42

Blumin, Stuart M., 132

Bodnar, John, 74

Bogue, Allan G., 39, 78, 101, 106, 132,
    134, 135

Borjas, George J., 83, 90, 91, 94, 157, 159,
    166

Bremen, 7, 14–18

Brush, T., 161

Busey, Samuel C., 162

business cycles before the Civil War, 37

Butcher, K. F., 158